Fishing
Central Florida

Kris Thoemke

Pineapple Press, Inc.
Sarasota, Florida

Inquiries should be addressed to:
Pineapple Press, Inc.
P.O. Box 3889
Sarasota, Florida 34230

www.pineapplepress.com

Library of Congress Cataloging-in-Publication Data

Thoemke, Kris W.
Fishing central Florida / Kris Thoemke.
p. cm.
Includes index.
ISBN 978-1-56164-479-7 (pb : alk. paper)
1. Fishing--Florida--Guidebooks. 2. Florida--Guidebooks. I. Title.

SH483.T483 2010
799.109759--dc22

2010035769

First Edition
10 9 8 7 6 5 4 3 2 1

Design by Jennifer Borresen
Printed and bound in the United States of America

To the many anglers who have taught me so much about fishing…
And, with love, to my wife, Marsha

Contents

FOREWORD

Kris Thoemke continues to impress me. He is a determined, methodical, relentless researcher, a person who deals in hard facts and shuns fantasy or speculation. These talents carried Kris through all of his academic work, culminating in a Ph.D. in marine biology, and they underscore the work he does today. When Kris talks about fishing in the Sunshine State, he speaks from firsthand experience or the latest and best research. When he tells you where to fish and which methods to use, you can be sure Kris is a reliable source.

Fishing Central Florida, and its companion volumes, *Fishing South Florida* and *Fishing North Florida,* loom as instant classics, the ultimate references for beginning and experienced anglers alike. These guidebooks are perfect for the resident who wants to expand his collection of hotspots, and for the visitor who wants to catch Florida fish and brag about it back home. Combined, Kris's three books describe over 600 specific sites based on extensive interviews with local specialists from all parts of the state. No other books provide even a fraction of the information contained in these three guidebooks.

Within the pages of each volume, you'll learn not only where and when to fish, but how to be successful when you get there. The introductory chapters detail angling ethics, safety factors, basic fishing tackle for all kinds of situations, and tips for hooking up with Florida's 24 most-sought-after species of game fish.

At least two million people visit Florida each year to enjoy its fishing potential. Add to that four million anglers within the state and the problem of finding the best fishing spots is magnified. Until Kris set his keenly analytical mind and innate curiosity to this monumental task, no one had ever attempted to collect in one place the incredible angling opportunities of Florida. In this guide you'll discover piers, bridges, and fertile waters accessible only by boat.

Fishing Central Florida is a working tool to be used repeatedly and frequently. For locating great saltwater fishing from Crystal River to Venice along the Gulf coast and from Daytona Beach to Ft. Pierce along the Atlantic coast and all freshwater points in between, it's just about as important as your rod and reel. All of us should commend Kris Thoemke for making many of Florida's so-called secret fishing spots common knowledge. My copy of this book will spend a lot of time out on the water with me. I know yours will, too.

—Mark Sosin, producer and host, *Mark Sosin's Salt Water Journal*

PREFACE

This is the first of three regional guides that, collectively, replace *Fishing Florida*, the statewide guide I wrote in 1995. While there have not been many groundbreaking changes in where to fish in Florida since 1995 or even the species that anglers catch, there is now a massive amount of information about fishing in Florida available to anglers on the Internet. Do a Google search of fishing in Florida and you will find hundreds of websites with information about recreational fishing in the Sunshine State. A word of caution about this information—some of it is very useful, some of it is biased, and too much of it is simply inaccurate.

The information presented in this book is a compilation of many sources, including thirty-seven years of my personal observations and experiences in Florida, as well as a distillation of useful information from the Internet and interviews with guides, bait and tackle store owners, avid anglers, and fisheries biologists. In this era of digital information, I even relied on old-fashioned printed materials. It's not all on the Internet yet!

No person, including myself, can claim to be the sole expert on fishing in the state of Florida. There are too many places to fish and too many species of fish to catch. That is why the Fishing Index information for each listing is based on interviews with knowledgeable anglers, my personal experiences, and other reliable and verified sources of information.

The directions to each site typically begin from a major town or road intersection that can be found on the State of Florida Official Transportation Map. Distances were calculated using the odometer in my vehicle, by measurement using the Florida Atlas and Gazetteer published by DeLorme Mapping Company, and by using Google Earth and Mapquest. You will also find the address of the sites that have an address. Enter this into your land-based GPS and those marvelous devices will guide you there.

The businesses mentioned in this book are not necessarily the only ones near each site. They are all places that I have visited or where I have spoken with the owners/managers over the phone. My endorsement of them extends only to saying that they provided information that was determined to be accurate for their areas. There are many other equally helpful and knowledgeable businesses that are not mentioned here. Their omission is not deliberate in any way.

I claim responsibility for compiling the information and assembling it in its final form. Not everyone reading this book who has intimate knowledge of a site may totally agree with the comments. Those discrepancies are, I believe, attributable to the many and varied perspectives of anglers. If there are errors of omission or inaccuracies of fact, I'm confident that I will hear about them.

Readers are encouraged to supplement what they read here with their personal experiences and whatever other credible information they can gather.

Change is constant and there is no doubt in my mind that some of the information on the following pages will need to be revised before we print the second edition. So I encourage you to do what I do with guidebooks; grab a pen and update the information that becomes out of date. And if you want to share your information with me, e-mail me at *kris@fishfloridaonline.com*.

For those who want to know more, I've included a list of credible websites at the end of the book. You will note that some of the listings are for websites of county property appraisers. These are geographic information system–based (GIS) websites that allow you to search for sites by address and other means and display aerial photos of the locations. I recommend you learn how to use these sites as they are very useful. You can also get similar results using Mapquest, Google Earth, and similar popular websites.

INTRODUCTION

Florida has a legacy of great fishing. I still have vivid memories of fishing the Everglades with my grandfather in the 1960s. We fished the canals along the eastern edge of the Glades under the watchful eyes of alligators, anhingas, and great blue herons. As a young teenager I spent most summers days from sunrise to well past sunset fishing off Anglin's Pier in Lauderdale-by-the-Sea, trying my luck from one of the many bridges in Fort Lauderdale, or spending a morning drift fishing on the Captain Bill or Dragon party boats.

For the past thirty-seven years I've had the opportunity to fish in every corner of this state. Most of the hot spots I've found are described in this book, along with dozens of new discoveries that I can't wait to try. In Florida you are never more than a few miles from fishable waters. The state is laced with hundreds of lakes, rivers, streams, and miles of freshwater canals that provide some of the best bass and panfish action that you will find anywhere there are fish.

Saltwater enthusiasts have thousands of miles of coastline and the blue waters of the Atlantic and Gulf of Mexico to angle for over 70 species of fish. Chum for yellow snapper in the Keys, kite fish for sailfish in the Atlantic Ocean, go grouper grabbing in the Gulf of Mexico, stalk snook among the mangroves, sight fish for redfish on the seagrass beds, test your skills on giant tarpon around Homosassa, and fish for cobia from the Panhandle's super piers. And that's just for starters! Florida is a land where your next cast could become the fishing adventure of a lifetime.

No matter how much or little fishing experience you have, *Fishing Central Florida* offers useful, accurate advice. With hundreds of site descriptions, tips on the tackle and techniques proven to catch fish in Florida, and numerous maps and tables, all the angling information that you need to enjoy fishing in Florida is at your fingertips.

When I completed the book *Fishing Florida* in 1995, we were about to enter a new era for fishing with passage of the "net ban" amendment to the state's constitution. With the state's multibillion dollar recreational fishery in danger, Florida's sport anglers took the initiative to remove entangling nets from the state's nearshore waters. As of July 1, 1995, commercial fishermen were no longer allowed to use these nets in state waters. Highly controversial at the time, supporters claimed that making the nets illegal would save overfished species, including striped mullet, spotted sea trout, pompano, bluefish, and Spanish mackerel.

Fast forward to 2010 and the article "What Happened After the Net Ban?" written by three University of Florida professors. Originally published in 2000 and reviewed in 2009, the article concluded the following:

- "The average annual commercial landings of 22 species of finfish reported by FDEP [Florida Department of Environmental Protection] to be impacted the most by the net ban declined in aggregate from 52 million pounds (mp) during 1992–1994 to 18 mp during 1996–1998 (data for 1995 was excluded since the ban was implemented mid-year). Average annual dockside value decreased from $21 million to $13 million during the same period."
- "Stocks of striped mullet are increasing. The mullet SPR* has increased since 1992 (18%–25%), and is expected to reach 35% by year 2000."
- "Stocks of spotted sea trout have remained steady following the net ban, but SPR* estimates ranging from 22% to 31% are still below target levels. The net ban has had less of an effect on spotted sea trout since this fishery has historically been predominantly recreational (i.e., hook and line)."
- "Spanish mackerel are primarily targeted by recreational fishers in the Gulf and commercial fishers in the Atlantic. However, following the net ban, Spanish mackerel are no longer overfished in the Gulf or Atlantic regions."

The report concluded: "Several stocks of fish historically targeted with entangling nets have exhibited an improvement since the net ban. For some species, such as mullet, stock improvement was already being reported as a result of management measures implemented before the net ban. For other

*"A measure of the health of fish stocks used by the FDEP is the *spawning potential ratio*, which is defined as the number of eggs that could be produced by an average female fish in the current fished stock *divided* by the same number for an unfished stock of fish. The spawning potential ratio, or SPR, is used as a proxy for the health of fish stocks."

species, such as Spanish mackerel, improvements in stocks have been accelerated following the net ban. And for others, such as spotted sea trout, bluefish, and pompano, the effect of the net ban is less clear." Based on this article, readers can judge for themselves whether the net ban is a success or failure. You can find the entire article at *http://edis.ifas.ufl.edu/.* Type in "net ban" in the search box.

Using This Guide

This book doesn't describe every place to fish in central Florida. Some sites are seldom fished except by locals and many other sites are nothing more than a place along a road by some water body where you can pull off the road and fish. It is not practical to include every place like this. *Fishing Central Florida* does, however, give a detailed overview of the fishing conditions for every county in central Florida and directions to over 145 productive places to fish.

The listings for central Florida are divided into the East Central and West Central. Each area is subdivided into sections based on natural geographic features and/or county lines. Entries for specific sites are numbered to correspond with the regional map accompanying each area.

Site entries adhere to the following format:

#. Name of site

Fresh or salt water; types of fishing (bank, boat, bridge, pier, etc.)—Ramp (if present)—$ (indicates a fee)

Description: General information about the site, a special nearby feature, and/ or amenities available at the site.

Fishing Index: Specific information about the best time to fish, the top species caught at the site, tips on how to fish the area, brief interviews, and other information about the site.

Directions: Directions relative to a city, intersection, prominent landmark, etc. Routes to many of the sites are well signed. In some instances, the signs may indicate different routes than the ones described in this book; the way you go is a matter of personal preference. State parks signs are usually brown with white lettering. Florida Fish and Wildlife Conservation Commission (FWC) boat ramp signs are small green rectangles with yellow lettering.

Access points: Some entries feature more than one access point. Additional descriptions and directions are provided as needed.

Address: Not every site has a street address but if it does, the listing will be here. Enter this into your GPS and follow the directions to the site.

For more information: A place or person to contact for additional information such as seasonal closures, up-to-the-minute bait or lure recommendations, and current conditions.

The locations described in this book include piers, bridges, beaches, bank and shore spots, and even locales for those who like to wade fish. When you reach a particular site, other nearby spots may look like good places to fish. The rule to follow is: Be safe and respect private property. There are many great places to fish, but if getting to them is dangerous or requires entering private property and you don't have permission from the landowner, don't go.

At the end of each chapter there is a month-by-month summary highlighting the top fishing action for the region. Also, a species availability chart reveals at a glance when a particular species of fish is present and whether it is a peak time of year for the species in the region.

Remember, before you go fishing know if you need a saltwater and/or freshwater fishing license and get that license. If in doubt, check with a local bait and tackle store, any tax collector office, or go online to *www.myfwc.com* and click on the link for fishing and then for licenses.

Many other websites are referenced in the listings in this book. They include county, chamber of commerce, state government, and a few private websites. You should be able to find the home page for most of these sites and then drill down into them to find any new or updated information.

Finally, readers can find more information about fishing in Florida by checking out *www.fishfloridaonline.com* and *www.fishingfloridaonline.com*

ACKNOWLEDGMENTS

As was the case for *Fishing Florida*, my previous book, there are literally hundreds of fishing guides and bait and tackle shop owners and anglers to thank for sharing their local knowledge with me. Unfortunately, it would take pages of text to list their names, so I have decided to give one huge collective thank-you to them all and not mention names.

Thanks are in order for June Cussen, the editor of this book, and Jennifer Borresen, who prepared the maps for this book. Their thoughtful comments and suggestions are much appreciated. Finally, a special thank-you to Duane Raver for his outstanding drawings of the fish described in the section on Florida's top game fish.

Fishing Fundamentals

The Responsible Angler

Beginning this book with a brief explanation on why anglers must be concerned about the aquatic environment is a deliberate act on my part. Here's why: **The present and future of fishing in Florida is and will continue to be largely dependent on how anglers interact with the environment when on and off the water.**

The survival of every sport fish species depends on that species having the habitat and food to survive and, at a minimum, living long enough to be replaced by one of its offspring. As a species, humans have impacted the habitat of every fish species described in this book. Our unique ability to fashion the environment to suit our needs has changed the freshwater and saltwater environments mainly through placing unwanted substances in these waters; i.e. pollution.

In some instances the source of the pollution is readily identifiable; a pipe discharging an effluent from a factory. More commonly, but far less obviously, many pollutants enter the water by the simple act of humans spraying or pouring them on the ground. While it may not seem significant, there is a good chance that these chemicals will eventually end up in Florida's lakes, rivers, or coastal waters. No matter how pollutants enter the water, their presence eventually has a negative impact on the environment, including the fish's habitat.

For anglers, the net result of pollution means there will be fewer fish to catch. Fortunately, just as humans have created these undesirable conditions, there is much they can do to help improve fishing conditions. Becoming educated about how your lifestyle might be contributing to pollution is a good place to start. If you are not informed, it is difficult to make a difference.

The National Marine Fisheries Service, in conjunction with angling groups, created a Code of Angling Ethics for anglers. The code not only encompasses protecting aquatic resources, it extends to the actions of anglers when on the water. If every angler were to follow these guidelines, fish stocks would be sustained and places to fish would definitely be around for this and future generations of anglers. Here it is:

The Code of Angling Ethics

- Promotes, through education and practice, ethical behavior in the use of aquatic resources.

- Values and respects the aquatic environment and all living things in it.

- Avoids spilling and never dumps any pollutants, such as gasoline and oil, into the aquatic environment.

- Disposes of all trash, including worn lines, leaders, and hooks, in appropriate containers, and helps to keep fishing sites litter-free.

- Takes all precautionary measures necessary to prevent the spread of exotic plants and animals, including live baitfish, into non-native habitats.

- Learns and obeys angling and boating regulations, and treats other anglers, boaters, and property owners with courtesy and respect.

- Respects property rights, and never trespasses on private lands or waters.

- Keeps no more fish than needed for consumption, and never wastefully discards fish that are retained.

- Practices conservation by carefully handling and releasing alive all fish that are unwanted or prohibited by regulation, as well as other animals that may become hooked or entangled accidentally.

- Uses tackle and techniques that minimize harm to fish when engaging in "catch and release" angling.

Fishing Regulations

Anglers have a legal and moral obligation to follow the state's saltwater and freshwater fishing regulations. The goal of the regulations is to maintain a sustainable stock of each species so that anglers will have fish to catch whenever they go fishing. The quality fishing experience that all anglers want cannot be sustained without anglers voluntarily adhering to the regulations.

The regulations spell out which species of fish an angler can keep, what months of the year they are legal to possess, and what size of a particular species is legal to possess. The Florida Fish and Wildlife Conservation Commission (FWC) uses the best science available to establish the regulations and to decide if changes are necessary. This also includes emergency closures of a fishery in response to such things as environmental factors and evidence of overfishing. Not everyone may agree with all of the regulations or decisions, but that does not excuse an angler from adhering to them. The FWC does, I believe, make an outstanding effort to manage the saltwater and freshwater fisheries for anglers.

It is essential that all anglers have a copy of the most recent regulations and a measuring device with them every time they go fishing. Like every other law, ignorance of the regulations is not a valid excuse if you happen to be stopped by a law enforcement officer when you are fishing. You can learn more about the regulations by picking up copy of the saltwater and freshwater regulations at any bait and tackle shop or tax collector's office. This information is also available at *www.myfwc.com* (click on the link to fishing).

Catch-and-Release Fishing

Not only do Florida's current fishing regulations require the immediate release of numerous species of fish, many anglers voluntarily release fish they could legally keep. If you practice catch-and-release fishing, here are some tips on how to increase the chances of survival for the fish you release.

- Wet your hand, or better, use wet gloves (or a towel if you don't have gloves) to handle the fish at all times. The slime that you don't like to get on your hands is part of the fish's protective barrier to the environment. Gloves and towels help preserve the slime layer.

- Use a barbless hook. In some anglers' opinion barbless hooks are just as effective in catching fish as traditional barbed hooks. The secret to keeping a hooked fish on the line is to keep the line taunt and not allow any slack. Anglers may have to look around for a store that sells barbless hooks or make a barbed hook barbless by pinching down or filing off the barb of a conventional hook.

- Use a circle hook. Long used by commercial fishermen, circle hooks are now common in the recreational angling world. The advantage of a circle hook is that when the fish takes the bait, the hook almost always ends up in the fish's jaw, the easiest place to remove the hook.

- Use a hook removal tool. These are simple but useful tools that allow you to remove a hook without touching the fish. They take a bit of practice to learn how to use but once you do, it will a part of your tackle box forever.

- If the fish swallows the hook, you can try to remove it using needle-nose pliers. If you can't get it out, it is better to cut the leader as close to the hook as can be safely done and let the fish go.

- Play a hooked fish quickly. If the fish is exhausted by the time you get it to the boat, leave it in the water and give it a chance to recover before releasing it.

- Hold fish carefully when photographing your catch. If you want a grip-and-grin photo of you and your fish, hold the fish horizontally and supported from its belly and lower jaw. Don't hold it vertically by the mouth. Have the camera ready before talking the fish out of the water to minimize the time the fish is out of its natural environment. About as long as you can hold your breath is how long a fish should be out of the water.

- When it is time to release the fish, don't throw it overboard. Place the fish headfirst in the water and release it. If the fish does not swim off right away, gently hold it by the tail and bottom lip. You may also depress the lower jaw to open it and move the fish forward (never backwards) in the water to help get more water passing over the gills. When the fish has enough strength it will swim away.

- Never gaff a fish that you plan to release. It can cause tremendous injury to the fish.

- Use of a venting tool may be advised when fish are brought up from depths greater than 30 feet. The air bladders of some species, especially snappers and grouper, may become distended and cause the fish's stomach to evert and come out through its mouth. Using a venting device has been shown to work well on groupers but is of questionable value for snappers and other narrow-bodied fish. Venting tools are hollow needles about 1 to 1½ inches long that are inserted into the body of the fish at the tip of the pectoral fin at an angle of 60 to 75 degrees. Insert the needle slowly and stop when you hear air escape and you can see the distended belly go down. Do not insert the needle into the everted stomach. It will not solve the problem.

Mounting a Trophy Fish

A long time ago, anglers who wanted to mount their prized catch took the fish to the taxidermist. He would make a mold of the body, skin the fish and mount it on the replica created from the mold. Today all the taxidermist needs is a photograph and the length and girth of the fish to create your trophy mount. That way you can release the fish. The mount you get will be a fiberglass body that matches the size of the fish you caught and is painted to look like the fish you caught.

Which Rod and Reel?

Anglers face a multitude of fishing conditions in Florida and a myriad of rods and reels to choose from. Choosing the right rod and reel can be daunting. Spend a few hours at a store with a large selection of rods and reels and you will find the choices are nearly endless. Because there is no single rod and reel combination that is better than all others, you might end up buying a sharp-looking rod and reel that is woefully inadequate for what you are trying to catch or, worse, mismatched and destined to function poorly. Unless you plan to turn pro, most anglers can catch plenty of fish with a few basic combinations. Here are some guidelines that will help you select the right equipment for the type of fishing you have in mind.

Fresh Water

Rod and reel choice matters more to bass anglers than those who just want to catch panfish or catfish. If the latter is your goal, just about any lightweight rod and reel combo will work. Bass anglers tend to take fishing more seriously, and the well-equipped bass angler is likely to have up to a half-dozen different combos. Most anglers find they can get by with the following three combos:

- A 6-foot medium-action spinning rod with a reel that can accommodate 6- to 12-pound test monofilament line. If you are only going to use one combo, this is it. Use this for casting lures, plastic worms, or live shiners.
- A 6½- to 7-foot stiff rod and a trigger grip paired with a bait-casting reel. This is the basic worm rod. In experienced hands this rod will give you good control, which is what you need when trying to cast a plastic worm to the precise spot you want it to hit the water. You can also use this for flipping, a technique used when fishing in heavy cover.
- A 7-foot fiberglass rod with a high-speed reel commonly referred to as a crankbait combo. This is used when you want to fish with lures designed to dive below the surface.

Some anglers like to fly fish for bass and panfish. Depending on your skill level, a 7½- to 8½-foot rod with a reel rated for 5- to 8-weight line will work. And for pure simplicity, the traditional cane pole is a great way to introduce kids to fishing or for adults to enjoy fishing the way their parents or grandparents did.

Salt Water

The saltwater environment is varied and the tackle needed to be successful changes with the place you are fishing. By location, here are some guidelines on the type of rods and reels to use:

Bay and Backwaters – A good all-around choice is a 6- to 7-foot medium-action spinning rod and reel. The reel should be balanced to the rod and be capable of holding at least 150 yards of 8- to 15-pound test monofilament line. With this combo you can fish with live bait, jigs, and lures for the most popular estuarine species, including snook, spotted seatrout, and redfish. If some of the larger redfish or tarpon over 50 pounds are your target, use a stiffer rod and matching reel with 15- to 25-pound test line.

Fly fishing is very popular and a 7- to 9-weight rod and matching reel will work for catching snook, redfish, and small tarpon. For the bigger tarpon a 12-weight combo is a good choice.

Bridges and Piers – A stout 8-foot rod and reel rated to handle 20- to 40-pound test line is a good choice when you are elevated above the water more than 10 feet. Some veteran bridge and pier anglers will use up to a 12-foot rod if they are looking to catch some of the bigger fish that frequent these locations. The stiffer combo is also beneficial in keeping a hooked fish from getting back into the pilings. Once the fish gets into some cover, you have lost and the fish has won. If the fish doesn't break the line, you will end up doing it. When you feel the fish bite, keep its head up in the first few seconds and you have a chance. That is where the stiff rod will help.

Using a lighter combo such as the ones recommended for bays and backwaters creates anther problem when it's time to haul your catch out of the water. If the fish is over a few pounds, the line can break as you raise the fish. And if you try to raise the fish while holding your rod perpendicular to the water and letting the rod flex, it can snap. In these instances, use a bridge net that you can drop down to the surface of the water and use to raise the fish.

Surf – Surf fishing is popular along both coasts. But there are significant differences in the type of gear that you use when fishing along the beaches of the Gulf of Mexico versus the Atlantic Ocean. From Tarpon Springs southward, Gulf coast surf anglers can use a 6½- to 7-foot fast- or medium-action spinning combo capable of handling 10- to 15-pound test line. Most of the fish are caught in the trough that parallels the shoreline and is only a few feet from the beach.

Along the Atlantic coast, surf anglers must be capable of casting much further offshore to reach the troughs and the fish. Consequently, surf anglers typically use stiff 9- to 12-foot "surf" rods with reels spooled with 15- to 30-pound test line. To increase the casting distance, add a 2- to 5-ounce sinker.

Offshore – Offshore angling requires a wider variety of rods and reels than other types of saltwater angling. Bottom fishing for grouper, snappers, and their allies is done using "boat tackle," short, stiff rods and heavy-duty open-face or spinning reels. The rods range from 5½ to 6½ feet in length with reels having 150 yards or more of 20- to 40-pound test line. When fishing for pelagic species such as permit, amberjack, dolphin, and king mackerel, a medium-stiff 6½- to

7-foot rod with a spinning reel capable of holding at least 200 yards for at least 15-pound test line is the preferred combo. Anglers can cast these rigs to fish that are close to the boat.

When trolling for big kings, dolphin, sailfish, and marlin, specially designed rods and reels with star drags and the capability to hold 200 yards or more of 20-pound (or more) test line are necessary. A warning about this type of fishing: A high-quality rod and reel will cost well over $1,000, and you will need at least two rigs; four would be better if you plan to troll for the big fish.

Terminal Tackle: The End of the Line

Terminal tackle is the stuff at the end of the line—hooks, leader line, weights (sinkers), floats, beads, rattles, snaps, and swivels. The hook size, sinker weight, type and length of leader line—and how to connect everything together using knots, snaps, or swivels—varies depending on the fishing conditions. The key to catching fish lies in knowing which combination is needed to catch what you are targeting. A good way to get the right terminal tackle for your fishing conditions is to consult with the staff at a bait and tackle store. Tell them what you are fishing for and ask for some suggestions.

Fresh Water

If you are fishing for panfish, the simplest of terminal rigs will work—a small hook tied to the end of the line. Often a float (bobber) is attached to the line so that it is easier to know when a fish is biting and it's time to set the hook.

The term "small hook" is relative, so keep in mind the species you are targeting. Small mouth equals small hook. Hook manufacturers use a sizing system with size 1 being in the middle of the range of sizes. Hook sizes 2, 3, 4, etc., get progressively smaller, while hooks progressively larger than size 1 are referred to as 1/0 (pronounced *one aught*), 2/0, 3/0, etc.

Bass fishing is the most popular type of freshwater fishing in Florida. Fishing for this highly prized gamefish is done using live baitfish, artificial lures, or plastic worms. If using live baits, the terminal tackle consists of 18–32 inches of leader line with a hook tied to the end of the leader. A small sinker may be used if fishing in deeper water to help get the baitfish down to the bottom and to keep it there. Some anglers may also use a float. If using artificial lures, simply replace the hook with the lure and remove the weight and float if using either. When fishing with lures most anglers tie the hook or lure directly to the leader and avoid using snaps and swivels.

When using a plastic worm, there are two common ways to rig the terminal tackle. The Texas rig uses a weight, usually a bullet-shaped one, threaded onto the line immediately in front of the hook. The worm is rigged on the hook, and the weight essentially rests against the leading edge of the worm. The other popular set-up is the Carolina rig. For this the weight is threaded onto the line and is kept from reaching the hook and worm by using a swivel to tie the leader line to the line on your reel. This is also an instance where anglers may want to use a plastic bead between the weight and the swivel to reduce fraying of the knot by the weight.

Salt Water

Leader line is an essential when saltwater fishing. For most species it will be a monofilament or fluorocarbon leader. When fishing for king mackerel, sharks, and other fish with a mouthful of sharp teeth, use a multistrand steel leader. About the shortest length of leader line used is 24 inches. It will be a higher pound test than the line on the reel. For popular species such as snook and redfish, 20- to 40-pound test is sufficient. When going after big tarpon, 40- to 100-pound test leader would be the choice.

Most saltwater fishing is done using live bait, a piece of cut bait, or an artificial lure. When bait fishing or using cut bait, the basic rig is simple—leader line with a hook at the end. Without a weight, the free-lined rig can be cast and retrieved much like an artificial lure. Add a weight and the rig can be fished on the bottom or in places where there is a strong current. Typically, an egg sinker is threaded onto the line above the swivel connecting the line and leader line. Anglers have a choice of offset (does not lie flat) or straight hooks (lie flat).

Two other variations of the bait fishing rig involve using floats. The fixed float rig involves adding a float at a fixed height above the hook. This sets the depth the bait will be suspended below the surface. The other variation is to use a popping cork float. It also suspends the bait at a fixed depth but has an added feature to attract fish. The cork makes a popping sound when the angler twitches the line. This sound attracts curious fish and is particularly effective when fishing for spotted seatrout.

When using artificial lures, the lure is typically tied directly to the leader line. There are many types of lures, but most fall into one of the following classes: jigs, soft-bodied lures, or hard-bodied lures.

Surf, bridge, and pier anglers might use a modified bottom rig called a pyramid rig. The line is tied to one part of a three-way swivel. A separate leader with a hook at the end is tied to the second part and another length of leader with a weight is tied to the third part.

A Dozen Tackle Tips

1. Learn how to tie good knots. Unless you are cut off when the fish runs the line across an oyster, rock, or other submerged structure, chances are you lost the fish because the knot connecting the line to the leader line or the leader line to the hook failed. There are dozens of knots and some are more popular in one region than another. The following are ones that are considered reliable and easy to tie: line to hook, swivel, or lure—Uni and Palomar; line to line—Uni to Uni and Albright.

2. Monofilament line stretches up to 20%. The advantage of this is that it reduces the sudden stress a fish puts on a line when pulling against the drag. The disadvantage is that it gives the fish a chance to head into cover before you can turn its head.

3. Braided and fused lines have virtually no stretch, which gives you a better chance of turning the fish's head towards you and away from the bottom. The disadvantage is that all of the shock of the fish on the line is transferred to the rod and drag on the reel. A poorly made rod or reel may not survive the shock of the initial strike.

4. Replace the line on your reels on a regular basis. The frequency with which you should do this depends on the number of times you fish and how many fish you are catching. When monofilament line stretches, it does not return to its original shape. Over time it will permanently stretch out. You can't see this, so err on the side of caution and change it sooner rather than later.

5. Examine the terminal end of your line frequently. Look for cuts, nicks, and abrasions in the line and leader line. At a minimum, do this every time you catch a fish or feel the line run over a rough bottom. Fishing line's strength is significantly reduced when the line is damaged. Often the damage is near the hook or lure and all that's necessary is to cut off the damaged portion and retie the hook or lure. It may take few minutes, but you will lose fewer fish this way.

6. Don't leave monofilament line exposed to the sun. The ultraviolet rays destroy the line. If your line looks or feels chalky, replace the line.

7. Don't discard fishing line in the water. For that matter, never throw any trash in the water. Fishing line does not break down over time and longer lengths of line, especially if dangling from a branch of a mangrove or other tree, can entangle a bird and lead to its death. Recycling boxes are found at many boat ramps and on piers and bridges. Additionally, most bait and tackle shops accept line for recycling.

8. Use a swivel to connect the leader line to the line if you are using a sliding sinker weight. If no weight or a split shot is used, tie the leader directly to the line.

9. When tying the leader line to a lure, use a loop knot to secure the lure to the line if you don't use a split ring between the line and the lure. If a split ring is used, a tight knot such as the Uni can be used to tie the line to the split ring.

10. Salt water corrodes metal. Always rinse off rods, reels, and lures after a day of saltwater fishing. Let everything dry before putting away. Follow the manufacturer's direction for keeping reels properly lubricated

11. Keep hooks sharp. Use a hook sharpener. Even fresh-out-of-the-package hooks can stand to be sharpened before using.

12. Buying quality tackle pays off. Pay special attention to the guides on the rod and the drag in the reel. Look to see if the guides are corrosion resistant and smooth on the inside. Make sure the drag is made from quality components. Don't be shy about asking the retailer to help you find the best quality for the money you plan to spend.

Baits: What Turns a Fish on?

The debate over which bait and lures work best will never be resolved because there is no best lure for a particular type of fishing. That said, there is a general consensus that for freshwater fishing live wild shiners are the bait of choice for trophy largemouth bass, and live Missouri minnows are the best bait for crappie. On the saltwater side, live shrimp would get the nod as being the most commonly used saltwater baits for inshore and nearshore species, and a trolled ballyhoo takes top honors as the best bluewater bait. When it comes to lures and flies, there as many opinions on what works best as there are anglers in Florida.

Fresh Water

Live bait – Live shiners are a good choice, especially for inexperienced anglers. The bait provides the action that attracts the fish and this gives the angler more time to focus on the bite and setting the hook. Native shiners are preferable to aquaculture-grown ones. Both are usually available at bait and tackle shops. Anglers can net their own shiners so long as they are eight inches or less in length. Alternatives to wild shiners include whole pickerel and panfish (bluegill, redear sunfish, redbreast sunfish, spotted sunfish, flier, and warmouth). If caught by the angler, he/she can use these fish whole or parts thereof. Other live baits used for bass include crayfish, frogs, and worms (large night crawlers are best).

If panfish are the target, small minnows, crickets, grasshoppers, freshwater shrimp, insect larvae, and red worms are the most popular baits. For crappie, which tend to run a bit larger, Missouri minnows are the live bait of choice.

Artificial lures – There is a huge selection of lures for largemouth bass, crappie, and panfish. Any one of them can catch fish if the conditions are right and the lure is presented in a way that attracts the fish's attention. For bass, plastic worms are one of the most popular choices. These baits come in a variety of colors, shapes, and lengths. Many now are also impregnated with scents designed to enhance their attractiveness. Plastic worms are fished on and beneath the surface. Darker colors tend to be more effective with black, grape, and root beer being some of the more popular colors.

Surface plugs, diving lures, and spinnerbaits are the other common choices for bass anglers. There are at least a dozen major manufacturers and many smaller companies that, when you throw in color patterns, provide bass anglers hundreds of options to choose from.

Surface plugs are a good choice early in the morning or late in the day during the hot summer months. Bass will feed on the surface when the water is cool and when a big bass busts your lure as it skims along the surface, it certainly provides an extra thrill. Diving lures, including spoons and shallow-and deep-diving crank baits work when the water is warmer because the bass will be in the deeper and cooler parts of lakes. They are especially popular when fishing submerged structures or along the edges of areas of vegetation.

Many of Florida's lakes are infested with excessive growth of exotic plants such as hydrilla. In severe cases, the weeds form large, dense floating mats that can cover much of a lake's surface. The state and most counties have ongoing programs to remove and control exotic plant species. Slowly and expensively, some progress is being made. Anglers have a love-hate relationship with exotic species. While they provide good cover for bass and other freshwater species, to effectively fish these weed patches, you need to cast accurately and use weedless hooks or be prepared to pull weeds out of your lure after every cast.

Flies – Fly fishing for bass and panfish is not as popular as saltwater fly fishing. That said, there is no reason why you can't fly fish for freshwater fish. Because these fish do not have flies presented them very often, anglers might be surprised with the results. Poppers, deceivers, streamers, and other fish-style patterns are common choices. But, there are no hard and fast rules on which flies to use when seeking bass, panfish, or crappie. Experiment with different patterns and colors and see what works best—something fly fishing enthusiasts like to do anyway.

Salt Water

Live bait – Live shrimp are the most commonly used saltwater bait because of their widespread distribution, abundant supply, and reasonable cost. They work well because shrimp are common inhabitants throughout the coastal waters of the state and naturally make up an important part of the diet for fish inhabiting these waters. The key to using shrimp is to keep them alive and allow them to continue their natural kicking motion once they are hooked. Shrimp will live the longest if hooked through the tail, but this restricts their natural movement. Hooking them in the head allows for a more natural action but anglers must be careful not to hook the shrimp through its vital organs. One method is to place the hook through the carapace (the large unsegmented piece of shell behind the eyes). The other method, and the one that allows for the best casting, is to hook the shrimp from beneath the head and bring the hook out through the top of the carapace just behind the eyes. In both instances, avoid the dark spots beneath the carapace as these include vital organs such as the heart and stomach.

Live shrimp are not the only live bait that works. Many anglers will pass up shrimp if they can get live baitfish. Most baitfish species are difficult to keep alive so they are seldom sold in bait shops. To get these prized baits, anglers must net their own using a cast net. One good cast can provide over a hundred baitfish. They can also be caught using a sabiki rig; a string of small gold hooks tied to a segment of light line with a weight at the end of the line. The rig is jigged up and down in a school of baitfish. They will readily strike at these shiny hooks. No matter how you catch them, a live bait well is required as these fish will not survive unless they are held in a tank where there is plenty of running water that is being constantly resupplied.

Schools of baitfish can be found around pilings and channel markers or in open water areas. Finding them is as simple as looking for the nervous water (ripples on the surface) created by a school of baitfish, visually spotting them in the water, or watching where birds such as pelicans and terns are diving into the water and feeding on the fish. There are numerous species of small fish and not every one is suited to be used as bait. Among the most popular baitfish found in the coastal waters are the scaled sardine, gulf menhaden, mullet (small ones are known as finger mullet), threadfin herring, blue runners, and ballyhoo. Pinfish don't form big schools like the others, but they are abundant and are in high demand by anglers seeking grouper and snapper.

There is a rule of thumb when saltwater fishing: The bigger the bait, the bigger the fish you can catch. Anglers fishing offshore often want larger baitfish such as grunts, pinfish, and squirrelfish in the 6- to 12-inch range. These are a preferred bait when fishing for 10-pound or larger grouper or snapper.

There are also a few specialty live baits that are preferred mainly by one species that deserve to be mentioned. Permit and tarpon love small crabs. Some bait shops sell them when they can get them. Otherwise, anglers may find small crabs attached to floating seaweed or debris that they can dip-net or catch using crab traps. Pompano will readily hit sand fleas, odd-looking crustaceans that anglers can dig up from the beaches (more commonly on the Atlantic coast) using a sand flea rake. Finally, sheepshead show a preference for fiddler crabs, which anglers can collect along muddy shorelines around mangroves.

Cut bait – Dead shrimp, squid, and chunks of fish make excellent bait for a large variety of fish. They have the advantage of being easy to use; simply stick it on your hook and toss it in the water. Cut bait works because the oils that are released attract nearby fish. Also, don't think that cut bait is only for catching small fish. A dead catfish with its fins cut off or a whole mullet are two of the better baits for catching large tarpon.

Small pieces of shrimp, the size of a pea or lima bean, are also used to tip the hook on a jig. This creates a particularly effective bait for species such as snook, redfish, and spotted seatrout. Don't use too large of a piece as it can interfere with the jigging action of the lure.

Chum – Saltwater anglers use chum to stir up the action by attracting fish and getting them in the mood to bite. Chum comes in an infinite variety of forms. Just about any leftover part of a fish can be ground up to make chum. There are dozens of recipes and any one that creates a stinky mess is bound to work. You can even use cat food (generally the cheapest stuff you can find) as chum. Fortunately, you don't have to make your own. Blocks of frozen chum are readily available at bait and tackle shops. When ready to chum, simply put it in a mesh bag and toss it overboard.

Artificial lures – The choices saltwater anglers face are staggering. Hard-bodied lures are made from plastic, wood, and metal and typically have one to three sets of treble hooks dangling beneath them. They include styles that float or dive to various depths. Jigs and spoons are other types of lures commonly used by saltwater anglers. Jigs come in a variety of sizes, colors, and designs. The hook can be tipped with a small piece of shrimp. The most popular spoons are metal with a gold or silver finish.

Soft-bodied lures are made from injection-molded plastics and a few other composite compounds. They are shaped to imitate baitfish, shrimp, marine worms, eels, crabs, and other natural critters. All are designed to look like the real thing and often have a scent that is cooked into the plastic while it is being molded. The key to using these lures is in the skill of the angler to make an inanimate object appear real enough to get a fish to bite.

Flies – Saltwater fly fishing is a popular sport in Florida. Most areas have at least one specialty shop that caters to the fly fishing crowd. These stores sell the most popular flies for the area and the materials to tie your own. Larger streamers, deceivers, and crab patterns are the most popular styles. The colors and material used in these patterns have some regional variation.

Tides

Anglers have a much better chance of catching fish if they know the times of the high and low tides. Fish are most active when the water is ebbing or flowing. In coastal waters this equates to the tide coming in and going out. It also applies offshore where the water does have a pattern of movement, but it is harder to detect. As a general rule there will be two high tides and two low tides each day. This is not a consistent pattern across the state, and there are times each month when an area may have one or three tides in a day. Additionally, tides can be enhanced, dampened, or even canceled by the wind blowing in the same or opposite direction as the water is moving.

What matters for anglers is knowing when the water is on the move. There is a longstanding debate as to whether fishing is better on an incoming or outgoing tide—or if it even maters. What may be more important is when, during the time the water is moving, is the better time to fish? Experienced anglers generally consider one to two hours before the high and low tides to be the best time to fish. Monthly tide charts are available at most bait and tackle stores. There are also several software programs that provide information on the tides. To maximize your chances of catching fish, always know the tides before you go fishing.

Fish Hangouts

Finding and catching fish is easier if you understand their habits. While fish's brains are no match for ours, their instincts allow them to win more than their fair share of the battles with anglers. The most important point to keep in mind is that, with the exception of a few open-water species such as sailfish and marlin, fish like to be around structures—reefs, pilings, rocky bottoms, or any other submerged object that provides refuge and/or may hold a meal for the larger fish.

In the aquatic ecosystem, there is no such thing as a free lunch. Small fish are consumed by slightly larger fish, and the slightly larger fish are merely a food source for fish that are a size-class larger. Only the largest fish need not fear being some other fish's lunch. Submerged structures provide habitat and a place for small and large fish to find another fish a bit smaller and suitable for the larger fish's next meal.

This is why so much effort goes into finding structure when fishing. Find structure and there is a very good chance there will be fish nearby. In fresh water, submerged logs, flooded timberland, submerged aquatic vegetation, and rocky areas tend to be where anglers find and catch fish. In salt water, mangrove shorelines, oyster bars, rocky bottoms, and artificial reefs and wrecks are where anglers catch fish.

A good bottom-profiling machine is one of the most effective tools an angler can have when fishing. These electronic devices are anglers' eyes below the surface. But finding structure is not always easy. There are thousands of square miles of potentially fishable habitat in Florida. Finding these locations offshore is a hit-or-miss proposition unless you have someone who is willing to share the locations of known fish hangouts with you.

For anglers who primarily fish in the estuarine waters of the many bays, lagoons, and estuaries and are willing to put forth the effort, one of the best ways to find submerged structure is to visit the area you plan to fish during times when the tide is lower than normal. In the shallow waters, many areas are exposed and you can see where the structure is located and store that information on your GPS for future reference.

Ten Tips on Techniques

1. When bottom fishing, use just enough weight to get the bait to the bottom and keep it there. Too much weight makes it difficult to feel a bite, and not enough weight allows currents to sweep your bait off the bottom and out of the strike zone.

2. When bottom fishing, let the bait drop to the bottom, and then reel in the line until you can see and feel tension on the line. Keep tension in the line at all times so you can feel the bite.

3. When fishing over any structure and you feel a bite, the first few seconds are critical to your chances of landing the fish. In one fluid motion, reel in any slack and then jerk upwards hard enough to set the hook but not so hard that you jerk it out of the fish's mouth. The goal is to turn the fish's head upwards towards the surface and not allow the fish to drag you into the structure. If the fish goes down, chances are very good you will never land the fish.

4. Casting requires accuracy, so practice, practice, practice. If there is one way that will guarantee you catching more fish, it is being able to place the bait in the zone where the fish are most likely to be found. Sometimes you can see the fish; other times you are relying on your knowledge that the fish will be around

the structure. In either case, if you can't cast to the spot you want the bait to be, you are not going to have a very high success rate of catching fish. The only way to get better is to keep casting.

5. If using an artificial lure, retrieval speed matters. A general rule of thumb is the colder the water, the slower the retrieve. Cold water slows down fish so they need more time to react. Exceptions to this rule apply to the open ocean species such as king mackerel, sailfish, and dolphin. They are fast swimmers and thus will be more likely to strike fast-moving lures.

6. When surf fishing, learn how to read the water along the beach. Most fish are in the troughs that parallel the shoreline and are often less than 25 feet offshore along the Gulf coast and 100 feet off the Atlantic coast. Along the Atlantic coast, there will be washouts perpendicular to the troughs that allow water to move out to sea. Washouts change location, but if you can find them, fish them.

7. Along the Gulf coast, try wading to the sandbar on the outside of the trough. It is usually less than 50 feet from the shoreline. Cast back toward the shore and begin the retrieve. This gives the bait the natural appearance of coming from the surf zone back into the waters of the trough as the waves recede.

8. Learn how to use a cast net. Like accurate casting, it takes practice. Live baitfish are one of the best baits, but you have to catch your own.

9. When fishing from bridges and piers, fish straight down near the pilings. Remember, fish like structure and you need to use stout tackle capable of turning the fish's head before it can take you into the structure and cut you off.

10. When fishing offshore for fast-swimming fish such as cobia, wahoo, permit, king mackerel, and amberjack, be aware and expect the fish to peel off a hundred yards of line in a matter of seconds. If you are at anchor, there won't be time to pull up the anchor so use a quick-release anchor system. This allows you to quickly release the anchor line and retrieve it later. This frees you up to drift or start the engine and follow a fish determined to run away and strip the line off your reel.

Protecting Yourself from the Sun and Heat

Florida is nicknamed the Sunshine State for good reason. The daily dose of sun may be good for tourism, but overexposure to the sun's ultraviolet (UV) rays is not good for your skin. Anglers should take appropriate precautions to prevent sunburn and reduce their risk of skin cancer. Remember to protect yourself from UV rays reflected off the water as well as from directly overhead—you can suffer sunburn even while standing in the shade of a boat awning or other cover. Also be aware that UV rays are present even on cloudy days. You will get a sunburn if you skip the sunscreen on an overcast day.

Use a good sunblock lotion with an SPF (Sun Protection Factor) of at least 15. If you're going to be fishing all day and there are no places to get out of the sun, or if you have very sensitive skin, use a sunblock with as high a rating as you can find. Some lotions are sweat- or water-proof, an advantage in most angling situations. To obtain the maximum benefit, apply the lotion to all exposed skin about twenty minutes before going outside. Don't forget ears, nose, face, back of the neck, and—if wearing sandals, or going barefoot—tops of feet. During the day, reapply as necessary, especially if you've been swimming or perspiring heavily. Overuse of sunblock is seldom a problem. Some people also use lip balm with sunscreen in it.

Consider wearing long pants and a long-sleeved shirt to minimize exposed skin. A hat (preferably with a wide brim) and sunglasses are as essential as a rod and reel. Most anglers swear by polarized sunglasses, which reduce glare off the water's surface and allow you to see beneath the surface.

Hot and humid weather also places people at risk of heat exhaustion or life-threatening heat stroke. Symptoms of heat exhaustion include feeling faint or dizzy; heavy sweating; skin that is cool, moist, and pale; headache; and heat cramps. If these symptoms are left untreated they can quickly lead to the more serious heat stroke, a life-threatening event. If you suspect someone has heat exhaustion, get the person out of the sun. If possible, lay the person down, loosen their clothing, and elevate their legs. Have the person drink cool liquids that are nonalcoholic and caffeine-free. A good way to cool someone is to moisten their skin or clothing and fan the person.

Heat strokes occur when the body's cooling mechanisms no longer work. The main symptom is an elevated body temperature above 104° F. Unless you have a way to measure this, look for the other signs: rapid heartbeat and/or shallow breathing, cessation of sweating, disorientation or confusion, headache and/or nausea, and fainting. A heat stroke is a medical emergency. If possible, call 911 and request help. Until help arrives, move the victim to a cool, shady spot and remove or loosen tight clothing. Apply cool water to the entire body and fan the person. If the person is conscious and can swallow, give sips of cool water.

Potentially Problematic Plants and Animals

Florida is blessed with an abundance of plants and animals. Fortunately, most of these are harmless, but a few species can turn a fun day outdoors into something less than a pleasant experience. Here's a brief rundown of some of the plants and animals to avoid.

Poison Ivy – This vinelike plant with shiny leaves in clusters of three grows along the ground and up trees and fence posts. Urushiol is the chemical in poison ivy that makes a person itch and develop a rash. Symptoms show up anywhere from a few minutes to several hours after contact. If you do come in contact with poison ivy, wash the oil off before it's absorbed into the skin. Use water (no soap—it removes protective skin oils) to thoroughly rinse the area. If a rash or blisters develop, treat them with a hydrocortisone cream. Don't worry about spreading the rash. Contrary to widespread belief, the blisters do not contain the oil from the plant, and the rash is not contagious. Do see a doctor if the rash is on your face, genitals, or covers more than one-quarter of your skin surface.

Brazilian Pepper – This exotic shrub, originally brought to this country for its ornamental value, is in the same family as poison ivy. Brazilian pepper can grow almost tree-sized and is common along the banks of canals in central and south Florida. Some people who are sensitive to poison ivy may also have a reaction to Brazilian pepper if they come in contact with the plant. Treat it the same way you treat poison ivy.

Mosquitoes – These pesky bugs can drive anglers to distraction, and they also carry diseases, including a potentially fatal form of encephalitis. But a good defense against them is as close as a can of insect repellent. Those with DEET in them seem to work best, but this harsh chemical is a skin irritant to some people. It should not be used excessively and is not recommended for children. Citronella-based and other natural repellents are also effective. If it's not too hot, wear long pants and a long-sleeved shirt with tightly woven cloth. These clothes can be sprayed with insect repellent. Treat bites with anti-itch topical creams or ointments. Ones with hydrocortisone and an antihistamine seem to be most effective.

No-See-Ums – No-see-ums are a type of insect known as a midge, and they rank at the top of the list of annoying critters for many anglers. If you're being bitten by something but can't find anything to swat at, say hello to the no-see-um. Use insect repellents to keep them off your body. If the wind is blowing over and off a wetland area such as a mangrove-covered island and you happen to be on the downwind side, it's possible for a mass of no-see-ums to blow your way and begin to bite. The best defense when this occurs is to move away as quickly as possible.

Fire ants – Another imported pest, the fire ant is now a problem for the entire southern half of the country. Fire ants build mounds that look like small piles of dirt. If you accidentally step on one, a swarm of ants will attack in seconds. The bites are about as painful as a bee sting and some people may suffer allergic reactions. Fire ant mounds are found along river and lake shorelines and even on sandy beaches.

If you feel one bite, expect more. The chances are good that you have more than one ant on you. Get them off as soon as possible. Be careful because many people get bites on their hands as they brush the ants off their feet and legs.

Relief comes from a benzocaine-based product for the pain and a hydrocortisone cream to relieve the itching. A puss-filled blister often arises at the site of the bite several days later. Resist the temptation to rupture the blister as that may lead to an infection and more pain.

Chiggers – Chiggers are the larval form of mites, a group of small but annoying arachnids. The chances of seeing or feeling a chigger crawling on you is essentially zero, but rises to 100 percent once they bite and inject their saliva, which contains strong digestive enzymes that destroy the surrounding tissue. The chigger then feeds on this. To protect yourself, spray your shoes and ankles with repellent specifically designed to be applied to clothing. At the end of the day, and hopefully before they bite, you can wash chiggers off your skin by taking a shower or bath. If itchy, irritated areas develop, an anti-itch cream and a few days' time will solve the problem.

Ticks – Ticks are gaining more attention thanks to the deer tick and Lyme disease, both of which occur in Florida. We also have the more familiar and larger dog tick, which can carry some diseases.

Watch for ticks on your clothing or skin whenever you walk through tall brush or grass. They typically hitch rides on feet and legs and begin crawling upward, searching for a warm site to dig in. Flick them off before they attach. Don't try to crush them between fingertips—this can release disease-carrying body fluids. A permethrin spray on your clothing, especially from the knees to the feet, helps keep ticks off.

If a tick attaches itself, carefully remove it by grasping as much of the head and mouthparts as possible with tweezers. Then gently pull out with a steady motion. Do not twist the tick when pulling it out. The goal is to make sure you get all of the tick, including its mouth parts. Do not try to remove the tick by burning it or smothering it with Vaseline, oil, or alcohol. Treat the wound to avoid infection and watch for flu-like symptoms that may signal a tick-borne disease.

Bees, hornets, yellowjackets, and wasps – Florida has them all, including a few killer bees. Reactions to the sting from one of these creatures range from mild to life-threatening, although the latter is rare. There is no bee and wasp repellent that you can apply to your skin or clothing. The best way to avoid being stung is to look for and avoid these insects and their hives or nests. You can also lessen your chances of attracting trouble by wearing white or earth-tone clothing. Avoid colognes, perfumes, and fruity or flowery shampoos. If stung, apply one of the sting-relief products that can be purchased at any pharmacy. For bee stings, make sure the stinger is removed as soon as possible. If necessary, apply ice to reduce swelling and take an antihistamine to relieve itching. Watch for signs of a serious reaction—excessive swelling, undue anxiety, shortness of breath, and itching or hives. Seek medical help immediately if these symptoms develop.

Scorpions – The few species of scorpions living in Florida prefer to remain hidden most of the time. Keep your hands out of dark crevices and shake out your shoes before putting them on. The sting of the most common scorpion in the state is on par with a good bee sting. It is not considered life-threatening unless you have a special sensitivity to the venom. If a scorpion does bite, apply ice to reduce swelling and take ibuprofen or acetaminophen for the pain. Watch for an allergic reaction and seek medical treatment if symptoms develop.

Spiders – All spiders can bite but only two are considered dangerous. The black widow's venom causes abdominal pain, muscle cramps, nausea, swelling around the eyes, and possibly shock. The brown recluse's venom destroys the tissue around the bite site, resulting in an open wound on the skin. It is subject to infection and can take months to heal. Spider bites are often relatively painless and may go unnoticed until secondary symptoms appear. If you suspect a black widow or brown recluse bit you, seek medical attention immediately.

Jellyfish – Jellyfish have transparent tentacles with thousands of stinging cells that can raise itching, burning welts on contact. Some stings are toxic enough to cause more severe reactions, including anaphylactic shock, which can be life-threatening. Be especially wary of the Portuguese man-of-war; its tentacles grow to more than 10 feet long and each is armed with thousands of stinging cells. The bluish to pinkish float is a distinguishing mark for this potentially dangerous species.

Wind may blow jellyfish and man-of-wars into the surf zone and onto shore. Wave action may break the nearly invisible tentacles into small pieces that can still sting. Staying out of the water is the only sure way to prevent being stung (also watch where you step when walking on the beach). If stung, rinse the affected area with seawater (freshwater ruptures the stinging cells, making matters worse). Then rinse again with vinegar or rubbing alcohol. If the pain is severe or covers a large portion of the victim's skin, seek medical help.

Stingrays – Some species of stingrays inhabit the shallow waters where surf and wade anglers like to tread. If a person accidently steps on one, the serrated barb at the base of the fish's tail can sting a person, usually in the foot or ankle. The puncture wound is painful, with pronounced swelling, and often becomes infected.

Wear an old pair of shoes when walking through shallow waters. It's also a good idea to do the "stingray shuffle"—shuffle your feet to avoid stepping directly on top of these bottom dwellers. If you are stung, flush the wound with fresh water and then apply hot water (as hot as the person can stand). The venom is protein-based and hot water denatures the protein and thus reduces the pain. Some people may have an allergic reaction or develop an infection after being stung. Monitor the wound and seek medical attention if any signs of an allergic reaction or an infection develops.

Barracuda and Amberjack – What makes two fish, one with a large mouth full of razor-sharp teeth and the other with a much smaller and basically toothless mouth, worthy of a listing in the dangerous plants and animals section? Rest assured it's not because the fish are likely to attack a person, although there are a few documented instances of barracuda leaping out of the water and striking anglers in boats. Actually, these fish are potentially dangerous because of what happens if you eat the meat from either of these species.

Both species, especially barracuda, can have high concentrations of ciguatera toxin, which is passed on to people who eat the meat of these fish. Ciguatera toxin is produced by microscopic organisms that live around coral reefs and other hard submerged structures. The toxin accumulates in the tissues of fish feeding around reefs. Barracuda and permit that feed on reef-dwelling fish can accumulate levels of ciguatera that can make humans sick.

The problem is that ciguatera has no taste or smell, you can't see it, and it isn't destroyed by cooking or freezing the meat. There's no simple way to tell if your catch of the day will make you sick, and the price for such uncertainty may be high. The toxin attacks the nervous system and intestinal tract. Symptoms include vomiting, diarrhea, and numbness or tingling around the mouth and in the arms and legs. There may also be pain in the teeth, painful urination, and blurred vision. A few people have a more severe reaction with muscle pain, dizziness, and sensations of temperature reversal. Most cases last two to three weeks, but some persons can suffer for months. A doctor can help ease the symptoms, but there is no known cure. Consequently, those who know about ciguatera don't eat barracuda and amberjack, especially ones caught in the Florida Keys.

Health Warning

Most fish caught by anglers are safe to consume, but since *Fishing Florida* was published in 1995, the list of fish to avoid or limit consumption of has grown. It is a shame that anglers who want to eat what they catch have to consult the state's Department of Health to determine if the fish they caught are safe to eat. This is especially true for young children and women of childbearing age as they can be more adversely affected by consuming tainted fish. There are many more warnings for this group, so it is advised to check the list and limit your consumption as indicated.

Mercury remains the primary contaminant of fish. However, there are also some warnings about specific pesticides, including dioxin. As more testing is done, the list of fish consumption advisories changes. The most up-to-date information can be found on the Florida Department of Health website, *www. doh.state.fl.us/floridafishadvice*. For most freshwater fish, consumption of once per week to once per month is commonly recommended. There are some areas where consumption by children and women of childbearing age is not advised at all. While there are DO NOT EAT sites throughout the state, many of the DO NOT EAT warnings are found at freshwater areas in southeast Florida.

For saltwater fish, most are safe to eat from once per week to once per month. For children and women of childbearing age DO NOT EAT warnings in 2009 existed for blackfin tuna, cobia, king mackerel, little tunny, all shark species, and crevalle jack (in Biscayne and Florida Bays and the Florida Keys). The DO NOT EAT advisory for all other individuals is limited to king mackerel over 31 inches fork length and all sharks 43 inches and longer.

Boating

While there are plenty of quality land-based fishing spots in Florida, fishing from a boat adds a new dimension. It allows you to search for the fish rather than have to wait for the fish to find you. A boat is also the best way to see and enjoy some of the scenery and other wildlife that the state has to offer.

This book lists dozens of boat ramps that provide access to every part of central Florida's coastal and offshore waters, as well as freshwater lakes and rivers.

Refer to the listings in this book for specific directions and, for many sites, addresses to all the major public boat ramps in each county. Additionally, many marinas rent boats ranging from canoes and simple jon boats to pontoon boats and cruisers large enough for a safe, comfortable day of offshore fishing.

Whether you use your own boat or rent one, safety on the water is taken seriously in Florida. In addition to FWC law enforcement officers, many coastal counties have their own marine enforcement units. Officers frequently stop anglers to check for safety equipment, fishing licenses, and violations of fishing regulations. Before you board any boat, make sure that it has the safety equipment required by the Coast Guard and the vessel's registration. It is also a very good idea to have the most current summary of the state and Gulf or Atlantic federal fishing regulations.

Boaters should also note that Florida has a strict DUI law for boaters. If you are suspected of drinking while operating a boat, a law enforcement officer can administer a field sobriety test. If you fail, they will take you to jail.

Fishing Guides

Fishing with a guide can make the difference between a fishing trip that is memorable and one that you'd just as soon forget. Guides have the local knowledge necessary to find and catch fish. Fifty years ago, just about anywhere you wet a line you could catch a fish. Fishing conditions are different now because there are more anglers and fewer fish. It is not difficult to catch fish in Florida, especially if you are fishing a specific area on a regular basis. Experienced guides may be on the water 200 or more days per year. The really good ones pay attention to where and when fish are biting and use the knowledge to put their anglers in waters where they know the fish are present. Then it is only the angler's skill that determines how many fish he or she can catch.

Finding a guide is as easy as going online and doing a search for fishing guides in a particular location. If you are old-fashioned and have a phone book, fishing guides are still listed in the yellow pages. Many hotels, motels, and even bed-and-breakfasts keep lists of guides that they recommend.

If you are going to use a guide, it is important to find one that will give you the fishing experience you want. Some guides like to take families fishing and others prefer only experienced anglers. If the information you need to know is not on a website or an advertisement, e-mail or call several guides. Don't be bashful about asking questions. The cost of a guided trip will be several hundred to over a thousand dollars, so you should make sure that the guide you plan to hire will be able to provide you with the kind of trip you want.

Special Species

Florida has a handful of threatened and endangered species, one former listed species, and one common species of special note to anglers.

West Indian Manatee – This endangered marine mammal is common in most central and south Florida coastal areas and some freshwater rivers. They can also be found in north Florida during the warmer months of the year. Collisions with boats are one of the leading causes of non-natural deaths for manatees. The state has enacted manatee speed zones throughout much of the area where boaters are most active and manatees are known to inhabit. Typically, there will be a posted speed limit inside marked channels with a slow speed zone outside the channel. In areas where manatees congregate, idle or slow speed zones are posted. Some areas have year-round restrictions, and for others the speed restrictions are seasonal. Be aware of any posted speed limits where you boat. You can obtain more information about manatee,s including maps showing the manatee protection zones, from the FWC's website, *www.myfwc.com*. Search the website for "Florida manatee program."

It is illegal to intentionally kill, molest, annoy, or disturb manatees. If you notice someone doing any of these, or if you find a dead or injured manatee or an orphaned juvenile, call the FWC at 1-888-404-3922 or *FWC (392) or #FWC on your cell phone.

Sea Turtles – Five species of sea turtles are found in Florida's coastal waters and nest on the state's beaches: loggerhead, green, leatherback, Kemp's ridley, and hawksbill. The loggerhead is threatened and the others are endangered in Florida. Anglers may notice sea turtles when offshore and even in estuarine areas. Plastic bags and other plastic items that anglers may throw overboard are a potential threat to sea turtles as they are known to mistake these items as prey and ingest them. Doing so can kill sea turtles, so anglers are strongly encouraged to keep all trash on board and throw it away when back on land.

Brown pelican – Once nearly wiped out but now thriving, pelicans like to hang out around fishing piers, bridges, fish-cleaning stations, and any other place where anglers congregate to fish. Over time some of these birds associate anglers with a potential meal and will compete with you for your baitfish (ones you have disregarded and ones that are hooked to your line) and remains of the fish that you are cleaning. If the bird does not get hooked, it may become entangled in your fishing line or that of another angler. When this happens, don't cut the line and let the bird fly off. The dangling line is a death sentence for most birds as it can become entangled on any structure or tree where the pelican lands, trapping the bird there until it dies. Instead, try to reel in the pelican and disentangle it. The bird won't be thrilled with this, but you can help ease the bird's stress and help prevent injury to you and the pelican by gently but firmly grabbing and holding the bird's bill closed while also holding the pelican's wings so it cannot flap around and possibly cause more injury. Two people can do this more easily than one. This also will allow one person to check to see if the line is wrapped around any part of the bird. If it is, carefully remove all the line. If a hook is through the flesh, cut or pinch down the barb before removing it. Don't try to remove imbedded hooks as this is likely to cause more damage. Cut all of the line off and leave the hook in place. When done, carefully release the bird. If there are other injuries, call a local wildlife rescue shelter for assistance.

Bottle-nosed Dolphin – Not to be confused with the dolphin fish, this is an air-breathing mammal that is a common sight in the state's nearshore waters and estuaries. Over the years, people have lured these mammals to their boats in order to give them a snack and get an up-close look. This has led to dolphins associating boats with food. And, as any angler who has had a dolphin around where he or she is fishing knows, when a dolphin is around, the fish won't be. If you encounter this situation, it is best to move to a new spot. Healthy wild animals, especially dolphin, do not need our help in getting a meal, so do not feed them or any other wild animal.

Central Florida's Top Game Fish

Some anglers have a knack for catching more fish than others. The reason for this may be simpler than you think; the ones who catch fish are dedicated anglers with keen powers of observation. They have studied the fish's biology and behavior and have experimented with a wide range of lures, baits, and techniques so they know what works and what does not. They also keep notes on when, where, and how they catch fish, and try to learn as much as they can about the behavior of each species. To help improve your angling success, here is some basic information as well as some tips on how to catch the most sought-after species in central Florida.

Saltwater Species

Barracuda

Sphyraena barracuda
GREAT BARRACUDA

Distribution – This is a widely distributed species in the coastal and offshore waters of central Florida. The larger fish are usually caught around just about any kind of submerged structure in the Atlantic Ocean and Gulf of Mexico. Juveniles, which spend time in estuaries, are occasionally caught around the mangroves, especially near passes. Barracuda are year-round residents throughout state, although they tend to be less common the farther north you go in the winter as they prefer warmer water.

Tackle and techniques – When fishing offshore, use spinning or bait-casting gear with a minimum 15-pound test line and a heavy monofilament or wire leader. The fish may also be caught when trolling for blue water species. Barracuda are most dangerous when hooked and being brought into the boat; beware the 'cuda's razor-sharp teeth.

Bait – Shiny baits—live or artificial—tend to attract these curious predators. A traditional lure that is very successful is the tube lure.

Food value – Barracuda are said to be tasty but few people eat the meat because of the risk of ciguatera poisoning (see page 22–22). As there is no way to know if the meat is tainted, it is best to avoid eating barracuda.

Bluefish

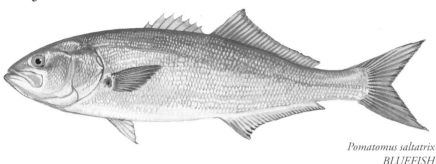

Pomatomus saltatrix
BLUEFISH

Distribution – The largest concentrations and the biggest fish are caught on the Atlantic side. Bluefish are most numerous in Florida during winter and stay close to shore, providing good action for surf and pier anglers. These fish tend to travel in schools of similar-sized fish.

Tackle and techniques – Surf fishing is one of the most popular methods of catching bluefish. When the surf is rough and the fish are farther offshore, use a big surf rod and reel. Anglers fishing from piers and from the surf on calm days can use a 6-foot rod and standard spinning or bait-casting reel with 12-pound test line. Bluefish have a row of razor-sharp teeth in their upper and lower jaws, so use a heavy monofilament or light-wire leader.

State regulations apply to this fish. Check the latest edition of the rules and regulations for size and bag limits and open and closed seasons.

Bait – Live baitfish, taken by cast net from the schools the bluefish are feeding on, is a sure way to catch one of these fish. Other small fish, when tossed into a feeding frenzy, will also work. Gold and silver spoons are very effective in schools of bluefish as the fish will strike at the lures thinking they are baitfish. Another reliable choice is a jig tipped with a piece of shrimp. Pieces of cut bait and large spoons work when trolling.

Food value – Bluefish meat is strong and on the oily side compared to many other species and is an acquired taste for many. It does not freeze well, so only keep what you plan to eat for dinner.

Cobia

Rachycentron canadum
COBIA

Distribution – Cobia are pelagic (open water) species that are widely distributed offshore and in large bays such as Tampa Bay. Cobia migrate north in spring and south in the fall (often accompanying large rays) but reside year-round in south Florida. More fish are caught along the Gulf coast than in the Atlantic Ocean. Cobia like to hang out around structure. Most are caught from boats, but some are taken from ocean piers. Cobia are aggressive feeders and can grow to 2 feet in length in their first years of life.

Tackle and techniques – Medium- to heavy-duty spinning tackle with 15- to 30-pound test line works best on these strong fighting fish. Use a heavy monofilament or fluorocarbon leader. When the water is warm, the fish may be close enough to the surface to sight fish for them. A reel with lots of line and a good drag system is essential as these fish can peel off 50 yards or more of line on their initial run. And it only takes a few seconds!

State and federal regulations apply to this fish. Check the latest edition of the rules and regulations for size and bag limits and open and closed seasons.

Bait – Cobia readily take small live fish or crabs. Hardhead catfish are an important part of their diet so try one of these as bait. If the cobia are near the surface, free-line the bait. If they are closer to the bottom, use just enough lead to get your bait down to where the fish are but not so much that it restricts the ability of the baitfish to move around. The most successful artificial lure is a big jig tipped with a piece of squid or other cut bait. If sight fishing, cast ahead of the fish and bring it toward them.

Food value – A meaty fish, cobia is good grilled. Because cobia feed heavily on crabs, the meat is rich and is sometimes described as having a lobster flavor to it.

Dolphin

Coryphaena hippurus
DOLPHIN

Distribution – Dolphin travel in schools in open water and are year-round residents in southeast Florida and the Keys. In central Florida, dolphin arrive in the late spring as they migrate up the Atlantic coast. They are sporadically found along the lower and mid-Gulf coast and are most likely to be caught from late spring to early summer. Dolphin are fast-growing oceangoing fish reaching up to three feet long in their first year. Dolphin less than 3 pounds are called "chickens." Three- to 8-pound fish are known as "schoolies." "Gaffers" are the ones you need to gaff in order to get in the boat. Big fish weighing more than 30 pounds are known as "slammers." Large males, known as "bull" dolphin, have a bony crest on their foreheads that is lacking in females.

Tackle and techniques – Look for schools of small- to medium-sized dolphin around any floating object. This includes lines or patches of seaweed and any type of floating debris. Cast to them using medium-weight spinning tackle. Dolphin of all sizes are also caught by trolling. Boat tackle with 20-pound test line or higher works when trolling.

State regulations apply to this fish. Check the latest edition of the rules and regulations for size and bag limits and open and closed seasons.

Bait – Trolling baits include a rigged ballyhoo, a piece of cut bait, or an off-shore lure designed for dolphin and other big-game species. When casting, use cut bait or ballyhoo. When a school is nearby and they are in a feeding frenzy, anything light colored and flashy will get a strike. When you catch the first fish, leave it in the water. Chances are good that other dolphins will show up to keep the hooked fish company.

Food value – This species is a highly regarded food fish. It is called mahi mahi in restaurants and retail stores. The slightly off-color flesh is mild and good grilled or fried. Try it with some mango chutney.

Flounder

Paralichthys albigutta
GULF FLOUNDER

Distribution – Flounder are caught statewide, but the bigger specimens are found from central Florida northward. There are three species of flounder caught in Florida but only two, the Gulf flounder and the southern flounder, are present in central Florida. The third species, the summer flounder, is found in northeast Florida. The Gulf and southern species live along the Atlantic and Gulf coasts. However, the southern flounder is more common north of the Loxahatchee River on the Atlantic coast and north of the Caloosahatchee River on the Gulf coast. Additionally, the two species have different habitats; Gulf flounder prefer a sandy bottom while southern flounder prefer a mud and silt bottom.

Tackle and techniques – A medium-duty spinning or bait-casting combination is sufficient. Use 6- to 20-pound test line and a monofilament leader. Light-duty boat tackle also works when fishing from a boat, bridge, or pier. A flounder's bite is light, nothing more than a soft tap. Unless you feel the fish begin to pull against the drag, try to wait several seconds before setting the hook. These fish will swim off with the bait before swallowing it. Once you are ready to set the hook, set it with a hard snap of the line.

State regulations apply to this fish. Check the latest edition of the rules and regulations for size and bag limits and open and closed seasons.

Bait – Small live fish are the bait choice. Along the Atlantic coast, anglers prefer finger mullet; along the upper Gulf coast, bull minnows are the top pick. Flounder are bottom feeders, so get your bait on or just above the bottom. Lures are seldom used to fish for flounder although they will occasionally hit a shrimp-tipped jig bounced along the bottom.

Food value – The white, flaky, delicate meat is one of the more popular fish featured on restaurant menus and in grocery stores and fish markets. Often topped with crab meat or shrimp, flounder is also great when fried, sautéed, or baked.

Grouper

Epinephelus morio
RED GROUPER

Distribution – There are over 10 species of grouper that are caught in Florida. Offshore of central Florida, black, gag, red, and goliath groupers are the most widely distributed and commonly caught species. Of these species, all but the goliath grouper are popular table fare. Goliaths, which can grow to well over 500 pounds, are a protected species and harvesting them is not allowed.

Adult groupers are offshore bottom dwellers. Younger fish are often caught in seagrass beds, around mangroves, and in the deeper holes of backwater tidal creeks.

Red grouper, the most abundant grouper species in the Gulf, may grow to three feet in length and average about 10 pounds. Gag and black grouper look similar, but the black grouper grow much bigger, often reaching over 100 pounds compared to less than 50 pounds for most gags.

Grouper have the ability to change sex later in their lives. Not all individuals make the switch, but when it happens, females become males.

Tackle and techniques – Grouper are bottom dwellers. However, they will come off the bottom if they see a meal overhead. Most are caught from boats anchored or drifting over submerged structure. In some places, slow trolling over hard bottom also produces fish. In either case, boat tackle with 20- to 40-pound test line with a 40- to 80-pound test leader is necessary to get these strong fish to the surface.

When a grouper bites, it is seldom more than a few feet from a place of refuge. Don't allow much slack in the line as the key to landing one of these fish is to turn the fish's head up to keep it from going under a rock or into a hole. If it gets back to the bottom, let your line go slack and wait at least 5 minutes, 10 would be better. If the fish thinks the threat is gone, you may have a chance to suddenly and quickly take up the slack and yank the fish from its hiding spot.

State regulations apply to this fish. Check the latest edition of the rules and regulations for size and bag limits and open and closed seasons.

Bait – Small live fish and dead whole or cut baits are the baits of choice. Grouper will eat anything that comes their way. Jigs can be used when at anchor or drifting. Deep-diving saltwater plugs work when trolling.

Food value – For many seafood lovers, grouper is their number one choice. As a result of its popularity, most species are considered overfished and there are strict state and federal regulations that include closed seasons. The firm, flaky meat is good fried, baked, and sautéed.

King mackerel

Scomberomorus cavalla
KING MACKEREL

Distribution – Along the Atlantic coast, king mackerel are caught year-round south of Jupiter Inlet; only during warmer months do they venture farther north. In the central Gulf and Atlantic waters, the fish migrate northward in the spring and southward in the fall. The run only lasts about two months in the spring and the same amount of time in the fall. Most fish are taken offshore, but some larger fish move into nearshore waters and are occasionally caught from ocean piers and in the surf.

Tackle and techniques – Fishing from a boat using standard boat tackle with 20-pound test line or higher is the preferred method. Most kings are caught when trolling for them. However, if you know that fish are in the area, you can also drift and cast to them. King mackerel have a mouthful of sharp teeth so a wire leader is preferable to reduce break-offs. These fish will be found at varying depths, and the best way to find out where they are on any given day is to set out an array of lines trolled at different depths. Jigging may also work once you've found a school and are drifting through it. From the surf or a pier, you will need a medium to heavy rod and reel with at least 20-pound test line on it to handle the big fish that come close to shore.

State regulations apply to this fish. Check the latest edition of the rules and regulations for size and bag limits and open and closed seasons.

Bait – When trolling, fish-shaped lures or plugs are preferable. Or try a piece of cut bait or a whole baitfish with a 4-to-6-inch-long plastic skirt.

Food value – King mackerel tend to have a strong flavor and are oily. This makes them good candidates to be brined and then placed in the smoker. Like other oily fish, it does not freeze well so plan to use it when fresh.

Marlin

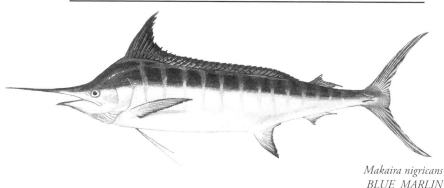

Makaira nigricans
BLUE MARLIN

Distribution – White and blue marlin spend their entire lives at sea. Both are warm water species. In Florida, they are found along the Atlantic coast from St. Augustine to the Florida Keys. The fish are also taken during the summer months offshore from the Panhandle and occasionally offshore 50 or more miles along the central Florida coast. If you really want to do battle with one of these great fish, and every angler owes it to himself or herself to do this at least once in a lifetime, head to one of these areas. The blue marlin is the larger of the two species, averaging about 300 pounds compared to a 60-pound average for white marlin. In both species, females are larger than males.

Tackle and techniques – Marlin are caught by trolling. Use 50- to 130-pound test line and tackle to match it (which tends to be expensive). Landing a blue marlin requires a special fighting chair or a stand-up belt for anglers with strong arms and back. The chair is preferable and safer. Anglers are strapped in so they aren't pulled out of the boat. The boat's captain is an integral part of the battle. He or she must maneuver the boat to keep the fish from breaking off. Unless you have the boat and equipment to do it right, charter a boat and captain.

State regulations apply to this fish. Check the latest edition of the rules and regulations for size and bag limits and open and closed seasons.

Bait – Trolling a live bait such as a bonita works, but you must troll at a relatively slow speed to keep the bait alive. Trolling with an artificial bait is a popular method of fishing. Specially designed blue-water trolling lures for big-game saltwater fish like marlin and sailfish can be towed at a much faster speed. This allows anglers to cover more territory, increasing the chances of a hookup. A typical lure has a hard plastic "fish" head with a soft plastic skirt attached. Rigged to this lure are the hooks. There are many ways to rig the lures with one or more hooks, typically 10/0 to 14/0 in size. If you don't know how to rig trolling lures, you can buy them in a ready-to-fish form.

Food value – Marlin are considered a sport fish and routinely caught and released.

Permit

Distribution – Permit are warm-water fish that are found year-round in south Florida and the Keys. They move northward in the summer months and comprise an important part of the offshore catch in the central Gulf and Atlantic. In addition to being found around offshore structure, permit are common inhabitanst of the seagrass flats in the Keys and Biscayne Bay.

Tackle and techniques – Offshore, fish for permit using at least a 7-foot spinning rod and a reel with 6- to 12-pound test line. Because these fish can easily reach 40 pounds, a beefier rod and reel with 12- to 20-pound test braided line will still produce a good fight and greatly increase your chances of bringing the fish to the boat. Permit usually swim close to the surface and often you will see them circling your boat. When this happens, cast ahead of where you think the fish will be and reel your bait in front of them. Unless you surprise the fish

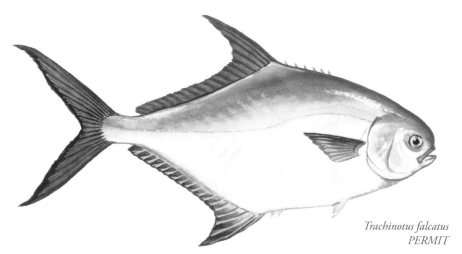

Trachinotus falcatus
PERMIT

and scare it off, it should take your bait. Permit have a tough mouth, so when you feel a bite, set the hook hard and do it a couple of times. In the shallower waters of south Florida, you can sight fish for permit using light spinning tackle or a fly rod. Fly fishers generally use a rod and reel rated for 7- to 9-weight line with at least 150 yards of backing.

State regulations apply to this fish. Check the latest edition of the rules and regulations for size and bag limits and open and closed seasons.

Bait – Permit love small live crabs. They will also hit live shrimp and cut bait, but crabs are much higher on their list of things to eat. You can buy crabs at some bait and tackle shops. It is also a good idea to have a long-handle dip-net on your boat. Look for floating clumps of seaweed on your way offshore and you may find small, 3- to 5-inch crabs clinging to the floating seaweed. If you find them, use the dip net to catch them. Keep them in your live well. The chances of a permit passing one by are very slim. Soft plastic artificial baits in a crab shape also work, as well as jigs tipped with shrimp. A crab imitation fly is a top choice for fly rodders.

Food value – Some anglers consider them a sport fish and always release what they catch. However, the fish is edible and the firm, slightly off-white meat is mild and lends itself to most types of cooking.

Pompano

Trachinotus carolinus
POMPANO

Distribution – Pompano are nearshore species common along both Florida coasts. A schooling fish, they are usually found along sandy beaches, in inlets, and around oyster bars or seagrass beds in estuaries. Surf and ocean pier anglers catch most of the fish. Pompano are migratory and are not as common in north Florida during the colder months of the year.

Tackle and techniques – Light spinning or bait-casting tackle is all you need to catch this fish. The fish are great fighters on ultra-light gear with 4-to 6-pound test line. A leader is recommended. Fly rodders can fish for pompano with a rod and reel rated for 7-weight line. Anglers fishing from boats should watch their wake when over potential pompano habitat. If any fish are around, they can often be seen skipping across the boat's wake. When you see this, slow down, turn around, and make some casts.

State regulations apply to this fish. Check the latest edition of the rules and regulations for size and bag limits and open and closed seasons.

Bait – Live sand fleas are the favorite bait for pompano. Some bait stores sell them, but you can easily collect your own. They live beneath the surface of the beach in the surf zone. On a receding tide look for ripples or bubbles coming from the sand and dig out the sand fleas. Pompano have small mouths, so use a #1 or 1/0 size hook. Around Melbourne and Cocoa Beach on the Atlantic coast, surf anglers like to use clams for bait. Live shrimp also works well.

Small jigs with a piece of fresh dead shrimp are the most effective artificial lures. Retrieve with a slow bounce across the bottom. The bouncing stirs up the sand and that attracts the attention of the pompano.

Food value – Pompano are highly regarded table fare. It is a mild fish that restaurants often serve whole, lightly battered and pan fried.

Redfish

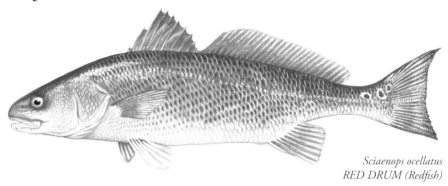

Sciaenops ocellatus
RED DRUM (Redfish)

Distribution – Also known as red drum, this widely distributed species is common throughout the state. Able to tolerate a wide range of salinities, redfish are common in estuaries and nearshore waters. Redfish grow quickly, reaching 12 inches in their first year. They can live up to 40 years and grow to 50 pounds. The area around Cape Canaveral is known for producing some of the largest redfish in the state. These bottom-feeding fish are not migratory; most tend to stay near the area where they were spawned. Since the end of commercial harvesting in 1989, redfish numbers have remained high, making it one of the most popular saltwater game fish.

Tackles and techniques – You can catch redfish using a variety of tackle. If you're fishing the flats where there is not much chance of the fish heading for cover and cutting you off, light tackle will add some challenge to landing the fish. If you fish deeper waters, around the passes, a heavier line is in order, perhaps a 12- to 15-pound test line with a 40-pound test leader. Fly fishers will find plenty of challenge using an 8- or 9-weight rig and varying the tippets from 2- to 12-pound test.

Finding redfish is easy once you understand their preferences. Look on the flats when the water temperature is above 70 degrees. The best time is when the water is coming onto or falling off the flats, making a shallow-draft boat the easiest way to reach the fish. Redfish are sensitive to noise and are easily scared off, so some anglers prefer to get out of the boat and wade. Protect your feet with an old pair of running shoes or other footwear.

When the water is less than 18 inches deep, the fish's tail often breaks the surface as it noses in the mud to feed—this is what anglers call *tailing* redfish.

When a redfish is tailing, wait for the fish to finish feeding and start moving to a new location. That's when you cast. Toss your bait ahead of the fish to intersect its path as you reel in the line. If you run the bait by when the fish is feeding, it could go unnoticed.

When fishing an incoming tide, eventually the water gets too high and signs of tailing activity diminish, but you can still locate fish by looking for humps of water created by schools of moving redfish. Cast ahead of them and bring the lure across their path.

Also look for redfish around stingray muds. When stingrays feed they stir up the bottom and create what anglers call a "mud." Redfish often follow close behind, looking for a meal of their own.

When the water cools below 70 degrees, redfish head for deeper water. Look for them in channels near the flats and in the passes. This pattern becomes even more apparent as colder weather approaches. When the fish head for deeper water, you won't be able to sight-fish for them. Try using a live bait or blind casting until you find fish. Many anglers use lures to cover a lot of territory until they find the fish, then switch to live bait.

Redfish tend to remain in the same area for extended periods. If you find fish on the flat or in a channel one day, there is a good chance that the fish will be there tomorrow.

State regulations apply to this fish. Check the latest edition of the rules and regulations for size and bag limits and open and closed seasons.

Bait – With an underslung mouth, the redfish prefers to feed on the bottom for small crabs and shrimp. A live shrimp under a popping cork is one of the most widely used baits. Experienced redfish anglers also know that these fish will eat just about anything presented to them if they are hungry, and they always seem to be hungry. Redfish go for small baitfish, jigs, spoons, and topwater plugs. The latter is an interesting bait to use when fishing the flats because the fish must come to the surface and partially roll over to get the bait. It makes for some exciting action.

Food value – Due to the abundance of redfish and the reluctance of many anglers to keep snook, redfish are the most popular nearshore and backwater species taken as a food fish. The slightly off-white meat is firm but flaky. It can be cooked almost any way you can cook a fish. Blackened redfish is one of the most popular ways to serve this fish.

Sailfish

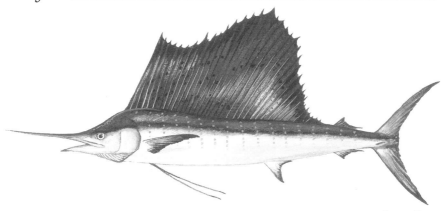

Istiophorus albicans
SAILFISH

Distribution – Sailfish are found offshore of Florida's Atlantic and Gulf coasts. In fact, this pelagic species has a worldwide distribution in temperate and tropical waters. Along the Atlantic coast, sailfish can be caught just about any month, but the action tends to slow during the coldest times of the year and in the heat of the summer, when the fish are present but scattered. In the fall, before the winter fronts arrive, anglers will have to travel farther offshore to reach the edge of the Gulf Stream, where the fish will be moving south for the winter. Top months in south Florida and the Keys are the winter months because the cold fronts sweeping down from the north cool the Atlantic waters and push sailfish south. In the Gulf, the best chance of catching sailfish comes during the warmer months and by venturing 50 or so more miles offshore. Some of the best reports come from anglers fishing off the Panhandle coast during summer. Occasionally one is hooked on the Lake Worth Pier near Palm Beach or from one of the ocean piers in the Panhandle.

Tackle and techniques – Slow trolling a live bait or trolling a bit faster with a dead bait or lure is the most effective way to catch sailfish. Once hooked, the fun begins as this fish is likely to put on an aerobatic display when it jumps. Most sailfish are less than 70 inches in length and not as heavy as the sailfish's blue-and-white-marlin cousins, so anglers can use boat tackle with line in the 20- to 50-pound range and a 6- to 8-foot length of 40- to 80-pound test leader. You can even use medium-weight spinning tackle for a real challenging fight. Make sure you have at least 200 yards of line on the spool or this technique probably won't work. Fly rodders using big 12-weight rigs can also tackle sailfish anywhere they can see one to cast to. Anglers will find sailfish by trolling lures along the edge of and in the Gulf Stream's blue waters. Anglers must also know the depth of the day for the sailfish. It can change daily and listening to your marine radio may give you a clue as to where other boats are finding the fish.

Unless you are experienced in fishing for sailfish, take a charter boat trip. Not only do the captains know how to find the fish, their mates are skilled at handling the fish at boatside. There is some danger involved when the fish is alongside the boat, and it is better for someone with experience to hold and release the fish.

State and federal regulations apply to this fish. Check the latest edition of the rules and regulations for size and bag limits and open and closed seasons.

Bait – Sailfish have a wide-ranging appetite. Live pinfish, blue runners, mullet, goggle eyes, and ballyhoo will attract a sailfish's attention. A rigged dead fish or large piece of cut bait also works. Blue water trolling lures, which come in many sizes and colors, are also effective. They can be used alone or rigged with a dead baitfish.

Food value – Sailfish are considered a sport fish and routinely caught and released.

Shark

Carcharhinus limbatus
BLACKTIP SHARK

Distribution – Collectively, sharks are widely distributed throughout the state. Anglers can catch sharks in the nearshore and offshore waters, in bays, and even on the flats. Some of the more commonly sought after and caught species are the blacktip, lemon, hammerhead, spinner, sandbar, and bull sharks. The future of shark populations is of increasing concern. Many species give birth to live young, only one or two at a time. As angling pressure on sharks increases, such a low reproductive rate may mean severe declines for some species unless further regulations are enacted.

Tackle and techniques – The tackle used depends on the size shark you're fishing for and where that species lives. Light spinning tackle and fly rods are adequate for small blacktip sharks caught on the flats and in the backwaters. The big sharks of the coastal and open waters require much stouter gear. Wire leaders and rods and reels capable of handling from 20- to 100-pound test line are the order of the day. Shark fishermen have their own subculture and you can learn more by doing an Internet search for shark fishing in Florida.

Go with an experienced shark angler before trying it on your own. Bringing a 5-foot or larger shark alongside or into a boat is dangerous no matter how many times you have done it.

State and Federal regulations apply to this fish. Check the latest edition of the rules and regulations for size and bag limits and open and closed seasons.

Bait – The bait of choice, with few exceptions, is a live fish or a freshly killed one. The bloodier species such as bonita make the best dead baits. What most anglers would consider a good-sized fish to catch makes a great bait for a shark.

Food value – Shark meat is firm and tends to have a light reddish color, although it is not overly strong. It holds up well when grilled. To make its flavor milder, try marinating shark in teriyaki sauce before grilling.

Sheepshead

Distribution – Sheepshead are year-round residents throughout the state. They are most commonly found around bridge and dock pilings, oyster bars, and nearshore reefs and wrecks. They are also caught over seagrass flats and, in the winter months, over offshore structures.

Tackle and techniques – Light to medium spinning and bait-casting tackle with 6- to 12-pound test line is sufficient. When fishing for bigger, stronger sheepshead on the offshore reef and wrecks, use boat rods and reels. Use a small, sharp hook and set it quickly when you feel the fish start to move off with the bait. You will feel a few light taps as the fish takes the bait into its mouth. Ignore those and wait a moment or two for a heavy feeling. That's when to set the hook. Use as little weight as necessary to get the bait to the bottom. The more weight you use, the less sensitivity you have in feeling the fish bite.

Archosargus probatocephalu
SHEEPSHEAD

State regulations apply to this fish. Check the latest edition of the rules and regulations for size and bag limits and open and closed seasons

Bait – Among the most popular baits are live fiddler crabs, live or dead shrimp, and sand fleas. Sheepshead are great bait stealers. Their small mouth and ability to nip bait off a hook before you can set it make them a challenge to catch. When fishing around a bridge, some anglers scrape barnacles off the pilings with a flat-blade shovel. This serves as a chum and attracts fish.

Food value – The white, firm meat is surprisingly mild and tasty. Lightly bread the fillets and pan fry or sauté.

Snapper

Distribution – Fifteen species of snapper live in Florida's waters. The top five are yellowtail, mangrove (also known as gray snapper), lane, red, and mutton. Mangrove snapper are found throughout the coastal waters from the mangroves and nearshore seagrass beds to the hard bottoms, wrecks, and coral reefs offshore. They can be caught any month of the year. Lane snappers are also widely distributed but are more abundant in the warmer offshore waters of south Florida. Lanes are the smallest of the top five, maturing when they reach 6 inches long. Red snapper are most common in the deeper, northern offshore waters. They are slow growers; a 20-year-old red snapper weighs about 35 pounds. Some red snapper are caught offshore in central Florida in the summer, but the best place to fish for this species is offshore in the Panhandle.

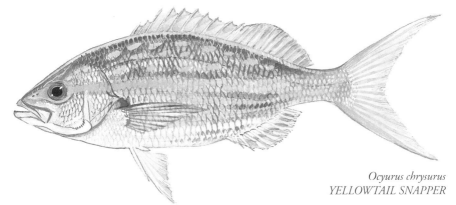

Ocyurus chrysurus
YELLOWTAIL SNAPPER

Some yellowtail snapper are found in most of the state's coastal waters but in significant numbers only in southeast Florida, especially the Keys. Mutton snapper are found around the state in moderate numbers, but the best fishing is in the Keys.

Tackle and techniques – When fishing inside waters for mangrove snapper and offshore for lane and yellowtail snapper, use light spinning or bait-casting tackle with 6- to 12-pound test line. For larger fish such as reds, big offshore mangroves, and muttons, boat tackle with 20- to 30-pound test and a heavy monofilament leader is necessary. There is no magic to the technique of catching snapper. You drop a bait down to the bottom, they bite, you set the hook and reel them in. Any fish over a few pounds gives a good fight. Just don't be too anxious to set the hook at the first nibble. Your best chance at catching your limit of these tasty fish is to fish for them offshore at night during the summer.

Mutton snapper are the only species that routinely visit the flats in the Keys. Anglers fishing for permit on the flats will have the right tackle for mutton that comes their way. Use a 7-foot spinning rod with a reel of 6- to 12-pound test line or a rod and reel rated for 7- to 9-weight line. Reels should have at least 150 yards of backing.

State and federal regulations apply to these species. Check the latest edition of the rules and regulations for size and bag limits and open and closed seasons.

Bait – Small live fish such as pinfish, squirrel fish, and ballyhoo are excellent snapper bait. Cut bait is also very effective, especially if used when chumming. It is the standard procedure when fishing for yellowtail in the Keys and for any night fishing offshore (snapper are active feeders after dark). When mutton fishing on the flats, use a small crab or a live shrimp. For artificial lures try a soft plastic crab lure, a fly designed to imitate a crab or shrimp, or a streamer in a small fish pattern.

Food value – Snapper meat is light, flaky, and mild. Because of the abundance of snappers and generous bag limits, this is one of the most popular food fish in Florida. Snapper can be fried, broiled, sautéed, or baked. There are dozens of recipes for this versatile fish.

Snook

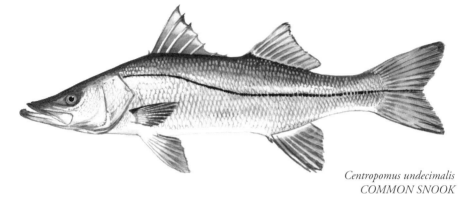

Centropomus undecimalis
COMMON SNOOK

Distribution – The common snook may be the perfect saltwater game fish—it is a great fighter and makes delicious eating. This species is found throughout the estuaries and coastal waters of central and south Florida. There are four species of snook, but three of them never get larger than 18 inches. And, unless you pay careful attention, you may not even notice that some of the smaller snook you catch are not the common snook species. All must be released if caught because of the current (2010) 28-inch minimum size limit on snook. The common snook is the big one, growing in excess of 40 pounds.

Snook are primarily inshore fish that don't migrate far from where they spawn. From April to October, adults move from the estuaries to spawn offshore. Juveniles and adults tolerate fresh water and often move into coastal canals and tidal creeks. Snook are tropical species and their northward distribution is limited by cold water. In general, Cape Canaveral on the Atlantic coast and Tarpon Springs on the Gulf coast mark the northern limits of this species. Some fish will move northward, especially if there is a sustained period during which the water does not drop below 60 degrees. Within its range when the water temperature drops below about 60 degrees, snook head for warmer waters. However, unusually cold snaps such as the one experienced in the winter of 2009–10 killed hundreds of thousands of fish within their range and led to an emergency closure of the fishery.

Look for snook around overhanging mangroves, dock pilings, and other submerged structures. In the summer you can also find them in the shore-parallel channels that are a few feet offshore along the sandy beaches of both coasts.

Tackle and techniques – A medium-weight spinning or bait-casting rod and reel with 8- to 20-pound test line is necessary for this strong fighting fish. Use heavier tackle when fishing around bridges. Snook are adept at running into cover and breaking lines. A heavy monofilament or fluorocarbon leader also helps to reduce break-offs caused from abrasion and the fish's razor-sharp gill covers.

Snook like to ambush their prey. They often wait in eddies for small fish or crabs to be carried by current. For this reason, snook fishing is usually good when the tide is moving in or out.

Night fishing is another good way to catch snook. The fish love to hang around lighted areas close to the water. Look for docks with lights or take a lantern and hang it just above the water's surface. Snook will dart in and out of light eating the small fish that are attracted to the light. When it is cold, snook move far up small tidal creeks, sometimes going into freshwater regions, or head towards the deepest water around. Because they are sensitive to the cold, they tend to become lethargic and unwilling to bite when as the water cools.

State regulations apply to this fish. Check the latest edition of the rules and regulations for size and bag limits and open and closed seasons. A special snook stamp is also required in addition to a saltwater fishing license.

Bait – Snook will eat anything that looks good and is easy to catch. Although they will eat small crabs and shrimp, their favorite food is small fish. Cast net your own bait, particularly if you can catch what the snook are feeding on locally. Free lining the baitfish is the most popular technique. In areas where the current is especially strong, a small weight may be necessary.

Casting artificial lures is also popular. Any of the fish-shaped lures, jigs tipped with shrimp, and gold or silver spoons are traditional favorites. Two legendary snook lures are the red-and-white MirrOlure and the red-and-white Zara Spook. Cast the lure as close to a structure as you can. A snook may not move from its spot unless the lure is dragged right across the fish's nose.

Food value – Snook meat is highly regarded as a food fish. However, a large percentage of anglers choose to release all the snook they catch because of the intense fishing pressure on this species. If you do decide to keep and eat a snook, the meat is mild, white, and flaky. It is best pan fried, broiled, or sautéed.

Spanish mackerel

Scomberomorus maculatus
SPANISH MACKEREL

Distribution – This species is commonly found along both coasts of Florida. The fish travel in large schools and are migratory. They overwinter in the offshore waters of south Florida. In the Gulf of Mexico, the northward migration to the upper regions of the Gulf of Mexico for the summer brings them to central Florida around April with a return trip through the region in the fall. Thus, this species may be around in great numbers one day and virtually gone the next. Spanish mackerel are caught from the surf, off ocean piers, and in boats within 1 or 2 miles of shore along the Atlantic coast and up to 5 miles offshore along the Gulf coast. Anglers may also find them in estuarine waters near the major passes.

Tackle and techniques – Medium-duty spinning or bait-casting tackle with 6- to 12-pound test line is suitable. Use a heavy monofilament leader or a small-diameter wire leader. This fish has a mouthful of small sharp teeth.

To find the schools of fish, look to the sky. Spanish mackerel like to feed on baitfish and so do pelicans, terns, and frigate birds. If you see a large patch of disrupted water and a number of birds diving into the area, you've located a school of bait. Get within casting distance of the baitfish and you will catch some Spanish if they are around.

If there are no signs of surface activity, troll with a spoon or jig. When you hook the first fish, throw a milk-jug marker buoy overboard. Return to the site and begin casting. Where there's one Spanish mackerel, there are bound to be more.

All the fish in a school will be close to the same size and age. If you are looking for bigger fish, try around the edges of the school you're fishing or look elsewhere for another school. If you are working a school and there isn't much action, try smaller bait or lures.

State and federal regulations apply to this fish. Check the latest edition of the rules and regulations for size and bag limits and open and closed seasons.

Bait – When fishing a school of Spanish, mackerel you can use a live baitfish or free-lined shrimp, but a spoon or jig works just as well and is easier to use. If the school is in a feeding frenzy, this fish will strike at any shiny object, including a bare hook.

Food value – Some people like Spanish mackerel and others avoid it. The fish is stronger flavored than many other saltwater species and that limits the number of people who like to eat this fish. The meat has a reddish tinge and is soft and slightly oily. Baking it produces the best results according to those who like to eat Spanish mackerel.

*Spotted seatrout*_____

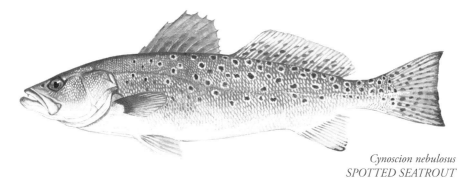

Cynoscion nebulosus
SPOTTED SEATROUT

Distribution – This is a common species in the estuarine and coastal waters of Florida. Recent research has concluded that there are five genetically distinct stocks of this species in Florida. Spotted seatrout are common throughout the state except from Lake Worth south to Miami. This species prefers estuaries, spawning there and growing up among the seagrass beds. The fish won't move far from the area in which they grew up. Females tend to live longer than males and eventually grow to a larger size.

Tackle and technique – Light spinning or bait-casting tackle is sufficient. Use a free-lined bait with or without a popping cork, troll or cast with spoons, slowly bounce a jig on or near the bottom, or cast a variety of hard and soft lures. Some anglers fly fish with a rod and reel rated for 7-weight line. Fish of similar size tend to school together. When you catch one fish, mark the site with a buoy and work the area.

State regulations apply to this fish. Check the latest edition of the rules and regulations for size and bag limits and open and closed seasons.

Bait – This species is an active predator with a wide-ranging appetite. A live shrimp is the most widely used bait. Dead shrimp, when used with a popping cork or tipped on a jig, are also effective. A variety of baitfish, including finger mullet, pinfish, and pigfish (small grunts), also work well. Deceivers, Bend Backs, and Dahlberg Divers are some of the fly rodders' choices.

Food value – The meat is white but is not as firm as other inshore species. If overcooked, it can become mushy. Try baking it with some lemon juice and butter or olive oil until it just flakes apart.

Tarpon

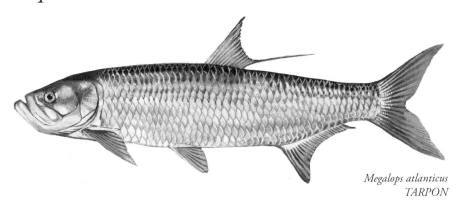

Megalops atlanticus
TARPON

Distribution – Tarpon are found along the entire Atlantic and Gulf coasts and in estuaries throughout Florida. Scientists believe the species migrate but the pattern is poorly understood. The general trend is for the species to avoid colder waters by moving south in the winter and then returning to northern parts of the state in the summer. This is evidenced by the arrival of the jumbo tarpon along the west central coast in the summer.

Tarpon also display an onshore to offshore movement during the mid-May to August spawning period. Breeding-sized fish will move offshore to spawn. Eggs hatch offshore and within 30 to 45 days the fish grow to about an inch long and move into the estuaries during the height of the rainy season. High water levels allow them to move far inland, and some become land-locked in small ponds and ditches as summer rains subside and mangrove forests dry out.

Tarpon take 10 to 13 years to mature. At that time males weigh about 40 pounds and females are close to 60 pounds. Once sexually mature, a tarpon can reproduce for up to 40 years.

Tarpon can also breathe air. The swim bladder connects to the fish's throat. Inside the bladder is a mass of lung-like tissue which can remove oxygen from air. One of the ways to scout for the presence of the "silver king" is to look and listen for tarpon to "roll" on the surface. That's when they gulp air and pass it into the swim bladder.

Tackle and techniques – A 7- to 8-foot stout rod rated for a minimum of 20-pound test with a reel capable of holding 150 to 300 yards of at least 12-pound test line is the type of spinning or bait-casting tackle to use. Most tarpon rigs use 15- to 30-pound test line. A good bass-flipping stick will work in lieu of buying a special tarpon rod. Fly rodders will want to use a rod and reel rated for 11- or 12-weight line. A 7- to 9-weight combination works for tarpon up to 30 pounds. Use a 30-pound test backing and have at least 200 yards on the spool in addition to the fly line.

Whether using a conventional or fly rod, use 20- to 40-pound leader to the end of the line. Attach a 1-foot piece of 100-pound test line to the end of the leader and tie the hook to that. The heavy line is necessary to prevent the fish from fraying or chewing through the line. Many anglers tie a Bimini Twist on the end of their spinning or plug rods and then tie the leader to that. This knot doubles the end of the line and makes a stronger connection with the leader. Use hooks ranging from 3/0 to 7/0 depending on the size of the bait.

Tarpon have very hard, bony mouths. Sharpen hooks before you use them, even ones fresh out of the package. When you feel a fish on the line, let it run with the bait for a few seconds, then set the hook hard.

Tarpon spook easily when there is noise in the water. Try to turn the motor off when close to your site and use a trolling motor or push pole to get within casting distance.

Let big tarpon have control the first few minutes. This is when they do the most jumping and all you can really do is hold on anyway. Dip your rod when the fish jumps. This gives the line some slack and makes you less likely to have the fish spit out the lure or break the line.

State regulations apply to this fish. Check the latest edition of the rules and regulations for size and bag limits and open and closed seasons.

Bait – Mullet or crabs are the preferred live baits. They are one of the tarpon's favorite natural foods and anyone with a cast net can catch some 5- to 10-inch mullet. Tarpon will also take other live baits, such as large shrimp, ladyfish, catfish, and pinfish. Don't rule out fishing with cut bait. When tarpon are feeding on a school of baitfish, they will stun some fish as they attack the school. A piece of cut bait apparently resembles a stunned fish close enough for a tarpon to go after it.

When using spinning or casting rigs, use lures that resemble mullet and other baitfish. Some of the more popular lures used by tarpon anglers are the

Zara Spook, Creek Chub Darter, Chartreuse Bomber Long A, 52m MirrOlure, Bagley Finger Mullet, Ratlin Flash, and Ratl' Trap. Experienced anglers usually replace the hooks that come on the lures with 3X-strength hooks because of the tremendous biting force of the fish.

Streamers are considered one of the best tarpon flies. Orange and red are the popular colors. The cockroach is another widely used fly.

When using artificial lures or flies, make your retrieve slow and straight. Don't retrieve the lure so that it is coming at the fish as this usually scares them off. Make a presentation that brings the lure across or at a quartering diagonal away from the direction in which the fish is swimming.

Food value – Virtually no one keeps a tarpon for eating. They are very bony and have a low food value. They are exclusively a sport fish. This helps prevent depleting the stock. So does the $50 special tag required for keeping a tarpon.

Freshwater Species

*Black crappie*_____

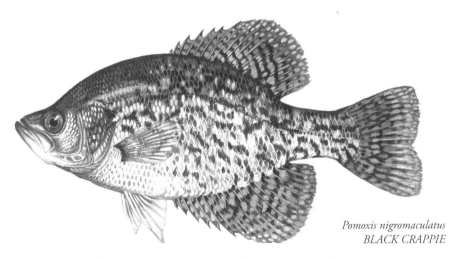

Pomoxis nigromaculatus
BLACK CRAPPIE

Distribution – This freshwater fish is found everywhere in Florida except the Keys. It prefers clear water and thus is more commonly found in lakes and a few of the large, slow-moving clear-water rivers. Specs, as some people call crappie, prefer water in the 70–75 degree F range. Reports from anglers suggest the species is more abundant in north and central Florida. However, Lake Okeechobee in the southern part of the state is famous for crappie fishing.

Tackle and techniques – Crappie average 1 to 2 pounds, so anglers can use any type of freshwater tackle, including cane poles, ultra-light spinning tackle, and fly rods. Crappies are an easy fish to catch once you locate a school of them. A baited hook and a bobber are all the terminal tackle needs. The best time of year to fish for crappie is during the December to early or mid-March spawning season.

State regulations apply to this fish. Check the latest edition of the rules and regulations for size and bag limits and open and closed seasons.

Bait – Missouri minnows are the most popular bait. Other small shiners will work as well. Experienced anglers looking for more of a challenge will use small jigs or spinner baits.

Food value – One of the most popular freshwater food fish. Larger ones can be filleted. However, pan dressing is another popular method. Scale the fish, and then remove the head, fins (except the tail), and entrails. When cooked, the skin and backbone can be easily removed. The meat is mild, white, and flaky.

Largemouth bass (Black bass)

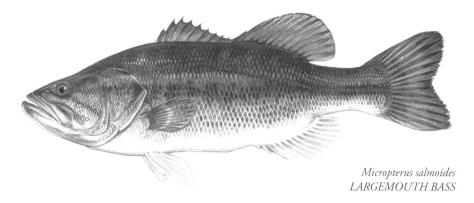

Micropterus salmoides
LARGEMOUTH BASS

Distribution – Largemouth bass, the largest member of the sunfish family, is found in almost every freshwater lake in the state that has some aquatic vegetation. Technically speaking, there are two subspecies of largemouth bass: northern largemouth and Florida largemouth. There are no pure northern largemouth bass in Florida. However, there are many genetic intergrades of northern and Florida largemouth bass in north Florida. The Florida largemouth bass is what anglers are catching in central and south Florida and is the subspecies that grows to trophy size.

Typically, largemouth bass prefer water temps less than 80 degrees and more than 65 degrees F. To keep in this range, bass will move from shallow to deeper water as the temperature changes. Anglers can use this to gauge where to locate these fish on any given day. Another clue on where to find this species comes during the winter spawning season when the fish are in shallow water, where the male makes a circular nest and the female lays her eggs and guards them.

Tackle and techniques – A variety of spinning and bait-casting rods and reels are used. A typical combination is a 6-foot rod with either a spinning reel rated to hold 4- to 20-pound test line or bait caster rated for 6- to 20-pound test line. The wide range of line strengths relates to the type of cover where you are fishing and the skills and preferences of the angler. Use heavier tackle in heavy cover to avoid break-offs.

Anglers can cast, flip, or pitch a bait to the fish. Bass anglers have dozens of variations of these techniques, and each angler seems to have one or two methods that he or she likes best.

State regulations apply to this fish. Check the latest edition of the rules and regulations for size and bag limits and open and closed seasons.

Bait – To catch a trophy fish, one over 10 pounds, your best chance for success is to use live wild shiners. Experienced anglers also use a wide variety of artificial lures for the big fish.

Soft plastic worms, rigged to run weedless, are the most popular lures for general bass angling. These worms come in dozens of colors, and there are almost as many theories on which color is best. Hard-bodied lures, including surface plugs, jigs, and diving baits, also work, and each is most effectively used at specific temperature conditions, water depth, and amount of floating or shoreline vegetation present.

Food value – Like snook, bass are edible but are more often released than eaten. If you want to cook one, the meat is slightly off-white and very flaky. Depending on where the fish is caught, it does have a mild but distinctive flavor that is described as being earthy, muddy, and a variety of other adjectives. Bass are known to contain mercury, an element that can be accumulated by humans and become toxic. Consumption advisories exist for bass in many of the state's most popular lakes. Pregnant women and children should pay special attention to and heed the warnings for consumption of bass. For the most up-to-date information, go to *www.doh.state.fl.us/floridafishadvice*.

Panfish

Distribution – Included in this group are bluegills, shellcrackers, (redear sunfish), stumpknockers (spotted sunfish), warmouth, fliers, and redbreast sunfish. While not every species is found throughout the state, there will be several species in just about every suitable location with the exception of the Florida Keys. Additionally, most species hybridize with other species, creating a melting pot of offspring.

The following is a summary of more commonly caught species:

Species	Distribution	Spawning	Habitat
Bluegill	Statewide	April–Oct	Lakes, ponds, slow-flowing rivers, and streams with gravel, sand, or mud bottoms
Shellcracker, (redear sunfish)	Statewide	March–Aug	Almost every freshwater aquatic system
Stumpknocker (spotted sunfish)	Statewide	May–Nov	Slow-moving streams with heavy vegetation and rivers with limestone, sand, or gravel substrates
Warmouth	Statewide	April–Aug	Swamps, marshes, shallow lakes, slow-moving streams, and canals that have soft, muddy bottoms
Flier	North and Central Florida	March–May	Coastal swamps, ponds, creeks, and canals with acidic water
Redbreast Sunfish	North and Central Florida	May– Aug	Coastal streams, rivers, and lakes with sandy bottoms and rocky areas

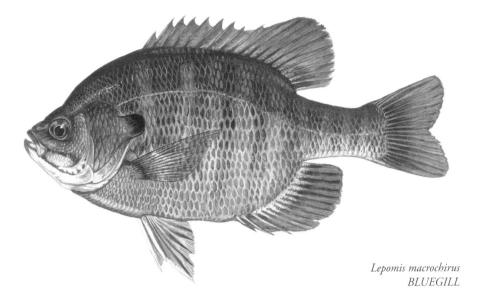

Lepomis macrochirus
BLUEGILL

Tackle and techniques – Light and ultra-light conventional tackle, a fly rod and reel rated for 5-weight line, or a cane pole are ideal for taking these small fish. The spring and summer spawning season provides the best action for native panfish, often reaching a monthly peak a few days on either side of the full moon.

State regulations apply to this fish. Check the latest edition of the rules and regulations for size and bag limits and open and closed seasons.

Bait – These fish will take live grass shrimp, earthworms, and crickets. Small lures such as spinner baits, popping bugs, and jigs are the most effective artificial baits.

Food value – It takes several panfish to make a meal. Fortunately, their abundance and liberal bag limits make these highly prized table fare. Most are too small to fillet and are typically pan dressed, seasoned, and fried in a pan. Try them with some eggs and grits for breakfast.

Striped bass

Distribution – Most of Florida's stripers are hatchery raised and are stocked in north Florida rivers and reservoirs and the St. Johns River. There may be some naturally reproducing fish in the rivers of northeast Florida as this is the southern limit of this well-known temperate coastal species. Because of its

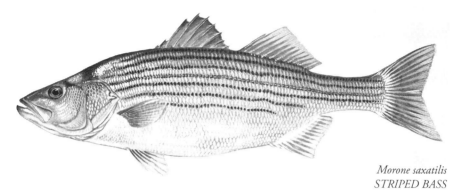

Morone saxatilis
STRIPED BASS

preference for cold water, this fish is seldom stocked or found farther south than Lake George on the St. Johns River. Additionally, striped bass in Florida rarely venture into saltwater like the Atlantic coast population.

Tackle and techniques – A stiff rod and a reel with 15- to 25-pound test line and a good drag will handle any big fish that decides to bite. One of the best times of year to fish for stripers is from February through April. During this time, stripers congregate at the tailraces (the area immediately downriver from the dam) of the dams on lakes Seminole and Talquin.

During warmer weather the fish head for cooler water and deeper holes. They will stay here from about June to October if the water remains warm. During summer, getting these fish to bite is tough. Your best bet is to fish for them at night or very early in the morning. Even then the fishing is nowhere near the quality it is in February and March.

State regulations apply to this fish. Check the latest edition of the rules and regulations for size and bag limits and open and closed seasons.

Bait – Live bait, especially live shad, is one of the most popular baits to use for trophy fish. For everyday angling, try yellow- or white-headed jigs. The weight used depends on how deep the fish are. Spoons also produce good results when deep jigging. The Redfin lure is effective if the fish are on the surface feeding on shad.

Food value – These full-flavored fish are best baked or grilled. If doing the latter, use a grilling basket because the meat is fine-grained and will easily fall apart once fully cooked.

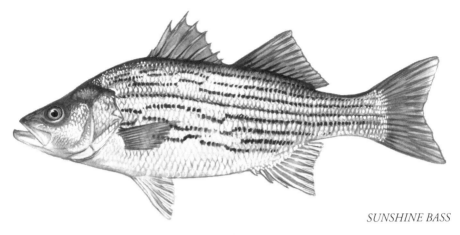

Sunshine bass_____

Distribution – Sunshine bass are a cross between male striped bass and female white bass. These fish don't grow as large as the stripers, averaging 3 to 4 pounds in north Florida and 1 to 2 pounds at the southern end of their range. Sunshine bass can tolerate warmer temperatures than stripers. As a result, these hybrids can be stocked in lakes as far south as Lake Manatee near Bradenton and Lake Osborne in West Palm Beach. The fishery is strictly a put-and-take effort; sunshine bass are sterile and cannot reproduce.

Tackle and techniques – Light-weight spinning or bait-casting tackle with 6- to 10-pound test line is sufficient for this species as the ones found in central Florida seldom weigh more than 2 pounds.

State regulations apply to this fish. Check the latest edition of the rules and regulations for size and bag limits and open and closed seasons.

Bait – Like striped bass, sunshine bass love live shad, white and yellow jigs, spoons, and some surface lures.

Food value – These full-flavored fish are best baked or grilled. If doing the latter, use a grilling basket because the meat is fine-grained and will easily fall apart once fully cooked.

Is It a Record?

Anglers dream of catching the big one, one that will enshrine their name in the record books. To determine if the fish you caught is a record fish, consult the Florida Fish and Wildlife Conservation Commission (FWC). The agency maintains the official state record list for freshwater fish. And, in cooperation with the International Game Fish Association, the FWC also maintains the state all-tackle saltwater records for conventional tackle and fly fishing.

Freshwater Records

If you've caught a fish that is a candidate for the list, it is important to follow the proper procedure to have your catch verified as a record fish. To qualify, the following criteria must be met:

- The fish must be caught by a legal sport fishing method.
- You must have a valid Florida fishing license or be exempt from needing one.
- An FWC biologist must identify the fish.
- The fish must be weighed on a certified scale.

To find an FWC biologist, refer to the listing of regional FWC offices (Appendix 2) or contact a local bait and tackle shop as they may be able to assist you. Time is critical, especially if you cannot keep the fish alive. The weight does decrease if the fish dies or is out of water for any period of time. If the fish is only a few ounces over the existing record, that weight can be lost if you have to delay certifying the weight. A list of the state freshwater records as listed on the FWC website *(http://myfwc.com/RECREATION/FW_record.htm)* as of August 2010 is provided in Appendix 1).

If your fish isn't quite big enough to break the current certified record, it may qualify for the FWC's "Big Catch" program. Anglers who catch a freshwater fish that exceeds the qualifying weight established by the FWC are eligible to receive a full-color Big Catch citation. There are 33 fish species that qualify for the Big Catch program. To be eligible for a citation, the angler must have a valid freshwater fishing license or be legally exempt from having one. The total length of the fish must be measured with a witness present. The angler then fills out an application and sends it to the FWC for approval. Applications can be obtained from any of the FWC regional offices or downloaded from *http://myfwc.com/docs/Freshwater/Freshwater_BigCatch_Application.pdf.* The application also has the qualifying lengths for the Big Catch program.

As a means to encourage kids to spend more time fishing, the FWC has a special program for children under the age of 16. The size limit to qualify for a Big Catch Certificate is lowered by 25% for all species. For the specific details on the kids and adult big catch programs, go to *http://myfwc.com/LEARNING/Learn_RecognitionPrograms_bigcatch.htm.*

Saltwater Fishing Records

The state record program for saltwater fish is administered by the International Game Fish Association (IGFA). This organization also maintains world records for the most popular freshwater and saltwater game fish. The state keeps records for more than 73 species of saltwater fish in two categories: conventional and fly fishing. The most recent state records listed on the FWC website at the time of this writing are as of July 2010 and are provided in Appendix 1. For updates to the records, go to *http://www.myfwc.com/RECREATION/Saltwater_FishRecords.htm.*

In order to qualify for a state record, anglers must follow the IGFA angling rules. These can be downloaded from the IGFA website *(www.igfa.org,* click on Go Fish, then World Records and then International Angling Rules) or you can send a request via mail to 300 Gulf Stream Way, Dania Beach, FL 33004. There is a small fee for the rules. You can also call IGFA at 954-927-2628. The requirements are very specific and if you are actively attempting to set a state or world record, it is essential that you be aware of the requirements beforehand.

Only fish caught in the state waters, within three nautical miles of the shoreline of the Atlantic Ocean or nine nautical miles of the shoreline of the Gulf of Mexico, are eligible for a state record. The fish must be weighed on an accurate scale, samples of the line must be provided, and photos must be included in the application form. Species which pose a problem of identity require determination by an ichthyologist or qualified fishery biologist.

Florida also has a Grand Slam Club for which anglers can qualify. This involves catching or catching and releasing three different species in one day. IGFA rules apply and you must submit an application to be eligible. The form is available at the FWC website, *http://myfwc.com/docs/RecreationActivities/SW_Application_GrandSlam.pdf.*

Four regional Grand Slams are offered:

North Florida Grand Slam: Spotted Seatrout, Red Drum (Redfish), Cobia

East Coast Grand Slam: Spotted Seatrout, Red Drum (Redfish), Tarpon

Florida West Coast Grand Slam: Red Drum (Redfish), Snook, Tarpon

South Florida Grand Slam: Bonefish, Permit, Tarpon

East Central Florida_____

Counties:
- Marion (eastern) • Putnam (southeastern) • Lake • Volusia
- Seminole • Orange • Osceola • Brevard • Indian River

Saltwater Fishing

The unique Indian River Lagoon system, less than one mile wide and three feet deep for much of its expanse, is the dominant coastal feature in east central Florida. Along with the Banana River and Mosquito Lagoon to the north, the three lagoons encompass 156 miles of Florida's coastline from Daytona to Stuart. With mangroves and salt marshes along the shoreline and extensive seagrass meadows in the shallow water, the entire lagoon is prime fishing grounds for redfish and spotted seatrout, with snook added to the mix south of Cape Canaveral.

The Indian River system contains about 700 saltwater and freshwater fish species, and is home to one-third of the state's population of manatees. It is also the source of 90 percent of the state's harvest of hardshell clams. Saltwater fishing contributes over $346 million to the east central Florida economy. The total economic benefit of a healthy Indian River Lagoon was estimated to be $3.7 billion in 2007.

After decades of urban growth from the mid-1900s onward, the lagoon's watershed was altered by numerous inland drainage projects that brought increased runoff and pollution to the lagoon. With urban development came the need for mosquito control. The method of choice was to dike and impound over 40,000 acres of marshes, separating them from the lagoon system and cutting off the vital role these marshes played in providing habitat for the fish, shellfish, and other wildlife that depend on the lagoon.

Fortunately, there has been an ongoing effort to monitor the health of the Indian River's ecosystems and develop programs to restore some of the damaged and lost habitat. Leading the way are the Indian River Lagoon National Estuary Program (NEP) and the St. Johns and South Florida Water Management Districts. For more information about the important programs and activities related to the lagoons, visit the water management district websites at *www. sjrwmd.com* and *www.sfwmd.com* or the Indian River NEP site at *www.epa.gov/ nep/programs/irl.html.*

The lagoons are linked to the Atlantic Ocean by five inlets that are magnets for fish and anglers. Snook, Florida's ultimate saltwater game fish, is one of the most sought-after inlet inhabitants from spring to fall. In winter, doormat-sized flounder show up, while snook seek out warmer waters in the creeks emptying into the lagoon.

Offshore, dolphin in the summer and sailfish in the winter give meat and sport anglers, respectively, something to fish for. Further enhancing the angling opportunities, this part of the coast benefits from the spring and fall run of king mackerel, cobia, dolphin, and blackfin tuna. Add year-round grouper and snapper action and anywhere you fish—from the beach to more than 50 miles offshore—the chances are really good that you will catch some fish. From the beach to more than 50 miles offshore, the chances are really good that you will catch some fish. It's almost guaranteed if you take a charter boat and rely on the captain's expertise.

East Central Regional Map

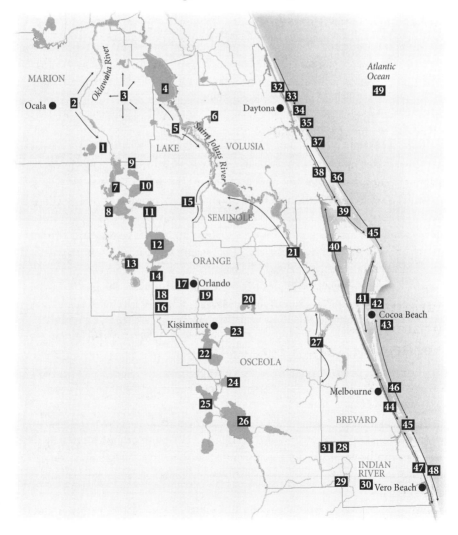

Freshwater Fishing

Many of the top lakes for trophy largemouth bass are in the central part of the state. Stick Marsh and Garcia Reservoir are two of the most famous bass fishing waters in Florida. The Kissimmee River begins in the swamps and lakes south of the Kissimmee–St. Cloud area and connects a series of bass filled lakes.

The Harris Chain of lakes surrounding Leesburg and the smaller Clermont Chain provide angling opportunities in scenic surroundings. The action on one or two lakes in each chain always seems to be really hot.

Fishing activity can be enhanced or tempered by the amount of the introduced aquatic plant, hydrilla—some provides good cover, but too much can make it too difficult to fish. Because conditions among these lakes vary widely from month to month it is a good idea to stop at a local bait and tackle shop to inquire on the current conditions.

The clear-water lakes in Ocala National Forest, even the small ones, are good places to fish for big largemouth bass and specs, the regional name for crappie. As the name implies, these lakes tend to have clear water and that gives the fish some advantages over the anglers. To even the odds local anglers use light line (in both pound test and color) and small baits when fishing these lakes. The clear water makes it easy for the bass to see the line attached to your bait. This, combined with the fact that these fish have seen every type of lure ever made, is what gives the advantage to the fish. But don't let this discourage you. Eventually the bass get hungry and patient anglers will reap the rewards.

The waters of Ocala National Forest are only the beginning of places to wet a line. The St. Johns and Ocklawaha rivers offer a number of well-known fishing holes. Rodman Reservoir on the Oklawaha River and Lakes George and Woodruff along the St. Johns River have long-standing reputations as great bass waters.

Marion (Eastern Portion), Putnam (Southeastern Portion), Lake (Northern Portion), And Volusia (Northwestern Portion) Counties

1. LAKE WEIR
Fresh – Boat – Ramp

Description: At over 5,600 acres this large lake is a popular place to fish. Weekends can be crowded, so if you want a more laid-back experience try fishing during the weekdays.

Fishing Index: Fish for largemouth bass, which is best in early spring. In

Marion (Eastern Portion), Putnam (Southeastern Portion), Lake (Northern Portion), and Volusia (Northwestern Portion) Counties

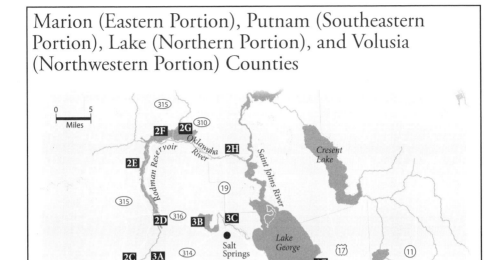

summer, fish for bluegills. There is a band of grass around the lake so there are plenty of good places to cast a shiner or lure.

Directions: The lake is approximately 14 miles southeast of Ocala.

Access Points:

1A. Carney Island Recreation/Conservation Area—*Boat — Ramp*
Directions: From the intersection of FL 25 and FL 464 in Oklawaha, drive west on FL 25 for 1.3 miles to SE 115th Ave. Turn left on SE 115th and follow the road across the train tracks to the ramp.
Address: 13275 SE 115 Ave., Ocklawaha, FL

1B. Hope Boat Ramp—*Boat – Ramp*
Directions: On the south shore of the lake. From the intersection of FL 25 and FL 42 in Weirsdale, drive west on FL 42 for 2.3 miles to the intersection with SE 115th Ave. Turn left onto SE 115th and drive south 1.2 miles to the ramp.

This is the largest and most developed ramp on the lake.
Address: 16050 SE 115 Ave., Weirsdale, FL

2. OKLAWAHA RIVER AND RODMAN RESERVOIR (LAKE OKLAWAHA)
Fresh – Boat and Bank – Ramp

Description: The Oklawaha River has its origins in the Harris Chain of lakes near Leesburg. The river flows north eventually joining the St. Johns River a few miles south of Palatka. Lake Oklawaha, commonly referred to as the Rodman Reservoir is an impounded portion of the river created by the upriver Eureka Dam and the downriver Rodman Dam. The river and lake form western and northern boundaries of the Ocala National Forest and some of the access points listed here are within the National Forest. Upriver of the Eureka Dam the Oklawaha is a winding scenic river that offers many good fishing opportunities. Boaters must always watch out for obstructions, as large branches and trees fall into the water and can block part of or the entire river.

The reservoir includes almost 13 miles of flooded timberland which provides great habitat for fishing and potential hazards for boat operators. Use caution, as submerged stumps and large branches are abundant especially along the edges of the reservoir. A remnant of the Cross Florida Barge Canal connects the Rodman Dam end of the reservoir to the St. Johns River.

A long-running feud over whether to remove the dams and restore the river has divided anglers and conservationists for many years. If it ever happens, it would lower levels on the lake up to 14 feet, effectively eliminating the lake and returning the water to the old river channel. Anglers, who mostly oppose the idea, say it would destroy a significant trophy bass fishery.

Fishing Index: Between Moss Bluff, the most upriver access point, and the Eureka Dam, there is good fishing for largemouth bass in the late winter and early spring. At other times of the year bluegills, shellcrackers, and catfish are the most common species caught. The current in this part of the river, where there are channelized sections, can be swift so you might need to use a sinker to get live baits down to where the fish are. It is also a good idea to seek out areas of protected waters within one of the numerous river bends and fish these areas using a live shiner with a bobber set to keep the bait a few feet off the bottom. The well-known reservoir has a reputation as a place to catch trophy largemouth bass, crappie, and bluegill. There is very good bass fishing throughout the year, but the best times are from February to April. Crappie fishing is good all year with bluegill action peaking between May and August. Look for these fish in places where they can get under some type of cover.

Directions: The river is in Marion and Lake counties east of Ocala.

Access Points between Moss Bluff Dam and Eureka Dam:

2A. MOSS BLUFF—*Bank, Pier, and Boat – Ramp*
Description: There are two ramps, one above the Moss Bluff Lock and Dam and the other below it. There is bank fishing and a fishing pier on the upriver (south) side of the lock and dam. The lock is operational and boaters can use it
Directions: From FL 25, along the north shore of Lake Weir, turn north onto FL 464 and drive 4.3 miles to the lock and dam. Or from FL 40 in Ocala National Forest turn south on CR 314A and go 7.6 miles to the junction with FL 464. Turn right and go 0.3 mile to the lock and dam.

2B. RAY WAYSIDE PARK (OCALA BOAT BASIN) —*Bank and Boat – Ramp*
Description: The ramp is located on a canal that connects to the Silver River just upstream from where it joins the Oklawaha River. This easy-to-reach facility provides access to the scenic portions of the Silver and Oklawaha rivers.
Directions: The ramp is on FL 40, on the west side of the river, about 9.5 miles east of the US 27 and FL 40 intersection in Ocala.

2C. GORE'S LANDING—*Boat and Bank – Ramp*
Description: The ramp is midway along the river between FL 40 and Eureka Dam. Camping is available at the site
Directions: From Silver Springs, drive 2 miles east on FL 40 and turn north on FL 315. Drive about 6.3 miles to NE 105th St. (Gore's Landing Road). Turn right and drive 2 miles to NE 130th Ave. Turn right onto NE 130th and drive 0.7 miles to NE 98th St. Turn left onto NE 98th and drive 0.8 miles to the ramp.
Address: 13750 NE 98th St., Ft. McCoy, FL

2D. EUREKA EAST AND WEST—*Boat and Bank – Ramp.*
Description: These two small ramps are within 0.1 miles of each other. The west ramp is on the north side of CR 316, and the east ramp is on the south side of CR 316.
Directions: From the intersection of FL 315 and FL 316 in Fort McCoy, take FL 316 east about 3.7 miles to NE 152nd Court Road. Turn left and drive north to 154th St. Turn right onto 154th and the ramp. To reach the east ramp, cross over the river on CR 316 and take the first right onto NE 152nd St. Follow it to the ramp on your right.

Access Points on Rodman Reservoir (Lake Oklawaha)
2E. Orange Springs—*Boat – Ramp*
Description: This facility is maintained by Marion County. Access to Rodman Reservoir is via a short canal leading to Orange Creek and then into the reservoir.
Directions: From the intersection of FL 19 and FL 310, take FL 310 west about 8 miles until the road ends at FL 315. Turn left and go 4.3 miles to the small settlement of Orange Springs. If you are approaching from the west, it is approximately 20 miles on FL 315 from the intersection of FL 315 and FL 40 near Silver Springs. Turn onto NE 245th Street Road (River Rd.) and follow it for 1.5 miles to the entrance to the ramp on your left.
Address: NE 245th Street Road, Orange Springs, FL

2F. Kenwood Ramp—*Boat – Ramp*
Description: A remote ramp that provides access to the lower part of Rodman Reservoir via a canal.
Directions: From the intersection of FL 19 and FL 310, take FL 310 west about 8 miles until the road ends at FL 315. Turn left and go 1.1 miles to the small settlement of Kenwood. FL 315 bends to the right. Look for the recreational area entrance sign and follow the access road to the ramp.

2G. Rodman Recreation Area —*Bank, Pier, and Boat – Ramp – $*
Description: This facility is operated by the state's Office of Greenways and Trails. The site provides anglers with access to Lake Oklawaha and the channelized segment of the Oklawaha River between the Rodman Dam and the St. Johns River. The pier is barrier-free and is located at Rodham Dam.
Directions: From the intersection of FL 19 and FL 20 in Palatka, drive south on FL 19 for approximately 8.7 miles. Just after crossing the Cross Florida Barge Canal, turn right onto Rodman Dam Road and follow this road 2.6 miles to the campground and ramp.
Address: 410 Rodman Road, Palatka, FL

Access Point between Rodman Dam and the St. Johns River:
2H. FL 19 Ramp—*Boat – Ramp*
Description: This ramp provides access to the natural portion of the Oklawaha River downstream of the Rodman Dam.
Directions: The ramp is about 9.2 miles north of the FL 19–Fl 314 intersection in Salt Springs. It is on the east side of FL 19 and the south side of the river.

3. OCALA NATIONAL FOREST

Fresh – Bank, Pier, Boat and Canoe – Ramp — $

Description: This 383,000-acre National Forest has 23 spring-fed streams and nearly 600 lakes. While most can be fished, many are accessible only on foot or with a 4x4 vehicle. The lakes have some vegetation around them but are acidic and usually low in nutrients. Nonetheless many of them have produced bass in excess of 10 pounds. The springs and lakes listed here are easily accessible by any type of vehicle. There are fees at some of the more popular boat ramps and most of the campgrounds. NOTE: Some of the directions for this listing refer to FR followed by a number. FR refers to "Forest Road" which are government roads within Ocala National Forest. Most are not paved.

Fishing Index: Fish the lakes for largemouth bass, bluegills, shellcrackers, and crappie, locally referred to as "specs." Some of the lakes are clear-water lakes and require some stealth as the fish can see you as well as you can see them. Try using a fluorocarbon leader or line. Small baits and lures are also recommended. Other lakes are colored-water lakes which are more familiar to anglers. The creeks emanating from the springs hold largemouth bass, bluegills, specs, and, in the springs feeding Lake George, striped bass can be caught.

Directions: Ocala National Forest begins about 10 miles east of Ocala.

For more information: Contact the Ocala National Forest (352) 625-2520 or visit their website at http://www.fs.fed.us/r8/florida/ocala/. For more detailed information on fishing in Ocala National Forest, inquire about how to purchase the book, *Fishing Opportunities in Ocala National Forest* by calling the number above.

Access Points:

3A. FORE LAKE—*Pier – Boat – $.*
Description: No gasoline engines are allowed on this 24-acre colored-water lake. Boats are allowed but they have to be small enough to be hand-carried to the launching site. Fishing is best around the vegetated shoreline. There is a campground next to the lake.
Directions: From the FL 40–FL 314 intersection, a few miles east of Silver Springs, take FL 314 east towards Salt Springs for about 5.4 miles to the entrance to the pier and ramp on your left.

3B. LAKE KERR—*Boat – Ramp*
Description: This 2,830-acre clear-water lake is shallow and has considerable

vegetation. It is the largest lake in the national forest. Most of the property around the lake is privately owned and the lake receives heavy use by water-skiers and personal watercraft. In 2010 FWC regulations *www.myfwc.com* had the following restriction: "Lake Kerr, Marion County, including Little Lake Kerr: No person shall kill or possess any black bass 15 inches or more in total length and less than 24 inches in total length. No person shall take in any one day more than three black bass of which only one may be 24 inches or longer in total length."

Directions: From the intersection of FR 88 and FL 314 a few miles west of Salt Springs take FR 88 3.8 miles to Moorehead Park Road. Turn right and drive 0.3 mile to the public boat ramp.

3C. Salt Springs Run—*Boat – Ramp – $*

Description: A popular place for anglers. The run empties into Lake George and is wide enough to accommodate large boats. Swimming in the spring and camping are also popular. Look for striped bass moving in from the lake. Bait, tackle, snacks, and rental boats are available on site from the privately run Salt Springs Run Marian and Landing.

Directions: The ramp is just off FL 19 in Salt Springs.

For more information: Call Salt Springs Run Marina and Landing at (352) 685-2255 or go to www.saltspringsmarina.com.

3D. Lake Bryant—*Pier – Boat – Ramp – $*

Description: This 765-acre colored-water lake is a popular fishing destination. Lake Bryant Camp is privately run with rental boats, cabins, and camp and RV sites for rent.

Directions: From the intersection of FL 40 and FL 19 take FL 40 about 12 miles west and look for Levy Hammock Road (SE 183 Ave.). Turn south and go 2.4 miles to Lake Bryant Camp.

Address: 5000 S.E. 183rd Avenue Road, Ocklawaha, FL

For more information: Call Lake Bryant Mobile Home and RV Park at (352) 625-2376 or go to www.lakebryant.com.

3E. Mill Dam Lake—*Boat — Ramp – $*

Description: A popular and convenient place to fish. The 168-acre lake is colored-water. The ramp may be unusable during low water. There is a parking fee.

Directions: From the intersection of FL 40 and FL 19 take FL 40 west about 11.2 miles. Turn north onto NE 196 Terrace Road, go 0.3 mile to FR 59, turn left, and follow the road 0.3 mile to FR 59A. Turn left onto FR 59A and drive 0.3 miles to the lake.

3F. Wildcat Lake—*Pier — Boat — Ramp — $*

Description: A 258-acre clear-water lake with vegetation that extends into the deeper water. It's a good place to find a big bass. This is a catch-and-release lake for bass according to the 2010 FWC freshwater fishing regulations.

Directions: From the intersection of FL 40 and FL 19 take FL 40 east 0.9 mile to the entrance road to the lake.

3G. Grasshopper Lake—*Pier – Boat – Ramp*

Description: A 147-acre clear-water lake with dense vegetation along the shoreline. There is a 20-hp limit on boat motors.

Directions: From the intersection of FL 40 and FL 19 take FL 19 south 2.7 miles to the entrance road to the lake on your left.

3H. Beakman and Sellers Lakes—*Boat – Ramp*

Description: These two lakes are linked by a waterway that is navigable except during low water. Both are exceptionally clear-water lakes that reportedly have some of the biggest bass in the region. These are difficult lakes to fish, requiring good angling skills and patience.

Directions: The ramp to Lake Beakman is just off FL 19 on your left, 3 miles south of the FL 19–FL 40 intersection. Access to Sellers Lake is via the channel connecting the lakes.

3I. Buck Lake—*Boat – Ramp*

Description: A 52-acre clear-water lake that supports trophy-sized bass. The lake has several brush attractors. Crappie are stocked here. There is a 20-hp limit on outboard motors.

Directions: From the FL 19–FL 40 intersection, go south 4.5 miles on FL 19 to FR 535. Turn right and follow FR 535 west. It becomes FR 595C after 0.5 miles. Continue another 0.9 miles to FR 595-2. Drive 0.6 miles and turn left. The ramp is 0.5 miles ahead.

3J. Alexander Springs—*Canoe – Ramp*

Description: This is one of the most popular sites in the national forest. It is a great place to launch a canoe and fish the swift moving creek. At the head of the creek is Alexander Springs, which features swimming and camping. Canoes can be rented on-site and there is a canoe launch. However, the area is usually congested with recreational users who are swimming, snorkeling, and diving, not fishing. Put in away from the recreational users at the FR 445 Bridge and head downstream.

Directions: From FL 19 about 12.5 miles north of Eustis, go east on FR 445 about 5 miles to the bridge over Alexander Springs Creek. The put-in spots for canoes are on either side of the bridge. The take-out is at the end of FR 552. To reach it from FR 445, drive 0.3 mile past the Alexander Springs Creek Bridge to

FR 552. Turn right and follow FR 552 about 4.5 miles to the take-out spot.

3K. Lake Dorr—*Pier – Boat – Ramp – $*
Description: The lake, despite a convenient location and nice campground, is not heavily fished. Try it in spring for largemouth bass and in fall for crappie.
Directions: There are two good ramps both off FL 19. One is 11.2 miles south and the other is 11.6 miles south of the FL 40–FL 19 intersection.

4. Lake George and Little Lake George
Fresh – Boat and Pier — Ramp

Description: Lake George is a 46,000-acre lake that is really a wide spot in the St. Johns River. It is a very popular place to fish. The depth seldom exceeds 10 feet and a shelf only 1 to 4 feet deep runs around the entire lake. These flats harbor eelgrass beds and are an excellent place to fish. Anglers also have good luck fishing around the pilings associated with the active military bombing range in the middle of the lake. The lake can become rough if the wind begins to blow – keep an eye on the weather. If it turns bad, return to home port or head up the spring runs along the lake's western shore. Salt Springs is one of the most popular destinations.

Fishing Index: Both lakes are well known for their largemouth and striped bass fishing. Largemouth bass spawn in the shallow waters around the edge of the lake in spring. Stripers run in the spring and some will move up the salt springs along the lake's western shoreline. They do not spawn in the lake. At other times of the year, anglers fish around the deeper water structures. Lake George has several brush attractors, small deep holes, and some jetties at the south end which are good places to try for both bass species. Crappie fishing is excellent in winter with Missouri minnows the preferred bait.

The naturally occurring high salt content in Lake George makes it suitable habitat for some saltwater species. The summer shrimp run often brings the crustaceans into the lower part of the lake. Redfish and blue crabs appear to be established in Lake George. Catching a redfish is not unusual and there are enough blue crabs to support a small commercial fishery. Anglers also occasionally catch mangrove snapper, flounder, and tarpon. On this lake, you might be in for a surprise when the fish gets to the boat.

Little Lake George, downriver from its larger cousin has a well-known fishing spot called the Croaker Hole. It is the place to catch stripers, especially in the spring.

For more information: Call the FWC Regional Office at (352) 732-1255 for a list of private fish camps around the lake.

Access Points: There are numerous commercial marinas and fish camps in Georgetown at the north end of Lake George and in Astor about 1 mile upriver from the south end of the lake. You can also access the lake for the ramp at Salt Springs Run in Ocala National Forest. The most popular public access points are:

4A. Blue Creek—*Boat – Ramp*

Directions: From the FL 40 bridge over the St. Johns River in Astor, drive 4.6 miles west on FL 40 to Blue Creek Road (FR 9983). Turn right and go 2.4 miles to Lake George Road (FR 9984). Turn left and follow Lake George Road 1 mile to the ramp.

4B. Butler Street Ramp—*Boat – Ramp – $*

Description: Head downriver to reach Lake George. Upriver leads to lakes Dexter and Woodruff.

Directions: In Astor, turn off FL 40 onto W. Michigan Ave. on the west side of the St. Johns. Drive 0.1 miles to the ramp.

Address: 55400 Butler St., Astor, FL

4C. Lake George Pier – *Pier*

Directions: From the intersection of FL 40 and US 17 north of DeLeon Springs, drive north on US 17 for 7.2 miles to the intersection with CR 3. Turn left and then make a right onto Ninemile Point Rd. Drive 5.1 miles to the end of the road and the pier.

Address: 770 Nine Mile Point Rd., Pierson, FL

5. St. Johns River (Astor to FL 44 Bridge including lakes Dexter and Woodruff)
Fresh – Bank and Boat – Ramp

Description: Heading upriver from Astor, it's a little more than 4 miles to reach Lake Dexter and the marshes of Lake Woodruff National Wildlife Refuge. Both lakes are totally undeveloped. Boaters just passing through can simply follow the channel markers. But to explore the wilderness, use a GPS or good map. Most of the local marinas and tackle stores have maps. Access to this stretch of the river is from Astor to the north, DeLeon Springs to the east, and off FL 44 to the south. Remember, the St. Johns River flows northward. Due to the presence of the endangered West Indian manatee, there are boat speed restrictions in this area.

Fishing Index: From Astor upriver to Lake Dexter, anglers fish for largemouth bass. Lake Dexter is the destination for crappie enthusiasts in fall and winter. The lake is considered a top spot for the tasty fish. In summer, lakes Dexter and Woodruff produce good stringers of big bluegills. The best times are roughly four days on either side of the full moon. Lake Woodruff is also noted for its bass fishing. Try for them around the many lily pads.

Access Points: The Butler Street Ramp (Site 4B above) in Astor is used by anglers approaching these lakes from the north.

5A. DeLeon Springs State Park—*Bank and Boat – Ramp – $*
Description: The park features swimming in the spring boil, the remains of an old sugar mill, and picnicking. Anglers can fish from the banks in Spring Garden Lake. Access to lakes Woodruff and Dexter is via Spring Garden Creek, a winding waterway that connects to Lake Woodruff.
Directions: From the intersection with US 92 in DeLand take US 17 north 7.2 miles to Ponce DeLeon Blvd. Turn left and go 0.8 mile to the park.
Address: 601 Ponce de Leon Blvd., DeLeon Springs, FL
For more information: Call the park office at (386) 985-4212 or go to *www. floridastateparks.org.*

5B. Ed Stone Park—*Bank and Boat – Ramp*
Description: A Volusia County facility adjacent to the St. Johns River Bridge on FL 44. Anglers can fish in the river off the seawall. Several commercial marinas are nearby.
Directions: From US 17 and US 92 in DeLand, take FL 44 west 5 miles to the park. The entrance is on the right before you cross the bridge over the river.
Address: 2990 West Highway 44, DeLand, FL

6.   Lake Dias
Fresh – Bank and Boat – Ramp

Description: This 711-acre dark-water lake is an FWC Fish Management Area. The land around the lake is relatively undeveloped.

Fishing Index: Fish congregate around the fish attractors in the lake, and anglers fishing near them generally have good luck. The lake is noted for its crappie fishing and has fair largemouth bass fishing. Spring is the best time of year.

Directions: From the intersection of FL 44, US 17, and 92 in DeLand, drive about 2.9 miles north on US 17. Where the highway bends left, go straight on FL 11 about 6.9 miles. The lake and ramp, at Candace Strawn Park, are on the left.

Address: 5320 S.R.11 DeLeon Springs, FL

For more information: Call the FWC regional office at (352) 732-1255.

Lake (southern portion), Orange, Seminole and Volusia (southwestern portion) Counties

7 – 12. Harris Chain of Lakes ———————————————
Fresh — Bank, Pier, Boat and Canoe – Ramp

Description: The Harris Chain of lakes (sometimes called the Oklawaha Chain) includes Lakes Beauclair, Dora, Eustis, Carlton, Denham, Griffin, Harris and Yale and the headwaters lake, Apopka. The fishing reputation of these lakes suffered in past years due to pollution problems. These issues are being aggressively addressed and the lakes, with the exception of Apopka, are now considered good places to fish.

Fishing Index: There is a diversity of water conditions on these lakes. Apopka remains the most polluted of the chain. However, ongoing efforts and millions of dollars are being spent to return the lake to its former status as a top bass fishing lake. The numerous canals connected to these lakes and canals connecting the lakes are prime fishing areas and should not be overlooked. They are usually deep and good places to fish when it is windy and rough on the lakes.

For more information: The website *www.lakecountybass.com* is a good source of information.

7. Lake Griffin ———————————————
Fresh – Boat, Bank, and Pier – Ramp

Description: This lake is the northernmost lake in the chain. From here water flows north into the Oklawaha River. Most of the land along the shoreline is undeveloped or minimally so. The lake is managed by the FWC as a Fish Management Area.

Fishing Index: The problems related to pollution that caused a decline in the quality of fishing in the 1990s are being addressed and fishing is considerably better. The eelgrass beds have recovered and big bass are now common, so don't be misled by old reports that fishing is not that great.

Access Points:
7A. Herlong Park—*Boat and Pier – Ramp*
Directions: From the intersection of US 27 and US 441 in Leesburg, drive east on US 441 about 1 mile. The park is on your left.
Address: 700 E. North Blvd., Leesburg, FL

Lake (southern portion), Orange, Seminole and Volusia (southwestern portion) Counties

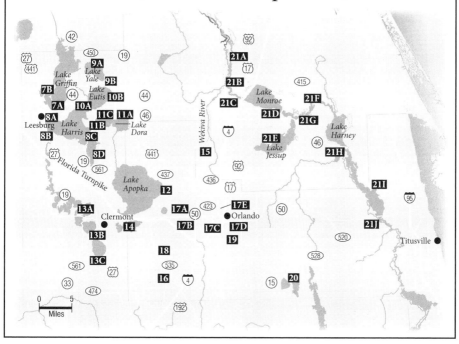

7B. LAKE GRIFFIN STATE PARK—*Boat and Bank – Ramp – $*
Directions: From the intersection of FL 44 and US 27 in Leesburg, take US 27 north about 3.5 miles to the park entrance.
Address: 3089 US 441/27, Fruitland Park, FL
For more information: Call the park office at (352) 360-6760 or go to *www. floridastateparks.org.*

8. LAKE HARRIS AND LITTLE LAKE HARRIS ——————
Fresh – Boat and Pier – Ramp

Description: Combined, the two lakes in the Harris Chain cover 15,500 acres.

Fishing Index: Lake Harris has more deep water than other lakes in the Harris Chain. To find them, you'll need one of the detailed topographic fishing maps that are widely available in the area and a good depth finder on your boat. Most of the shoreline of both lakes is lined with reed and Kissimmee grass, making these areas a good place to find bass. In the winter, crappie fishing is popular. The best crappie fishing, according to many anglers, is at night.

Access Points:

8A. Venetian Gardens—*Pier and Boat – Ramp*
Description: A City of Leesburg facility
Directions: In Leesburg, from the intersection with US 27, US 441, and FL 44 (Dixie Ave.), take FL 44 about 1 mile east. The ramp is just off the highway.
Address: 109 E. Dixie Ave., Leesburg, FL

8B. Singletary Park—*Pier and Boat – Ramp*
Description: A FWC facility, the pier is barrier-free.
Directions: In Leesburg. From the intersection of US 27 and FL 44, drive about 2.5 miles south on US 27. The park is just off the highway.
Address: 1902 S. 14th St., Leesburg, FL

8C. Hickory Point—*Pier and Boat – Ramp – $*
Description: This is an outstanding facility for anglers. Operated by Lake County, the site features 12 boat lanes and can accommodate deep-draft boats. Parking is ample. The combination dock and fishing pier is barrier-free and open to anglers at night.
Directions: From the intersection of FL 19 and US 441 in Tavares, take FL 19 south 4.7 miles to the park entrance. It is on the north side of the lake just before the FL 19 bridge.
Address: 27341 State Road 19, Tavares, FL

8D. Astatula Park—*Boat – Ramp*
Description: Provides access to Little Lake Harris
Directions: From the intersection of FL 19 and FL 561 south of Tavares, drive south on FL 561 approximately 5.5 miles to Florida Ave. Turn left onto Florida Ave. and drive 0.8 miles to the ramp.
Address: 12703 Florida Ave., Astatula, FL

9. Lake Yale
Fresh – Boat and Bank – Ramp

Description: The 4,000-acre lake is northwest of Eustis.
Fishing Index: As on other lakes in the Harris Chain, fishing on Lake Yale has improved. The FWC reports crappie, bluegill, and redear sunfish in areas where there are lily pads. Bass fishing is not as good as other Harris Chain lakes, but it is improving. Try the ledges around the deeper holes.

Access Points:
9A. Lake Yale East Ramp—*Boat – Ramp*
Directions: From the intersection with FL 44 in Eustis, take FL 19 north 5.5

miles to CR 450. Turn left onto CR 450 and go 1.8 miles to Lake Yale Rd. Turn left on Lake Yale Rd. and drive 1.4 miles to Yale Hammock Rd. Turn right onto Yale Hammock Rd. and drive 0.1 miles to Lake Yale Boat Ramp Rd. and follow this road to the single paved ramp.
Address: 39400 Lake Yale Boat Ramp Rd., Eustis, FL

9B. Marsh Park—*Boat and Bank – Ramp*
Directions: From the intersection with FL 19 in Eustis, take FL 44 west about 1.7 miles to CR 452. Take CR 452 0.6 mile to Yale Retreat Rd. (Old Chisholm Trail). Turn right and follow the road to the ramp on your left.
Address: 36545 Yale Retreat Rd., Eustis, FL

10. Lake Eustis
Fresh – Boat, Bank and Pier – Ramp

Description: A 7,806-acre lake that connects to Lake Griffin via Haines Creek and to Lake Harris via Dead River.

Fishing Index: The lake shoreline is fringed in cypress and maidencane, making it a productive home for largemouth bass. Try fishing for them around the mouths of the canals connecting this lake to lakes Harris and Griffin, especially when the weather is cooler.

Access Points:
10A. Tavares Recreation Park—*Boat, Bank and Pier – Ramp*
Directions: The ramp is off US 441, about 0.9 mile west of the US 441–FL 19 intersection in Tavares. It's adjacent to the Dora Canal (also known as Dead River) connecting lakes Eustis and Harris.
Address: 2030 W. Burleigh Blvd., Tavares, FL

10B. Lakeshore Drive Boat Ramp—*Boat and Pier – Ramp*
Directions: In downtown Eustis this city facility is on Lake Shore Drive 0.6 miles west of the FL 44 and Lake Shore Dr. intersection.

11. Lakes Dora, Beauclair, and Carlton
Fresh – Boat, Bank, and Pier – Ramp

Description: Lake Dora, a mid-size lake and the smaller Lake Carlton connects to Beauclair which connects to Lake Dora.

Fishing Index: These lakes have a reputation for holding a good number of trophy-sized bass, especially in the spring and fall, and good summer bluegill fishing.

Access Points:
11A. GILBERT PARK—*Boat, Bank and Pier – Ramp*
Directions: From the US 441 and CR 46 (E. 1st Ave.) intersection in Mount Dora, drive west on E. 1st Ave, for 0.6 miles to the intersection with N. Highland St. Turn left onto N. Highland and drive 2 blocks to Liberty Ave. Turn right on Liberty Ave. and drive 3 blocks to the park.
Address: Tremain Ave. and Liberty Ave., Mount Dora, FL

11B. SUMMERALL PARK—*Boat – Ramp*
Directions: From FL 19 on the south side of Tavares, turn onto Dead River Rd. or Wells Ave. and drive 0.2 miles to the ramp. Suitable for smaller boats, canoes, and kayaks.
Address: 1001 Wells Ave., Tavares, FL

11C. WOOTEN PARK—*Boat and Pier – Ramp*
Directions: In Tavares, from the intersection of FL 19 and W. Main St. (CR 452) drive east 0.9 miles to N. Rockingham Ave. Turn right onto N. Rockingham and drive 1 block to the park.
Address: 200S. Rockingham Ave., Tavares, FL

12. LAKE APOPKA
Fresh – Boat – Ramp

Description: This lake is too large and too well known to not mention. Unfortunately, its reputation, which was once as a great bass fishing lake, is now a different story. The lake is highly polluted and despite a significant effort to clean it up, the work is far from done and Apopka is not the fishing mecca many would like it to be. Hopefully conditions will improve in the years to come

Fishing Index: The only bright spot for anglers who want to fish in this lake is the southeast corner of the lake known as Gourd Neck. An active spring pumps enough fresh and unpolluted water into the lake to allow for a decent crappie fishery during the winter months
Directions: Magnolia Park, an Orange County facility, has a boat ramp. From US 441 west of Apopka, drive south on CR 437 approximately 5.2 miles to Magnolia Park and ramp.
Address: 2929 S. Binion Rd, Apopka, FL

Fish around lily pads and you're likely to find largemouth bass.

13. CLERMONT CHAIN OF LAKES
Fresh – Boat, Bank, and Pier – Ramp

Description: This chain of 11 small and mid-size scenic lakes surrounds the city of Clermont. Some lakes are surrounded by cypress trees and are tannin stained. Those without cypress, notably Lake Minneola, have somewhat clearer water. Jet skis and weekend cruisers make these lakes harder to fish on Saturday and Sundays.

Fishing Index: All lakes in the Clermont Chain are FWC Fish Management Areas signifying that the commission actively manages these areas to benefit anglers. January to April are the best months for catching largemouth bass. That's when the fish move into the shallow water and spawn. The lakes also have some big channel catfish in them, up to 40 pounds. Crappie fishing is popular in winter and where you find one you'll usually find more because the fish school up when the water is cold.

For more information: Go to *www.lakecountybass.com* or call Clermont Bait and Tackle at (352) 394-7000.

Access Points:
13A. CLERMONT BOAT RAMP—*Pier and Boat – Ramp – $*
Description: For access to Lake Minneola, anglers can fish for free from the fishing pier but must pay a fee to launch a boat. A couple of fish attractors are near the pier to help increase angler success.

Directions: From the intersection of FL 50 and Lake Minneola Shores (12th St.) in Clermont turn north onto Lake Minneola Shores and drive 0.3 miles to the intersection with Lake Minneola Dr. Turn right onto Lake Minneola Dr and go 0.1 miles to the park on your left.
Address: 930 West Minneola Ave., Clermont, FL

13B. PALATLAKAHA RIVER PARK— *Pier and Boat – Ramp*
Directions: This ramp provides access to lakes Minnehaha and Louisa. From the

A nice-size largemouth bass that, if released, has the chance to grow bigger before being caught again.

intersection of US 27 and Hammock Ridge Rd. in Clermont, drive west on Hammock Ridge Rd. for approximately 1.5 miles. Bear right onto Lake Louisa Rd. and drive 1.1 miles to the intersection with Hull Rd. Turn left onto Hull Rd. and drive 1.0 miles to the park.
Address: 12325 Hull Rd., Clermont, FL

13C. LAKE LOUISA STATE PARK—*Bank and Pier – Canoe Launch – $*
Description: This park on the south shore has camping, a swimming beach, and picnic areas. Anglers can launch canoes and kayaks from the Lake Louisa beach and can access four other smaller lakes in the park. Dixie Lake is the largest of these lakes. Gasoline motors are prohibited at all lakes, but trolling motors are allowed. The lakes offer good fishing in a quiet setting with the opportunity to see plenty of wildlife.
Directions: From the intersection of FL 50 and US 27 in Clermont, drive south on US 27 for 7.0 miles to the park entrance.
Address: 7305 US Highway 27, Clermont, FL
For more information: Call the park office at (352) 394-3969 or go to *www. floridastateparks.org.*

14. JOHNS LAKE
Fresh – Boat and Bank – Ramp

Description: What a difference a mile makes! Located just under a mile south of the south shore of Lake Apopka, John's Lake has been a good producer for largemouth bass. The FWC put over 200,000 bass in the lake in 2003.

Fishing Index: Fish along the weedlines using any of the standard bass baits—live shiners and spinnerbaits. Or use your depth finder to locate some of the rocky bottom in the lake.

Directions: From the intersection of US 27 and FL 50 in Clermont, drive east on FL 50 for 4.9 miles. Turn right on Lake Blvd. and follow the road 0.1 miles to the single paved ramp on your left.

15. WEKIVA RIVER
Fresh – Boat

Description: The river originates in Wekiwa Springs State Park and flows north to the St. Johns River, joining it at DeBary. Don't be confused about the different spelling—it is Wekiwa Springs State Park on the Wekiva River.

Fishing Index: Try fishing the river close to its junction with the St. Johns for largemouth, sunshine, and striped bass. The upper part of the river is not heavily fished and is a good place for fishing from a canoe or kayak.

Directions: The easiest access is from the ramps near Blue Spring State Park, Highbanks Ramp, or Lake Monroe Park (see below). Take the St. Johns River upriver to the confluence with the Wekiva. Paddlers can also launch at Wekiwa Springs State Park and paddle downstream. To reach the park, exit I-4 at the CR 434–Altamonte Springs Exit. Drive west on CR 434 for 1.1 miles. Bear right onto Wekiwa Springs Rd and drive 3.5 miles to the park on your right.

Address: The park's address is 1800 Wekiwa Circle, Apopka, FL.

For more information: Call Wekiwa Springs State Park at (407) 884-2008 or go to *www.floridastateparks.org.*

16. DISNEY WORLD
Fresh – Boat and Bank – $

Description: Yes, you can fish at Mickey's place and for real fish, too! All trips are on Disney boats and all fishing must be done with a member of the "cast," as they call their guides. The fee includes a one-year membership to the Bass Anglers Sportsman Society (BASS). Everything is provided and all fish caught are always released.

Fishing Index: Anglers can fish Bay Lake and Seven Seas Lagoon, Crescent Lake, World Showcase Lagoon, or Village Lake for largemouth bass. You can also fish from the banks at The Cabins at Fort Wilderness Resort, The Campsites at Fort Wilderness Resort, and Port Orleans Resort.

Directions: Disney World is just west of Orlando. The main entrance is off of I-4 just south of Lake Buena Vista.

For more information: Call Walt Disney World at (407) 939-2277 or go to *http://disneyworld.disney.go.com/recreation/fishing/.*

17. ORLANDO AREA
Fresh – Boat, Bank, and Pier – Ramp

Description: There are many places for freshwater enthusiasts to wet a line in the Orlando area and vicinity. The Harris and Clermont Chains of lakes described above are less than 30 minutes away from Orlando as are hundreds of other lakes. But anglers can also find top-notch fishing in lakes that anglers would have never thought possible. It's all due to Fish Orlando, a cooperative program between the FWC and the Cities of Orlando, Ocoee and Winter Park, Orange County, Bass Pro Shops and other groups.

Fish Orlando has two components – The Fab Five and the Urban Ponds. The Fab Five lakes are intensely managed by the FWC to produce big fish and a quality fishing experience and are described in more detail below. The Urban Ponds program is also managed, but the emphasis is on providing quality fishing experiences for less experienced anglers and those who want to eat what they catch. The Urban Ponds include Lake Santiago (Demetree Park), Bear Creek, Barnett Park Frog Pond, and Lake Island Park. These sites feature an abundance of bank and pier fishing sites. These are small water bodies so there are no ramps and boats are not allowed.

For more information about the Urban Ponds program and a description of the sites go to *http://www.myfwc.com/RECREATION/FW_Offices_Orlando_UrbanPonds.htm.*

The Fab Five Lakes include:

17A. STARKE LAKE, MUNICIPAL LAKEFRONT PARK—*Boat, Bank and Pier – Ramp*

Description: Starke Lake, a 225-acre lake in the City of Ocoee is managed for largemouth bass. The lake produces many 24-inch or less bass and a few that are bigger than this. This is a deeper than average lake and anglers sometimes have trouble finding and catching the fish. There are also crappie, redear sunfish, and brown bullhead catfish. Good catches of the latter can be had on the fishing pier which is barrier-free and has fish feeders designed to attract the fish to the pier.

Directions: From the intersection of FL 50 and FL 439 (Bluford Ave.), drive north on FL 439 for 1.5 miles. The park is on your right.

Address: 150 N. Lakeshore Drive, Ocoee, Fl

For more information: Go to http://www.myfwc.com/RECREATION/FW_Offices_Orlando_index.htm. A topographic map is available at http://myfwc.com/docs/Freshwater/FW_Offices_StarkeLakeTopographicalMap.pdf

17B. TURKEY LAKE PARK—*Boat, Bank and Pier*

Description: Turkey Lake, a 339-acre lake in the city of Orlando, is managed for largemouth bass and crappie. It is located less than 2 miles north of the Universal theme park. There is plenty of bank fishing and five piers with fish feeders and/or attractors near the piers. Anglers wanting to fish from a boat must rent one of the Bass Tracker boats Bass Pro Shops makes available at the park. For a small charge ($15 in 2010) you can rent one of the four boats allowed on the lake and can fish from 6:30 to 11:00 A.M. on Thursday to Sunday. There is no ramp and the public has no other access to the lake except the bank and pier fishing sites. Camping and primitive cabins are also available.

Directions: From the exit off I-4 at Kirkman Rd., drive north on Kirkman 1.3 miles to the intersection with Conroy Rd. Turn left onto Conroy Rd. and drive west for 1.4 miles to the intersection with S. Hiawassee Rd. Turn right onto S. Hiawassee Rd. and drive 0.8 miles to the park on your right.

Address: 3401 S. Hiawassee Rd, Orlando, FL

For more information: To reserve a boat, call (407) 299-1248. Additional information about this lake is available at *http://www.myfwc.com/RECREATION/ FW_Offices_Orlando_index.htm.* For a topographic map of the lake go to *http:// myfwc.com/docs/Freshwater/FW_Offices_TurkeyLakeTopographicalMap.pdf*

17C. CLEAR LAKE, GEORGE BARKER AND CLEAR LAKE PARKS—*Boat, Bank, and Pier – Ramp*

Description: These City of Orlando parks provide access to the 313-acre Clear Lake which is managed for hybrid striped (sunshine) bass. There is a ramp and pier at George Baker Park along the northeast shore and a pier at Clear Lake Park along the southeast shore.

Fishing Index: In addition to the intensive sunshine bass stocking program, the lake is also known to have numerous large crappie and a good population of largemouth bass. Look for the sunshine bass fishing to be best during the cooler months. Fish the deep holes in the lake and fish with a shiner or crappie minnow.

Directions: To George Baker Park: From the East-West Expressway exit onto US 441. Drive south on US 441 for 0.4 miles to the intersection with Monte Carlo Trail. Turn right and go 0.5 miles to the park. To Clear Lake Park: Exit I-4 at US 441 and drive north for 0.1 mile to the intersection with 29th St. Turn left onto 29th St. and drive 0.6 miles to the park entrance on your left.

Address: George Baker Park: 2000 Monte Carlo Trail – Clear Lake Park: 2301 29th St. Both are in Orlando.

For more information: Call (407) 246-2283. Additional information about this lake is available at *http://www.myfwc.com/RECREATION/FW_Offices_ Orlando_index.htm.* A topo map is available at *http://myfwc.com/docs/Freshwater/ FW_Offices_ClearLakeTopographicalMap.pdf*

17D. LAKE UNDERHILL, COLONEL JOE KITTINGER PARK—*Boat and Bank – Ramp*

Description: The 147-acre Lake Underhill on the east side of the city of Orlando is managed for largemouth bass. The lake has a reputation for producing a high number of 20-inch-plus bass. Anglers can bank fish along the southern shoreline or launch a boat from the ramp at the park. This lake is best fished during the weekdays or early in the morning on the weekends as the lake is also popular with jet skiers. This is a catch-and-release lake for all bass.

Directions: From the intersection of FL 50 (E. Colonial Dr.) and N. Bumby

Ave., drive south on Bumby for 0.9 miles to the intersection with E. South St. Turn left on South St. and drive east for 0.6 miles to S. Crystal Lake Dr. Turn left onto S. Crystal Lake Dr. and look for the entrance to the park on your right.
Address: 305 South Crystal Lake Dr., Orlando, FL
For more information: Call the FWC office at (407) 246-2283. Additional information about this lake is available at *http://www.myfwc.com/RECREATION/FW_Offices_Orlando_index.htm.*

17E. Lake Ivanhoe, Gaston-Edwards Park—*Boat and Bank – Ramp*
Description: Lake Ivanhoe is a 125-acre lake in the heart of downtown Orlando. The lake is comprised of three lobes, two of them west of Interstate 4 and the other on the east side. The lake is a favorite for water–skiers, so anglers need to take advantage of the early morning or cooler winter days when skiers will be inside either asleep or keeping themselves warm. Besides the bass, anglers may also hook up with some three–pound-plus channel catfish.
Directions: In downtown Orlando, exit Interstate 4 at Ivanhoe Blvd. and drive east on Ivanhoe for 0.1 miles where Ivanhoe joins N. Orange Ave. Continue on N. Orange Ave. for 0.2 miles to the intersection with N.E. Ivanhoe Blvd. Turn left onto N.E. Ivanhoe Blvd. and the ramp will be on your left.
Address: 1236 N. Orange Avenue, Orlando, FL
For more information: Call the FWC office at (407) 246-2283. Additional information about this lake is available at *http://www.myfwc.com/RECREATION/FW_Offices_Orlando_index.htm*

18. Butler Chain of Lakes
Fresh – Boat – Ramp – $

Description: Also known as the Windermere Chain these 11 interconnected lakes are just to the northeast of Disney World. Virtually all of the shoreline on these lakes is privately owned so bank fishing is not an option.

Fishing Index: These lakes have a reputation for producing some big bass. Try fishing the shoreline around the abundant submerged vegetation or search for some of the deep (20–40) holes. In some of the lakes schools of two- to four-pound bass make for some interesting fishing.

Directions: The boat ramp at R.D. Keene Park provides the only public access to this chain of lakes. From the intersection of I-4 and FL 535 (the Downtown Disney exit) take FL 535 north for 7.5 miles to the intersection with Chase Rd. Turn right onto Chase Rd. and drive1.2 miles where it turns to the left and continue another 0.9 miles to the park on your right.

Address: 10900 Chase Rd, Windermere, FL

19. CONWAY CHAIN OF LAKES
Fresh – Boat – Ramp

Description: Four clear-water lakes comprise this chain just to the northwest of the international airport. Bank fishing is nonexistent since nearly all land along the shorelines is privately owned.

Fishing Index: These lakes are noted for their schooling bass especially in the fall and winter. Just as saltwater anglers watch the surface of the water for movements of schools of redfish or look for terns and pelicans dive bombing schools of bait, anglers on these lakes should scan the surface for similar signs of schools of bass.

Directions: There is a small ramp at the end of Randolph Ave. two blocks east of FL 547 (S. Orange Ave.). From the intersection with McCoy Rd. (Sand Lake Blvd.) and FL 547, drive north for 0.7 miles to Hoffner Ave. Turn right onto Hoffner and drive two blocks to Randolph Ave. Turn left and follow the road to the ramp.

20. MOSS PARK
Fresh – Boat and Bank – Ramp

Description: This 1550-acre Orange County Park is located between Lakes Hart and Mary Jane. It has a campground, swimming area, and abundant wildlife.

Fishing Index: Fish the lakes for largemouth bass, bluegills, and crappie

Directions: Exit the Bee Line Expressway (FL 528) onto FL 15 and go south 2.6 miles to Moss Park Rd. Turn left and go 4 miles to the park.

Address: 12901 Moss Park Rd., Orlando, FL

For more information: Call the park office at (407) 254-6840.

21. ST. JOHNS RIVER (FL 44 BRIDGE TO FL 520 BRIDGE
Boat, Bank, and Pier

Description: Moving upriver from the FL 44 bridge, the river splits into two branches forming Hontoon Island between them. The island is a state park with camping, rustic cabins, and an observation tower. Once the branches rejoin, the St. Johns meanders for several miles and then opens to form lakes Monroe, Jessup, and Harney with short stretches of river surrounded by marshes separating the lakes. The section between lakes Jessup and Harney is the Lemon Bluff area, one of the most scenic parts of the river. Above Lake Harney, the St. Johns has numerous sloughs branching off the main course, and the land around the river is totally undeveloped. The Econlockhatchee River, which originates southeast of Orlando, enters the river a few river miles upstream of Lake Harney. Continuing upriver, the stretch from the FL 50 bridge to the FL 520 bridge is sometimes unnavigable due to low water.

Fishing Index: From roughly January to mid-April each year, American shad, a saltwater species that migrates from as far away as Canada, swims up the St. Johns to spawn. Most of the action is between Lake Monroe and Puzzle Lake which is a small lake a few miles upriver from Lake Harney. Fish for the 1- to 5-pound shad with live minnows, minnow-shaped lures, gold and silver spoons, and small jigs. Fly fishers also target this species with lightweight rigs. Largemouth bass fishing is good along all parts of the river. In spring, good numbers of striped and sunshine (hybrid) bass are also taken.

Access Points:
21A. BLUE SPRING STATE PARK—*Bank and Pier – Ramp*
Description: The park has a campground, cabins, swimming in the spring boil, and nature trails. Endangered West Indian manatees are present in winter and early spring and are easily observed from shore. The ramp is not part of the park, though it is adjacent. It accesses the St. Johns River. The pier was destroyed in 2006 when it was hit by a barge. There are plans to rebuild it. Canoes can be rented at the park.
Directions: From US 17/92 in Orange City (4.6 miles south of DeLand), turn west onto French St. and go 2.6 miles to the park. To reach the ramp, go past the park entrance and follow French St. until it ends at the ramp and the river.
Address: 2100 W. French Ave., Orange City, FL
For more information: Call the park office at (386) 775-3663 or go to *www. floridastateparks.org.*
21B. HIGHBANKS RAMP—*Boat – Ramp*
Directions: From US 17/92 in DeBary (4.3 miles south of Orange City), turn west onto Highbanks Rd. and go 2.9 miles to the ramp.
Address: 499 W. Highbanks Rd., DeBary, FL

21C. LAKE MONROE PARK—*Pier and Boat – Ramps*
Description: A Volusia County facility with camping and nature trails.
Directions: The park is on US 17/92 on the north side of the river where it

widens to become Lake Monroe. Exit I-4 onto US 17/92 at Sanford and go north 0.5 miles to the park. Another ramp is across U.S. 92 from the I-4 exit ramp.

Address: 975 US 17/92, DeBary, FL

For more information: Call the park office at (386) 668-3825.

21D. CAMERON WRIGHT PARK—*Boat and Bank – Ramp*

Description: A Seminole County Park with picnicking.

Directions: From the intersection with US 17/92 take FL 46 (Old Geneva Rd.) east for 5.3 miles to the park. It is on the west side of the FL 46 bridge.

Address: The street address is 5502 Old Geneva Rd., Sanford, FL

21E. LAKE JESSUP PARK—*Boat and Bank – Ramp*

Description: A Seminole County park with picnicking.

Directions: From the intersection with US 17/92 take FL 46 (Old Geneva Rd.) 0.5 mile to Sanford Ave. Turn right and go south 4 miles to the park.

Address: 5951 S. Sanford, Ave., Sanford, FL

21F. LEMON BLUFF—*Boat – Ramp*

Directions: From the intersection with US 17/92 in Sanford, take FL 415 north about 6.9 miles to Lemon Bluff Rd. Turn right and go 3.7 miles to the ramp at road's end.

Address: 907 Lemon Bluff Rd., Osteen, FL

21G. MULLET LAKE PARK—*Boat and Bank – Ramp*

Description: This 151-acre Seminole County park has a campground. It is on the shores of Mullet Lake, part of the St. Johns River.

Directions: From the intersection with US 17/92 in Sanford, take FL 46 east 7.8 miles to Mullet Lake Park Rd. Turn north and drive about 1 mile to the ramp.

Address: 2368 Mullet Lake Park Rd., Geneva, FL

21H. C.S. LEE PARK—*Boat – Ramp*

Description: A Seminole County park with picnicking.

Directions: From the intersection with US 17/92 in Sanford, take FL 46 east 15.8 miles to the bridge over the river. The park is on the west side. Or from I-95, exit onto FL 46 at Mims and drive west 11.2 miles to the park.

Address: 4600 East State Rd. 46, Geneva, FL

21I. HATBILL PARK—*Boat – Ramp*

Description: This Brevard County ramp may not be accessible when the water level is up on the river.

Directions: At Mims, exit I-95 onto FL 46 and go west 4.1 miles to Hatbill Park Rd. Turn left and go about 7.5 miles to the ramp.
Address: 100 Hatbill Rd., Mims, FL

21J. State Road 50 Ramp—*Boat – Ramp*
Description: An Orange County facility that provides access to a meandering stretch of river between lakes Harney to the north (downriver) and Poinsett to the south (upriver).
Directions: From Interstate 95 take the SR 50 exit south of Titusville and drive west on SR 50 for 4.9 miles to the ramp on the south side of the road.
Address: 28500 E. Colonial Dr, Orlando, FL

Osceola, Brevard (Western portion), and Indian River (Western portion) Counties

22 – 26 Kissimmee Chain of Lakes ──────────
Fresh – Boat/Canoe, Bank, and Pier – Ramp

Description: These lakes, connected by man-made canals and natural waterways, comprise the headwaters of the world famous Everglades. The system is managed by the South Florida Water Management District, which has been actively working to restore more of the lake's natural functions that were altered when the lakes became part of an earlier regional water management plan that focused on flood control at the expense of natural functioning. The FWC conducts periodic drawdown of several lakes and uses bulldozers to remove muck and aquatic vegetation. Local governments are also actively working to reduce the amount of nutrients entering the water. Combined, these actions have resulted in much improved fishing conditions.

Fishing Index: The consensus is that the big bass, which were once the hallmark of these lakes, are back. Big-time bass tournaments have returned and reports of 7- to 10-pound bass are common. Bluegill and crappie fishing is also good on these lakes.

For more information: Go to *http://www.myfwc.com/RECREATION/FW_Sites. htm* and click on the link for interactive maps. Lakes Toho, East Toho, and Kissimmee are listed.

Osceola, Brevard (western portion) and Indian River (western portion) Counties

22. LAKE TOHOPEKALIGA
Fresh – Boat – Ramp

Description: At 22,700 acres, over 40 percent of the lake is shallow, less than five feet deep. The lake has 33 miles of shoreline and where there is emergent or floating vegetation, fishing should be good. Because few can pronounce Tohopekaliga, most people simply say Lake Toho.

Fishing Index: Look for the bass along the edges of the dense patches of hydrilla that periodically plague the lake especially in the summer. Fish the deeper locations and get your bait or lure down in the strike zone. It will be near the bottom as that is where the cooler water and the fish will be.

Access Points:
22A. LAKE FRONT PARK—*Boat – Ramp*
Description: A City of Kissimmee park with plenty of parking.
Directions: From the intersection where US 17, 19, 92, 192, and 441 converge in Kissimmee, go south 0.9 mile on US 17/92 (John Young Prkwy.) to Emmett

St. and turn left. Go 0.4 miles on Emmett to Ruby Ave. Turn right on Ruby and drive two blocks to Lake Shore Blvd. Turn right onto Lakeshore and the ramp is ahead 0.1 miles on the left.
Address: 250 Lakeshore Blvd., Kissimmee, FL

22B. GRANADA RAMP—*Boat – Ramp*
Directions: From the intersection where US 17, 19, 92, 192, and 441 converge in Kissimmee, go south about 3.8 miles on US 17/92 (John Young Prkwy.) to Pleasant Hill Rd. (CR 531). Turn left onto Pleasant Hill and drive about 4.5 miles to Granada Rd. Turn left again and go to Ridgeway Dr. Turn right and go to the ramp.
Address: 2605 Ridgeway Dr., Kissimmee, FL

22C. SOUTH PORT PARK—*Boat – Ramp*
Directions: From the intersection where US 17, 92, 192, and 441 converge in Kissimmee, go south about 3.8 miles on US 17/92 (John Young Prkwy.) to Pleasant Hill Rd. (CR 531). Turn left and go about 8 miles to Southport Rd. Turn left again and go 5.5 miles to the ramp on the south end of the lake.
Address: 2001 E. Southport Rd., Kissimmee, FL

22D. WHALEY'S LANDING—*Boat – Ramp*
Directions: From the intersection where US 17, 92, 192, and 441 converge in Kissimmee, go south about 6.9 miles on US 192/441 to the intersection with Old Canoe Creek Rd. Turn right on Old Canoe Creek Rd. and drive 2.1 miles to Kissimmee Park Rd. (CR 525). Turn right and go south 4 miles to Lake Toho Rd. (CR 525A). Turn left on Lake Toho Rd. and go 1.4 miles to the ramp.
Address: 3759 Lake Tohopekaliga Rd., St. Cloud, FL
For more information: Call East Lake Fish Camp, (407) 933-5822.

22E. PARTIN TRIANGLE PARK—*Boat – Ramp*
Description: This Osceola County park provides access to Lakes Toho and East Toho via the C-31 canal connecting the two lakes.
Directions: From the intersection of US 441 & 192 and CR 523 (Canoe Creek Rd.) in St. Cloud, drive northwest on US 441 & 192 for 1.2 miles to the intersection with Neptune Rd. Turn left onto Neptune and drive 1.2 miles to the park on your left, – just across the canal.
Address: 2830 Neptune Rd., Kissimmee, FL

23. EAST LAKE TOHOPEKALIGA ————————
Fresh – Boat – Ramp

Description: The city of St. Cloud is along the south shore of this nearly circular 13,550-acre lake. The clear-water lake is a good place for night fishing.

Fishing Index: There is plentiful bulrush and torpedo grass along the shoreline making this lake a great place to catch largemouth bass. If you want a chance at a 10-pound or larger bass, this is a lake to fish.

Access Points:

23A. EAST LAKE BOAT BASIN—*Boat – Ramp*
Directions: From US 441 & 192 in St. Cloud, drive north on New York Ave. for 0.9 mile to the ramp.

23B. CHISHOLM PARK TRAIL—*Boat – Ramp*
Directions: From the intersection of US 192/441 and Narcoossee Rd. (FL15) just east of St. Cloud, drive north on Narcoossee Rd. for approximately 2.3 miles to Chisholm Park Trail. Turn left on Chisholm Park and follow the road to the park and ramp.
Address: 4700 Chisholm Park Trail, St. Cloud, FL

24. CYPRESS LAKE
Fresh – Boat – Ramp

Description: Far from civilization, cypress trees surround much of the shoreline. In addition to the ramp, anglers access this lake via the canals from Lake Hatchineha and Lake Toho. The ramp is maintained by Osceola County and is popular with airboaters.

Fishing Index: At just over 4,000 acres, this lake can be fished on those cooler windy days of the winter when Lake Toho will be too rough to safely navigate. Crappie (specs) provide good action in winter, and bluegills and shellcrackers are biting in spring and summer.

Directions: From the intersection of Canoe Creek Rd. (FL 523) and US 192/441 in St. Cloud, take Canoe Creek Rd. south 11.2 miles to Lake Cypress Dr. Turn right and go 2.3 miles to the ramp.

Address: 3301 Lake Cypress Rd., Kenansville, FL

For more information: Cypress Lake Fish Camp & RV Park is adjacent to the ramp. Call (407) 957-3135.

25. LAKE HATCHINEHA
Fresh – Boat – Ramp

Description: Many consider this 6,665-acre lake the prettiest in the chain. Much of the undeveloped shoreline is lined with cypress.

Fishing Index: Another good largemouth bass lake in the Kissimmee Chain. The waterway connecting this lake to Lake Kissimmee is also a good place to fish. This lake has some current and that helps hold down the hydrilla. Fish the shoreline using traditional bass angling techniques.

Access Points:
25A. Port Hatchineha Park—*Fresh – Boat – Ramp*
Description: The park and ramp are in Polk County, but once you enter the lake you are in Osceola County. It is the only public access on the lake.
Directions: From the intersection of US 27 and Dundee Rd. (about 6 miles south of Haines City), turn onto Dundee and drive east for 0.9 miles to the intersection with Center St. Turn left on Center and drive north for 1.2 miles to the intersection with Lake Hatchineha Rd. Turn right onto Lake Hatchineha and follow the road for about 9.8 miles to the end of the road and the ramp.
Address: 15050 Hatchineha Rd., Haines City, FL

25B. Camps Lester and Mack—*Fresh – Boat – Ramp*
Description: These two fish camps are local landmarks and have been in the area for years.
Directions: There is a ramp at Camp Lester on the waterway connecting lakes Hatchineha and Kissimmee. From US 27 in Lake Wales, go east 9.2 miles on FL 60 to Boy Scout Camp Rd. Turn left and go north about 3.2 miles to Camp Mack Rd. Turn right and go about 6 miles to Camp Lester Rd. Turn left to the camp. Camp Mack is adjacent to Camp Lester.
Address: Camp Lester: 14400 Reese Dr., Lake Wales, FL – Camp Mack: 14900 Camp Mack Road, Lake Wales, FL
For more information: Call Camp Lester at (863) 696-1123 or Camp Mack at (863) 696-1108.

26. Lake Kissimmee
Boat and Bank

Description: This is the largest lake in the chain at 35,000 acres. Water exits the lake at the south end and enters the Kissimmee River which flows to Lake Okeechobee. An aquatic vegetation management program, coordinated by the FWC, has been in place since the 1990s.
Fishing Index: This lake has been a prime largemouth bass lake for many years. There is abundant cover including native vegetation and dense mats of hydrilla. As in all the lakes in the lower Kissimmee Chain, fishing with a live shiner offers the greatest chance of catching a bass. This is a good tactic when the water is cooler, especially in the winter when lake water temperatures can drop below 60 degrees.

Access Points:

26A. Lake Kissimmee State Park—*Boat and Bank – Ramp – $*

Description: The park has a campground and a living history demonstration of an 1876 cow camp. The park's ramp is at the end of a winding road.

Directions: From US 27 in Lake Wales, drive east 9.2 miles on FL 60 to Boy Scout Camp Rd. Turn left and go north about 3.2 miles to Camp Mack Rd. Turn right and go about 6 miles to the park entrance.

Address: 14248 Camp Mack Rd., Lake Wales, FL

For more information: Call the park office at (863) 696-1112 or go to www.floridastateparks.org.

26B. Overstreet Ramp—*Boat – Ramp*

Directions: From the intersection of Canoe Creek Rd. and US 192/441 in St. Cloud, take Canoe Creek Rd. south 20.8 miles to Overstreet Rd. Turn right and go 5.5 miles to the ramp at road's end.

Address: 4900 Overstreet Rd., Kenansville, FL

26C. FL 60 Ramp—*Boat – Ramp*

Directions: There are two ramps, one on each side of the lock leading to the Kissimmee River. Turn off FL 60 on the west side of the bridge where it crosses the southernmost part of the lake. From the Florida Turnpike drive 19.8 miles west on FL 60. Or from US 27 in Lake Wales drive 26.5 miles east on FL 60.

For more information: Go to http://www.myfwc.com/RECREATION/FW_Sites.htm and click on the link for the interactive map for this lake.

27. St. Johns River (Lake Poinsett to Lake Helen Blazes)
Fresh – Boat, Bank, and Pier

Description: This part of the river includes lakes Poinsett, Winder, Washington, and Sawgrass and leads to the St. Johns River headwaters in Lake Helen Blazes and the surrounding marshes. While there is good fishing in these parts, access points are limited. Shallow water and extensive marshes make this an area where airboats have the advantage over conventional watercraft.

Fishing Index: Lake Poinsett has the best largemouth bass fishing along this part of the river. The river between lakes Poinsett and Winder is also pretty good, but Lake Winder has had a severe hydrilla problem. In 2000 the lake was treated and that has helped, but once hydrilla invades a water body all you can do is continue to control it. Elimination is not an option. Fish the vegetation lines with a weedless lure or plastic worm. Lake Washington is not heavily fished and is lined with bulrush, the place to look for bass. Upstream of this lake are lakes Sawgrass and Helen Blazes, two smaller lakes that produce some bass and plenty of bluegills and crappie. Hydrilla can be a problem in both lakes and when it is present, fish along the edges of the weedline or the part of the river that connects these two lakes.

Access Points:

27A. JAMES BOURBEAU PARK —*Boat and Bank – Ramp*
Description: Provides access to the north end of Lake Poinsett and a meandering stretch downriver (to the north).
Directions: Exit I-95 onto FL 520 (at Cocoa). Drive about 4.5 miles west on FL 520. The park is on the north side of the road. Lone Cabbage Fish Camp is on the south side.
Address: 8195 King St. (Hwy. 520), Cocoa, FL
For more information: Call Lone Cabbage Fish Camp at (321) 632-4199

27B. LAKE POINSETT LODGE—*Bank and Boat – Ramp*
Description: This fish camp allows bank fishing along its canals. Ask for an area map.
Directions: Exit I-95 onto FL 520 and go west 0.6 mile to Lake Poinsett Rd. Turn left and follow the road 1 mile to the lake.
Address: 5665 Lake Poinsett Rd., Cocoa, FL
For more information: Call Lake Poinsett Lodge at (321) 636-0045.

27C. LAKE WASHINGTON PARK—*Boat and Pier – Ramp*
Description: This Brevard County facility has a launching ramps for boats and airboats.
Directions: From US 1 near Eau Gallie, drive 5.8 miles west on Lake Washington Rd. to the ramp.
Address: 6000 Lake Washington Rd., Melbourne, FL

27D. CAMP HOLLY—*Boat – Ramp*
Description: This fish camp is a popular launch for airboats and is the closest ramp to Sawgrass Lake and Lake Washington. The owners offer airboat rides to the public.
Address: 6901 W. US 192, Melbourne, FL
Directions: Exit I-95 onto US 192 and go west about 3 miles to the fish camp.
For more information: Call Camp Holly Fish Camp at (321) 732-2179.

28. Stick Marsh and Farm 13
Fresh – Boat – Ramp

Description: These are two adjacent water bodies created in 1985 by flooding old farm fields. The area is closely managed by the FWC and is one of the commission's Top Ten Trophy Bass Spots. It has this rating in part because all largemouth bass caught must be immediately released unharmed. Plenty of guides along the central east coast fish this site. Check at a local bait and tackle shop or contact Stick Marsh Bait and Tackle. One note of caution: There are numerous underwater hazards present in these impoundments and boaters must exercise caution, especially if not familiar with the sites.

Fishing Index: These two sites offer some of the best bass fishing in Florida. The biggest fish are caught in spring using live wild shiners. Other species, including crappie, bluegills, and catfish, can be harvested according to state regulations. In the summer look for the big bass to be in the submerged ditches and drainage canals. These structures are also good places to fish for crappie. Finding them requires local knowledge or the use of a fish finder.

Directions: Exit I-95 at Fellsmere onto CR 512 and go west 2.9 miles to Fellsmere. Turn right on CR 507 and go north 4 miles to Fellsmere Grade Rd. Turn left onto the Grade, which parallels the C-54 Canal on the canal's south side. Follow the road 6 miles to the ramp.

For more information: Call Stick Marsh Bait and Tackle in Fellsmere at (772) 571-9855 or go to www.stickmarshbaittackle.com.

29. Lake Blue Cypress
Fresh – Boat – Ramp

Description: The undeveloped shoreline of this 6,555-acre lake is surrounded by marsh and cypress swamp. The FWC has placed fish attractors in the lake and they are marked by buoys. Primitive camping is allowed at Blue Cypress Park.

Fishing Index: The lake has a respectable reputation as a place to catch crappie, bass, bluegill and redear sunfish. In addition to fishing the shoreline, there are several fish attractors in the open water areas where bass and panfish will hang out.

Directions: To reach Blue Cypress Park, an Indian River County facility, drive east on FL 60 about 6.6 miles from the intersection of FL 60 and US 441 in

Yeehaw Junction to Blue Cypress Rd. Turn left on Blue Cypress and follow it 4.3 miles to the park and ramp.

For more information: Call Middleton's Fish Camp (adjacent to the county park) at (561) 778-0150 or go to *www.middletonsfishcamp.com*.

30. ANSIN-GARCIA RESERVOIR
Fresh – Boat – Ramp

Description: This 3,150-acre reservoir is only a few miles south of Stick Marsh. This is another flooded farm field. It is shallow and boaters should be careful as there are numerous underwater hazards. Dense hydrilla can make it difficult to operate a boat. Check with Stick Marsh Bait and Tackle ((772) 571-9855 – *www.stickmarshbaittackle.com)* for the current conditions.

Fishing Index: A very good place to fish for largemouth bass. However, the fish tend to run slightly smaller than at Stick Marsh. Bluegill and crappie are also targeted.

Directions: From the FL 60 exit off I-95, drive 7.5 miles west to FL 512 (Armory Dr.). Go north on FL 512 for 1.5 miles to the ramp on your left.

For more information: Call Stick Marsh Bait and Tackle in Fellsmere at (772) 571-9855.

31. KENANSVILLE LAKE
Fresh – Boat – Ramp

Description: This former cattle pasture was flooded in 1991. When it was flooded, the fences, berms, and other structures were left in place to create fish habitat. They also can be underwater hazards if you hit them with your boat. Average depth is three feet. However, there are some deeper areas in the northwest portion of the lake.

Fishing Index: This impoundment is best known for its crappie and bluegill fishery. In an effort to increase the quantity and quality of the largemouth bass, this is a catch-and-release lake. All bass must be immediately released.

Directions: From the Yeehaw Junction exit of the Florida Turnpike, drive north on US 441approximatley 13.5 miles to Kenansville. Turn right onto Fellsmere Rd. and drive east approximately 12 miles to the ramp.

VOLUSIA COUNTY (COASTAL AREA)

This section includes the Halifax River, which is really a tidal lagoon, Ponce de Leon Inlet, and the upper part of Mosquito Lagoon, all of which are to the north of Cape Canaveral. The water bodies separate the land from the barrier islands that front the Atlantic Ocean. The listings begin at the north and move to the south.

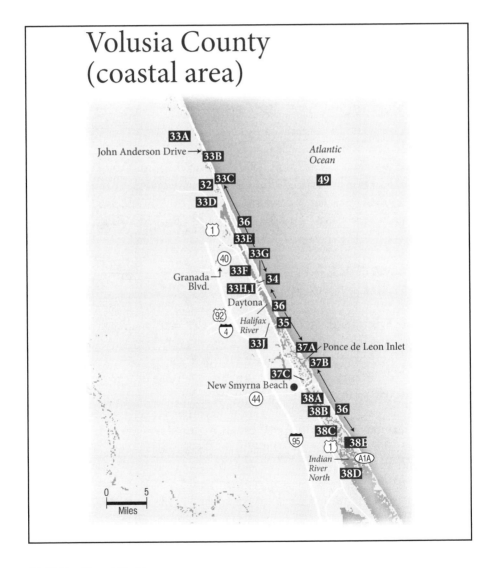

32. TOMOKA STATE PARK

Salt – Bank and Boat – Ramp

Description: A scenic park with big oak trees on a peninsula between the Tomoka and Halifax rivers. There is a campground, picnic area, and cultural museum. The park is the site of an old Timucuan Indian Village. The ramp provides access to the Tomoka River, which flows into the upper part of the Halifax River.

Fishing Index: Black drum and refish can be caught in the Tomoka River and Basin during the winter months. Live bait works best but a dead shrimp will entice the black drum to bite. In summer, fish for spotted seatrout, flounder, and small snook and tarpon. Land-bound anglers can fish from the banks of the Tomoka River or off the North Beach Street bridge. Fly fishers who like to catch small tarpon, in the 15- to 20-pound range, should try the creeks around the park. The action can be very good.

Directions: From FL 40 in Ormond Beach, take Beach St. north 4.1 miles to the park entrance.

Address: 2099 North Beach St., Ormond Beach, FL

For more information: Call the park office at (386) 676-4050 or go to www.floridastateparks.org.

33. HALIFAX RIVER

Salt – Boat, Bank, Bridge and Pier – Ramp

Description: This coastal river begins near Tomoka marsh and is joined from the north by the Intracoastal Waterway. Daytona Beach and surrounding communities line much of both shores.

Fishing Index: The shallows of the Halifax provide good year-round angling for redfish and sheepshead. Snook fishing is fair in all but the coldest months and peaks in summer and early fall. Spotted seatrout is best from April through June. Numerous piers and boat ramps make this part of the coast one of the most angler-friendly places in Florida.

Access Points:
33A. HIGHBRIDGE PARK—*Boat, Bank and Pier – Ramp*
Description: This Volusia County day-use park is along the scenic banks of

Halifax Creek at the upper end of the Halifax River. Fish from the pier or from the creek bank.

Directions: From FL 40 in Ormond Beach, take A1A north 8.5 miles to Highbridge Rd. Turn left and go 0.3 miles to the park.

Address: 39 Highbridge Rd., Ormond Beach, FL

33B. SEABRIDGE RIVERFRONT PARK— *Pier*

Description: A Volusia County park on the island side of the river across from Tomoka State Park. The 175-foot-long pier parallels the shoreline. Parts of it are shaded.

Directions: From FL 40 (Granada Blvd.) in Ormond Beach, turn north onto John Anderson Dr. and go about 5.7 miles to the park.

Address: 3570 John Anderson Dr., Ormond Beach, FL

33 C. HALIFAX RIVER FISHING DOCKS—*Pier*

Description: These four fishing docks offer land-bound anglers places to fish the Halifax River. Parking is limited at each site.

Directions: All are along John Anderson Dr.

San Jose Fishing Dock—2591 John Anderson Dr., Ormond Beach, FL

Bicentennial Park Fishing Dock—1800 N. Oceanshore Blvd., Ormond Beach, FL

Briggs Drive Fishing Dock—2500 John Anderson Drive, Ormond Beach, FL

Roberta Drive Fishing Dock—199 Roberta Dr., Ormond Beach, FL

33D. SANCHEZ PARK—*Boat and Pier – Ramp*

Description: This is a City of Ormond Beach park. The ramp provides access to Strickland Creek, which flows into the Tomoka River. The area is an idle-speed zone, making it a quiet place to fish and a good place for canoe or kayak fishing.

Directions: From FL 40 (Granada Blvd.) in Ormond Beach, take Beach St. north about 2.5 miles to Sanchez St. Turn left and follow the road until it ends at the park.

Address: 329 Sanchez Ave., Ormond Beach, FL

33E. CASSEN PARK—*Boat and Pier – Ramp*

Description: The park is in Ormond Beach on the mainland side adjacent to the Granada Blvd. bridge. The 1,500-foot pier, beneath the road bridge, is popular with anglers.

Directions: From US 1 in Ormond Beach, take FL 40 east 0.4 mile to the park.

Address: 1 South Beach St., Ormond Beach, FL

33F. Ross Point Park—*Pier*
Directions: In Holly Hill. From FL 40 in Ormond Beach, take Beach St. south about 3.7 miles to the park.
Address: 611 Riverside Dr., Holly Hill, FL

33G. Seabreeze, Main Street, US 92, and Orange Avenue Bridges—*Boat and Bridge – Ramp*
Description: Within a 1.4-mile stretch, these four bridges cross the Halifax River in Daytona Beach. Fish around the bridge pilings.
Directions: Seabreeze bridge is at the end of Mason Ave. (CR 430). Main Street bridge is between Seabreeze and the US 92 bridge. And Orange Avenue bridge is just south of the US 92 bridge. All are accessible from A1A and US 1. The ramp is located on the Daytona Beach side of the Halifax River at the base of the bridge.

33H. Halifax Harbor Marina—*Boat and Pier – Ramp*
Description: The full-service municipal marina is owned by the City of Daytona Beach and privately managed.
Directions: From the west end of the US 92 (Volusia Ave.) Bridge in Daytona Beach, turn south on Beach St. for 0.3 miles to Basin St. Turn left onto Basin and follow it to the marina.
Address: 450 Basin St., Daytona Beach, FL
For more information: Call the marina office at (386) 671-3601 or visit the website www.halifaxharbor.net.

33I. Bethune Point Park—*Boat and Pier – Ramp*
Directions: From the west end of the US 92 (Volusia Ave.) bridge in Daytona Beach, turn south on Beach St. The park is 0.5 mile down Beach St.
Address: 101 Bellvue Ave. Daytona Beach, FL

33J. Port Orange Causeway Park—*Boat, Bank and Pier – Ramp*
Description: Fish from the pier or along the shoreline. There are multiple ramps to launch from.
Directions: This is the A1A bridge (Dunlawton Causeway) over the Halifax River in Port Orange. From the intersection with US 92 in Daytona Beach, take US 1 south 4.9 miles to the A1A bridge. Turn left.
Address: 93 Dunlawton Ave., Port Orange, FL

34. MAIN STREET PIER
Salt – Pier – $

Description: This 1,006-foot pier in Daytona Beach sits at the site of the original pier built in 1917. It has a bait and tackle shop and rod and reel rentals for pier patrons.

Fishing Index: Fish year-round for whiting and sheepshead. In summer add redfish, flounder, and black drum. Spanish mackerel and a few snook appear around the pier in fall. By the end of October, whiting become abundant and bluefish arrive. They are the staples on the pier through winter.

Directions: The pier is in Daytona Beach at the end of Main St. From the intersection with US 1, take US 92 to the beach. Turn north on Atlantic Blvd. (A1A) and go 0.3 mile to the pier.

Address: 1200 Main St., Daytona Beach, FL

For more information: Call the pier office at (386) 253-1212.

35. SUNGLOW PIER
Salt – Pier – $

Description: This pier is in Port Orange, south of Daytona Beach. It extends 1,500 feet into the Atlantic. There is a restaurant at the beginning of the pier. Rod and reel rentals available.

Fishing Index: Whiting and bluefish are the main targets in winter. In spring, Spanish mackerel arrive along with some big flounder, redfish, and pompano. In summer, the mackerel leave, the flounder get smaller, and some small sharks are caught. Spanish mackerel return in fall for a brief visit.

Directions: From Daytona Beach, take A1A south 5.2 miles. A1A turns and goes back to the mainland via the Port Orange Causeway. Continue down the beach for three blocks to the pier.

Address: 3701 S. Atlantic Ave., Daytona Beach, FL

For more information: Call the pier office at (386) 788-3364.

36. VOLUSIA COUNTY BEACHES
Salt – Surf

Description: Almost every mile of the county's beaches is accessible to surf anglers. There are numerous beachfront parks and smaller pull-off areas where you can park and walk to the beach. In the Daytona Beach area, driving on the beach is permitted.

Fishing Index: Whiting is one of the year-round favorites of surf anglers. Pompano are around when the water is above 68 degrees. The best action comes in fall when baitfish begin their run. Starting around mid-September, big redfish, jacks, and bluefish show up to feed on the schools of small baitfish. High tide is the better time to fish the surf, and low tide is the time to go to the beach and look for the troughs and runouts—the places where the water moves back out to sea.

Directions: Access to the beach is from A1A, which runs from the Volusia-Flagler county line south to Ponce de Leon Inlet. It crosses over to the mainland in Port Orange and begins again south of the inlet in New Smyrna Beach. Anywhere you can legally park and get to the beach is worth trying.

Volusia County beachfront parks include:

Tom Renick Park—1575 Oceanshore Blvd., Ormond-by-the-Sea
Bicentennial Park1800 N. Oceanshore Blvd., Ormond Beach
Frank Rendon Park—2705 Atlantic Ave., Daytona Beach Shores
Sun Splash Park—611 S. Atlantic Ave., Daytona Beach
Winterhaven Park—4589 S. Atlantic Ave., Ponce Inlet
Flagler Avenue Park—Flagler Ave., New Smyrna Beach
Mary McLeod Bethune Beach Park—6656 S. Atlantic Ave., New Smyrna Beach
Smyrna Dune Park—2995 N. Peninsula Ave., New Smyrna Beach
27th Avenue Park—3701 S. Atlantic Ave., New Smyrna Beach

37. PONCE DE LEON INLET
Salt – Boat, Bank, Pier, and Surf

Description: Inlets are great places to fish, and land-bound and boating anglers have easy access to this inlet. Water moving through Ponce de Leon Inlet enters the Halifax River and the northern end of Mosquito Lagoon. It is the only inlet for these two bodies of water. For boaters, the ramp beneath the North Causeway in New Smyrna Beach is the closest one to the inlet.

Using a sand-flea rake to find pompano bait

Fishing Index: Snook, redfish, seatrout, flounder, sheepshead, mangrove snapper, and black drum are the mainstays here. They don't all gather here at the same time, but every month has one or two "hot" species.

Access Points:

37A. LIGHTHOUSE POINT PARK—*Pier and Surf – $*
Description: The barrier-free pier is a 1,000-foot paved portion of the inlet's north jetty. Surf fishing is popular on the park's beach.
Directions: From US 92 in Daytona Beach, take A1A south about 10.3 miles to the intersection where A1A turns right and heads back to the mainland at Port Orange. Take the A1A spur that continues south and go 5.5 miles to the park.
Address: 5000 S. Atlantic Ave., Ponce Inlet, FL

37B. SMYRNA DUNE PARK—*Bank and Surf – $*
Description: Fish along the beach or off the south side jetty, but exercise caution on the rocks. They can be slippery.
Directions: From New Smyrna Beach, take the A1A Causeway toward the beach. Just across the bridge, turn left onto North Peninsula Dr. and drive 2.1 miles to the park. It is about a 0.5-mile walk

37C. NORTH CAUSEWAY RAMP—*Boat and Pier – Ramp*
Description: There are two ramps and a fishing pier. It is the closest ramp to the inlet.
Directions: From the intersection of US 1 and Canal St. in New Smyrna Beach, drive east on Canal St. approximately 0.3 miles. The road ends at Riverside. Turn left and go 0.1 mile to North Causeway. Turn right and go about 0.4 mile to the ramp on your right.

38. MOSQUITO LAGOON, NORTH
Salt – Boat and Pier – Ramp

Description: South of Ponce de Leon Inlet and between the barrier island and the mainland is the Mosquito Lagoon. From the Inlet southward for about 12 miles to the small community of Oak Hill, the area is a maze of waterways and small mangrove islands. It is a great place to fish. Fifteen tidal creeks, each 2 miles or longer, feed into this labyrinth of mangrove islands. Boaters share these waters with the endangered West Indian Manatee. There are numerous speed zones, so it is important to pay attention to the signs and observe the posted boat speed limits. The North Causeway Ramp (37C above) also provides access to the north end of the lagoon.

Fishing Index: This is redfish central for anglers. The area is known for producing some huge bull redfish in the 30- to 40-pound range. This great sport fish is caught all year, with big fish being possible at any time. There are plenty of opportunities to sight-fish with spinning or fly tackle. This is also one of the top spots in the state for canoe/kayak fishing. A good website for more information about paddling in this area is *www.suncoastpaddling.com.*

Access Points:

38A. GEORGE KENNEDY MEMORIAL PARK—*Boat – Ramp*
Directions: On the mainland side. From US 1 in New Smyrna Beach, go south 2.3 miles on US 1 to Edgewater. At the intersection with Park Ave., turn left and go 0.2 mile to the City of Edgewater's ramp.
Address: 103 N. Riverside Dr,, Edgewater, FL

38B. MENARD-MAY PARK—*Pier*
Directions: On the mainland side. From US 1 in New Smyrna Beach go south 2.4 miles on US 1 to Edgewater. At the intersection with Ocean Ave., turn left and go 0.2 mile to the City of Edgewater's park.
Address: 413 S. Riverside Dr., Edgewater, FL

38C. VETERANS PARK—*Pier*
Directions: On the mainland side. From the intersection of US 1 and FL 44 in New Smyrna Beach, take US 1 south 3.9 miles to Edgewater. Turn left onto Riverside Dr. and go 0.25 mile to the City of Edgewater's pier.
Address: 1811 S. Riverside Dr., Edgewater, FL

38D. RIVER BREEZE PARK— *Boat and Pier – Ramp*
Description: This Volusia County facility is on the mainland side of the lagoon in the community of Oak Hill. Fishing is allowed on the pier but not the banks.
Directions: From the intersection of FL 44 and US 1 in New Smyrna Beach, take US 1 south about 11.5 miles to Oak Hill. If coming from Titusville, it is about 19 miles from the US 1 and FL 406 intersection. In Oak Hill, turn east on Birch Rd. and follow it 0.5 mile to the park.
Address: 250 H.H. Burch Rd., Oak Hill, FL

38E. SHIPYARD ISLAND—*Boat – Ramp*
Description: This ramp is on the barrier island side of Mosquito Lagoon just before you enter the northern end of Canaveral National Seashore.
Directions: To reach this paved ramp, drive south from the intersection of US 1 and A1A in New Smyrna Beach on A1A approximately 9.2 miles to the ramp. It is before the National Seashore's visitor center.

Brevard County (northern portion, coastal area)

39. Mosquito Lagoon, South
Salt – Boat, Bank, Wade, and Pier – Ramp

Description: The open-water portion of Mosquito Lagoon is within the boundaries of Merritt Island National Wildlife Refuge and Canaveral National Seashore. Most of the lagoon is 3 feet deep or less and the tidal range is less than a foot. Shallow-water boats, canoes, or kayaks are the way to get around. Wind often influences how much water is in this part of the lagoon. It can literally blow the water in or out of an area. IMPORTANT NOTE: You must have a self-issued fishing permit while fishing inside of the Refuge. You can download a printable copy at *http://www.fws.gov/merrittisland/fishing/06permits.html*.

Fishing Index: This may be the best place for redfish in the entire state. Extensive seagrasses grow in the shallows—perfect cover for redfish. They are present all year and the big bull reds, in excess of 20 pounds might be the fish you hook up with on your next cast. Spotted seatrout, some pompano, and jacks are also possible catches in the lagoon. There is a Pole/Troll Zone along the east side of the lagoon and the northern boundary of the refuge. For information on the rules and regulations governing this area, go to *http://www.fws.gov/merrittisland/fishing/index.html*.

Access Points:
39A. WSEG Ramp—*Boat – Ramp*
Description: This ramp provides the closest access to the pole and troll zones in the mid portion of Mosquito Lagoon.
Directions: From the intersection of US 1 and Courtenay Parkway (CR 3) south of Oak Hill, drive south on Courtenay Parkway for 4.1 miles to the intersection with Taylor Rd. Turn left onto Taylor and follow it 0.9 miles to the ramp. If approaching from the south, drive north on Courtenay Parkway for 4.1 miles from where the road crosses the Haulover Canal to Taylor Rd.

39B. Haulover Canal—*Boat and Bank – Ramp*
Description: The ramp is in Merritt Island National Wildlife Refuge. The canal connects Mosquito Lagoon and the upper part of Indian River—a good spot for bank fishing.
Directions: From US 1 in Titusville, drive 6.9 miles east on the Max Brewer Parkway to CR 3 (Courtenay Parkway). Turn north and go 4 miles to the ramp on the left.

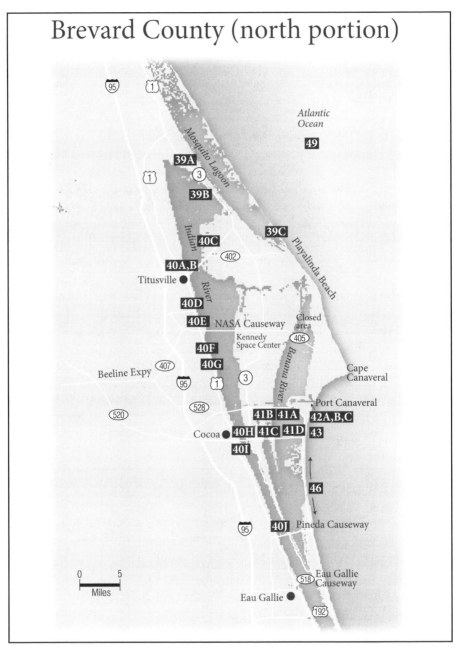

Brevard County (north portion)

Atlantic Ocean

Mosquito Lagoon

39A

39B

39C

Playalinda Beach

Indian

40C

40A,B

Titusville •

River

40D

40E NASA Causeway

Kennedy Space Center

Closed area

40F

40G

Beeline Expy

Banana River

Cape Canaveral

Port Canaveral

41B **41A** **42A,B,C**

Cocoa • **40H** **41C** **41D** **43**

40I

46

40J Pineda Causeway

Eau Gallie Causeway

Eau Gallie •

0 5
Miles

39C. CANAVERAL NATIONAL SEASHORE EDDY CREEK—*Boat – Ramp*
Description: This dirt ramp allows access to the south end of the lagoon for boats less than 16 feet in length. The ramp and other facilities in the area may be closed for short periods of time before and after rocket launches.
Directions: From US 1 in Titusville, take Max Brewer Parkway across the

Indian River. Go to FL 402 (Playalinda Beach Rd.). Turn right onto FL 402 and go 8.6 miles to Playalinda Beach. Turn north on the seashore road and go about 2 miles to the ramp.
For more information: Call the Merritt Island National Wildlife Refuge (321) 861-0668 or go to *www.fws.gov/merrittisland.*

40. UPPER INDIAN RIVER (VOLUSIA-BREVARD COUNTY LINE TO DRAGON POINT)
Salt – Boat, Bank, and Pier – Ramp

Description: Compared to Mosquito Lagoon, the amount of seagrass diminishes as you move south, but there is no shortage of places to fish along this portion of the river. Fishing is allowed from the relief bridges (smaller bridges on one or both sides of the main bridge) described below, on the causeways connecting the mainland to Merritt Island, and the beaches. These places are very popular with land-bound anglers, though parking is a problem; resist temptation and obey the posted no-parking signs. Fishing is not permitted on the NASA Causeway.

Fishing Index: Not as famous for fishing as nearby Mosquito Lagoon, but there are enough seagrass beds, especially along the river's eastern shore, to hold fish. This is a good place to fish for redfish and spotted seatrout.

Access Points:
40A. MARINA PARK—*Boat and Bank – Ramp*
Description: A City of Titusville facility adjacent to Sand Point Park.
Directions: From the intersection with FL 406 in Titusville, take US 1 north about 0.3 miles to Marina Park Rd. Turn right and go to the ramp.
Address: 501 Marina Rd., Titusville, FL

40B. VETERANS MEMORIAL PARK—*Pier*
Description: This free city pier extends into the Indian River. From September through the end of April, nighttime shrimping is popular. The pier was reopened in 2010 after being closed for several years due to storm damage. To catch shrimp you need a long-handled net and a light to hang over the surface of the water.
Directions: The pier is on the mainland side of the Indian River in Titusville at the base of the Max Brewer Causeway (FL 402).

40C. PARRISH PARK— *Boat and Pier – Ramp*
Directions: The park is 1.0 mile east of U.S. 1 on the Max Brewer Causeway (FL 402) bridge over the Indian River.
Address: 1 Max Brewer Causeway, Titusville, FL

40D. ROTARY RIVERFRONT PARK—*Pier*
Directions: From the intersection of US 1 and FL 50 in Titusville, drive north on US 1 for 0.6 mile to the park.
Address: 4141 South Washington Ave., Titusville, FL

40E. KENNEDY POINT PARK—*Boat and Bank – Ramp*
Directions: From the intersection of FL 50 and US 1 in Indian River City south of Titusville, drive south on US 1 for 0.25 mile.
Address: 4915 South Washington Ave., Titusville, FL

40F. MANATEE HAMMOCK PARK—*Bank and Pier*
Description: A county park with a developed campground, swimming pool, and outdoor game area.
Directions: From the intersection with FL 50 south of Titusville, take US 1 south 3.5 miles and look for the campground on the left.
Address: 7275 South US Highway 1, Titusville, FL

40G. PORT ST. JOHN RAMP—*Boat – Ramp*
Description: A popular, sometimes crowded ramp, heavily used by commercial clammers. Parking can be a problem.
Directions: From the intersection with FL 50 south of Titusville, take US 1 south 4.3 miles and look for the ramp on the left.
Address: 6650 North U.S. Hwy. 1, Port St. John, FL

40H. INTERCOASTAL WATERWAY PARK—*Boat, Bank and Pier*
Description: This Brevard County park is along the FL 520 (Merritt Island) Causeway from Cocoa to Cocoa Beach. Fish from the pier or along the shoreline.
Directions: From US 1 in Cocoa, take FL 520 east 0.7 miles and cross the Hubert Humphrey Bridge. Turn onto the access road to enter the park area.

40I. LEE WENNER PARK—*Boat, Bank and Pier – Ramp*
Description: A Brevard County facility on the mainland at the start of the Hubert Humphrey Bridge over the Indian River.
Directions: The park is at the base of the Merritt Island Causeway (FL 520) on the mainland side of the river in Cocoa. Turn off FL 520 onto Riveredge Blvd.

The park is on the south side.
Address: 300 Riveredge Blvd., Cocoa, FL

40J. POW/MIA Park (Pineda Landing)—*Boat and Bank – Ramp*
Description: Fish from the embankments around the bridges that are part of this causeway. Use caution when pulling off the roadway and parking as this is a busy road.
Directions: From the intersection with FL 520 in Cocoa, take US 1 south 11 miles to FL 404 (Pineda Causeway). Or from the intersection of US 1 and FL 518 in Eau Gallie, take US 1 north 5.5 miles. The Brevard County–maintained ramp is immediately north of the causeway on US 1.
Address: 1232 A St., Cocoa, FL

41. BANANA RIVER
Salt – Boat, Bank Bridge and Wade – Ramp

Description: This lagoon separates the east side of Merritt Island from the Canaveral Peninsula. The space shuttle launch pads are at the headwaters of this coastal waterway. The area north of NASA Parkway (FL 405) is closed to boating and fishing for security. Before launches from the Cape Canaveral Air Force Station there may be additional closures. The portion of the Banana River north of FL 528 is within the Merritt Island NWR and a refuge fishing permit is required (see Mosquito Lagoon, Site 39 above, for details).

Fishing Index: From the FL 405 Parkway south to the FL 528 Causeway (FL 528) is a manatee refuge. No motor boats are allowed. This is an excellent place to fly fish for big redfish either from a canoe or by wading in the grass flats. South of the FL 528 Causeway to the end of the Banana River at Dragon Point is also excellent year-round for redfish. Boats are allowed here and the preferred method is to sight-fish for them in the shallow waters.

Access Points:
41A. FL 528 (Bennett Causeway) —*Bridge and Wade*
Description: This segment spans the Banana River from Merritt Island to Port Canaveral. Fish from the seawall around the bridges and wade the flats on the north side of the road.
Directions: From the FL 528–FL 3 intersection on Merritt Island, take FL 528 east for 2.7 miles to the bridge. Pull off onto the dirt side roads.

41B. Kelly Park—*Boat and Bank – Ramp*
Description: A Brevard County park. Good bank fishing on the Banana River.

Directions: From the FL 528–FL 3 intersection on Merritt Island, take FL 528 east for 2.4 miles to the intersection with Banana River Dr. Take Banana River Rd. south for 0.1 mile to the park. Bait and tackle are available at the convenience store across the street.

Address: 2550 N. Banana River Dr., Merritt Island, FL

41C. KIWANIS ISLAND PARK—*Boat – Ramp*

Description: The park is on Sykes Creek on Merritt Island.

Directions: Take the Merritt Island Causeway (FL 520) from Cocoa toward Cocoa Beach. Cross the Indian River and go another 1.2 miles east on FL 520 from the intersection with FL 3 (Courtney Parkway). The park entrance is on the left.

Address: 951 Kiwanis Island Park Rd., Merritt Island, FL

41D. CONSTITUTION BICENTENNIAL PARK—*Boat – Ramp*

Directions: This City of Cocoa Beach park is located on the south side of the Merritt Island Causeway. From the intersection of FL 3 (Courtenay Causeway) and the Merritt Island Causeway, drive east on Merritt Island Causeway for 4.4 miles to the park entrance, on your right. If approaching from AIA, drive west on Merritt Island Causeway for 1.0 mile to the park on your left, just past the Cape Canaveral Hospital.

42. PORT CANAVERAL
Salt – Boat, Bank, Surf, and Pier –Ramp

Description: Port Canaveral is a cruise and cargo port. The Port Authority operates three parks—two with two boat ramps and one with a fishing pier. All are free and open to the public. The ramps provide access to the Atlantic Ocean. Jetty Park also has a campground and offers a spectacular vantage point for watching rocket launches. Reservations are suggested during the winter tourist season. Call Jetty Park at (321) 783-7111 for reservations. Numerous charter boats operate out of the Port Canaveral area.

Fishing Index: Fish from the jetty or along the beach. Snook, flounder, Spanish mackerel, bluefish, and mangrove snapper are common catches.

For more information: Visit the Port Authority's website at *www.portcanaveral.org*.

Access Points:
42A. RODNEY KETCHAM PARK (FORMERLY PORT'S END PARK)—*Bank and Boat – Ramp*

Directions: From FL 3 and FL 528 in Merritt Island, drive 5.2 miles to the intersection with George King Blvd. Turn left onto George King, drive 0.1 mile and turn left onto Dave Nisbet Dr. Go 0.1 mile and turn left onto Mullet Rd. Follow Mullet Rd. 0.7 mile to the park on your left.

42B. FREDDIE PATRICK PARKS—*Bank – Boat – Ramp*
Description: This park is about midway along the south shore of the Port Canaveral Channel. Access is to the Atlantic Ocean and the Banana River.
Directions: From FL 3 and FL 528 in Merritt Island, drive 5.2 miles to the intersection with George King Blvd. Turn left onto George King, drive 0.2 mile and turn left onto Flounder Street. Take Flounder north 0.2 mile to the park on your right.

42C. JETTY PARK—*Ban, Surf, and Pier*
Description: This park features the 1,200-foot paved, universally accessible Malcolm E. McLouth Fishing Pier at the opening of the port's channel to the Atlantic.
Directions: From FL 3 and FL 528 in Merritt Island, drive 5.2 miles to the intersection with George King Blvd. Turn left onto George King, drive approximately 1.4 miles to the park.
Address: 9035 Campground Circle, Cape Canaveral, FL

43.　COCOA BEACH PIER
Salt – Pier – $

Description: This 800-foot pier is for more than just fishing. With five restaurants, four bars, and several gift shops, it's a tourist destination.

Fishing Index: Fish for mangrove snapper and sheepshead year-round, and seasonally for Spanish mackerel, redfish, and snook.

Directions: From the A1A–FL 520 intersection in Cocoa Beach, drive 0.5 mile north on A1A to the pier.

Address: 401 Meade Ave., Cocoa Beach, FL

For more information: Call (321) 783-4050 or visit the pier's website, *www.cocoabeachpier.com*

Brevard (South Portion) and Indian River Counties

44. North-central Indian River (Eau Gallie Causeway to Sebastian Inlet) ———————
Salt – Boat, Bank, Bridge, and Pier – Ramp

Description: In this 18-mile stretch of the Indian River Lagoon, seagrasses are limited to a narrow fringe along the shoreline and around the shallow waters of most of the spoil islands.

Fishing Index: In developed areas, fish around dock pilings for snook and sheepshead. Fish for trout and redfish wherever there is seagrass. Fishing tends to be better closer to Sebastian Inlet. Around the bridges and causeways, anglers have good luck with mangrove snapper, sheepshead, redfish, black drum, and spotted seatrout.

Access Points:

44A. Eau Gallie Causeway Park Bridge—*Boat and Pier – Ramp*
Description: Fish from the catwalk beneath the main span of the bridge.
Directions: From US 1 in Eau Gallie, take FL 518 east 0.6 mile to the start of the causeway. The park is on the causeway.

44B. Ballard Park—*Boat and Bank – Ramp*
Directions: From the intersection with the Eau Gallie Causeway, take US 1 south about 1 mile to Thomas Barbour Dr. Turn left and go 0.5 mile to the park.
Address: 924 Thomas Barbour Dr., Melbourne, FL

44C. Claude Edge Front St. Park—*Boat and Pier – Ramp*
Description: This City of Melbourne park has a multilane ramp.
Directions: From the intersection of US 1 and US 192 (Melbourne Causeway), drive one block south on US 1 and turn left onto E. New Haven Ave. Drive two blocks to Front St. and turn right. The park is on your left.
Address: 2210 Front St., Melbourne, FL

44D. Melbourne Causeway—*Boat and Bank*
Description: The causeway connects Melbourne to Indialantic and Melbourne Beach. There is no relief bridge, but anglers can fish off the banks under the bridge. During the shrimp run, recreational shrimpers work traps from the banks beneath the bridge.

Brevard (south portion) and Indian River Counties

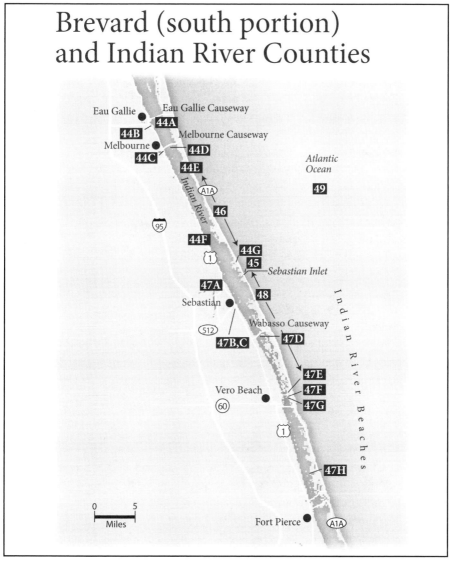

Directions: From US 1 in Melbourne, take US 192 east 0.25 mile to the entrance road to the causeway parking area on your right.

44E. Melbourne Beach Pier—*Pier*

Description: This 654-foot pier on the eastern shore of the Indian River has a covered area at the end. In summer, fish for spotted seatrout and redfish; in winter, whiting and sheepshead provide the action.

Directions: From US 192 in Indialantic, take A1A south 1.6 miles to Ocean Ave. Turn right and go two blocks to the pier.

Address: Ocean Ave. and Riverside Dr., Melbourne Beach, FL

44F. John Jorgensen and First Street Landings—*Boat – Ramp*
Description: These ramps are 0.3 mile apart along US 1. The multi-lane Jorgensen ramp is north of the single-lane First St. ramp.
Directions: From Melbourne, drive approximately 11 miles south on US 1 to the ramps. The ramps are 2.0 and 2.3 miles south of Valkaria Rd.
Address: Jorgensen Ramp: 5045 Highway 1, Grant, FL; First Street Landing: 4727 First St., Grant, FL

44G. Long Point Park—*Boat, Bridge, Surf, and Pier – Ramp*
Description: This Brevard County park has a campground with riverfront campsites, a swimming pond, and many other amenities. Reservations are accepted and recommended.
Directions: From US 192 in Indialantic, drive 15.2 miles south on A1A to the park. It's another 1.7 miles south to Sebastian Inlet.
Address: 700 Long Point Rd., Melbourne Beach, FL

45. Sebastian Inlet State Park
Salt – Boat, Bridge, Pier and Surf – Ramp

Description: The inlet is one of the best-known places to fish along Florida's east coast. The park has two ramps, with the main one on the south side of the inlet adjacent to the campground. The smaller ramp is on the north side of the inlet. Land-bound anglers can fish from the walkways on the north and south jetties or from the catwalk beneath the A1A bridge over the inlet. All are barrier free.

Fishing Index: The current in the inlet roars through so you will use more lead than usual if you are planning to fish the bottom or even to drift a bait at mid-water depth. Snook is a popular species for jetty anglers. But lots of other species feed in the pass including redfish, pompano, and occasionally sharks.

Summer snook fishing is great but snook season is closed, so it's strictly catch and release for this species. In fall, the bait-run along the beach begins and the action in the inlet can be frantic. Anglers may catch some big snook, redfish, sharks, tarpon, and any other species that happens to be around. In winter, big flounder provide the top action. Fish for them on the bottom using a live shrimp or finger mullet for bait.

Directions: From US 192 in Indialantic, drive about 17.2 miles south on A1A to the park. Or from FL 60 in Vero Beach drive 15 miles north on A1A.

Address: 9700 S. State Rd. A1A, Melbourne Beach, FL

Sand fleas, also known as mole crabs, are found in the surf zone. They are abundant along the Atlantic coast in central Florida.

For more information: Call the park office at (321) 984-4852 or the on-site Inlet Marina at (321) 724-5424. Or go to *www.floridastateparks.org.*

46. BREVARD COUNTY BEACHES
Salt – Surf

Description: Beginning at the county's northern boundary, surf anglers can enjoy the beautiful, undeveloped beaches of the Canaveral National Seashore. Beach access is restricted at the J.F.K. Space Center, but south of Port Canaveral Inlet the beach is open to the public all the way to Sebastian Inlet.

Fishing Index: Pompano and whiting are present year-round. Bluefish are the winter staple. Many seasoned surf anglers say that fall, when the baitfish make their run south, is the best time to surf fish. There's no telling what may bite. Snook, big redfish, tarpon, crevalle jack, and even a few king mackerel may take the bait. Big surf rods are essential to reach the fish, which are farther offshore from late fall to spring. Come summer, switch to light tackle and fish only a few feet from shore.

Directions: Wherever A1A runs along the beach, be on the lookout for a place to park and fish. When in Canaveral National Seashore, you must park in the designated parking lots and use the wooden walkways over the sand dunes to reach the beach. South of Port Canaveral, A1A is never more than a block or two from the ocean. Beginning with the beach at Jetty Park, numerous parks provide access to the beach. Anglers must be careful not to fish too close to swimmers and not to fish at all in the beach areas reserved exclusively for swimming. Besides the parks listed below, there are other local town and city parks that provide beach access.

Brevard County Beach Parks include:

> **Cherie Down Park**—8492 Ridgewood Avenue, Cape Canaveral
> **Lorie Wilson Park**—1500 N. Atlantic Avenue, Cocoa Beach
> **Robert Murkshe Memorial Park**—1600 Atlantic Avenue S., Cocoa Beach
> **Bonsteel Park**—8455 Highway A1A, Melbourne Beach
> **Canova Beach Park**—3299 Highway A1A, Indian Harbour Beach
> **Coconut Point Park**—3535 S. Highway A1A, Melbourne Beach
> **Howard E. Futch Memorial Park at Paradise Beach**—2301 N. Highway A1A, Melbourne
> **Irene H. Canova Park**—2289 Highway A1A, Indian Harbour Beach
> **Juan Ponce de Leon Landing**—4005 Highway A1A, Melbourne Beach
> **S.P.R. A. Park**—499 Highway A1A, Satellite Beach
> **Seagull Park**—285 Highway A1A, Satellite Beach
> **Spessard Holland North Beach Park**—2525 Highway A1A, Melbourne Beach
> **Spessard Holland South Beach Park**—2545 Highway A1A, Melbourne Beach

47. SOUTH-CENTRAL INDIAN RIVER (SEBASTIAN INLET TO VERO BEACH)
Salt – Boat, Bank, Surf, and Pier – Ramp

Description: A 21-mile stretch of the Indian River within Indian River County. Vero Beach is the largest developed area. This is manatee country and there are numerous speed zones. Be on the watch for the signs. Because there are no inlets between Sebastian and Fort Pierce connecting this part of the Indian River to the Atlantic, there is not much tidal flushing. Thus the salinity can vary greatly and is strongly influenced by the amount of rainfall.

Fishing Index: Trout and redfish are the staples of this part of the lagoon. Large trout, locally known as gator trout, can exceed 10 pounds. When the water warms up, snook and some tarpon will boost the action.

Access Points:

47A. Dale Wimbrow and Donald MacDonald Parks—*Boat – Ramp*
Description: These two Indian River County parks have small ramps that provide access to the Indian River via the Sebastian River.
Directions: Both parks are on Roseland Rd. From the intersection of US 1 and Roseland Rd. in Sebastian, drive approximately 1.7 miles to MacDonald Park and 2 miles to Wimbrow Park.
Address: MacDonald Park: 12315 Roseland Rd., Sebastian, FL; Wimbrow Park: 11805 Roseland Rd., Sebastian, FL

47B. Sebastian Ramp—*Boat and Pier – Ramp*
Directions: From the intersection with FL 60 in Vero Beach, take US 1 north 12.5 miles to Sebastian. Turn right onto Main St. and follow it 1 block to the ramp and pier.
Address: 700 Main St., Sebastian, FL

47C. Sebastian Yacht Club & Riverside Park—*Boat and Pier – Ramp*
Directions: From the intersection with FL 60 in Vero Beach, take US 1 north 12 miles to Sebastian. Turn right on Sebastian Blvd. and drive one block to Indian River Dr. The ramp is 1 ½ blocks north on Indian River Dr., and the pier is 1 ½ blocks south.
Address: 820 Indian River Dr., Sebastian, FL

47D. Wabasso Causeway Park—*Boat, Bank and Pier – Ramp*
Description: A popular spot for boaters and land-bound anglers alike. Anglers can fish from the shoreline or off the piers that parallel the Wabasso Causeway. The next ramp to the south is in Vero Beach.
Directions: From the intersection with FL 60 in Vero Beach, take US 1 north 7.8 miles to Wabasso. Turn right on FL 510 (Wabasso Causeway). The ramp is on the island side of the causeway.
Address: 3150 Wabasso Bridge Rd., Vero Beach, FL

47E. MacWilliam Park—*Boat – Ramp*
Directions: From the intersetion of US 1 and FL 60 in Vero Beach, follow FL 60 for 3.0 miles to the intersection with Indian River Dr. to the north and Memorial Island Dr. to the south. This is just across the bridge on the east side of the Indian River. Turn left onto Indian River Drive and then make an immediate left onto the park road leading to the ramp. A City of Vero Beach park.
Address: 3250 Riverside Park Dr., Vero Beach, FL

47F. FL 60 Bridge—*Pier*

Description: The old FL 60 bridge, or Merrill Barber Bridge, was relocated and replaced in 1994. A catwalk from the east side was built to provide anglers with a place to fish.

Directions: From the intersection of US 1 and FL 60 in Vero Beach, follow FL 60 for 3.0 miles to the intersection with Indian River Dr. to the north and Memorial Island Dr. to the south. This is just across the bridge on the east side of the Indian River. Turn right onto Memorial Island Dr. and then take an immediate right onto Bridge Plaza Dr.

47G. Riverside Park—*Boat – Ramp*

Directions: From the intersection of US 1 and FL 60 in Vero Beach, follow FL 60 for 3.0 miles to the intersection with Indian River Dr. to the north and Memorial Island Dr. to the south. This is just across the bridge on the east side of the Indian River. Turn right onto Memorial Island Rd. and go 0.1 mile to Dahlia Lane. Turn right on Dahlia and go one block to the ramp. A City of Vero Beach park.

Address: 350 Dahlia Lane, Vero Beach, FL

47H. Round Island Riverside Park—*Boat, Bank, Surf, and Pier – Ramp*

Description: This park on the island side of the river encompasses the land from the river to the Atlantic Ocean. Anglers can surf fish or launch a boat in the Indian River. Just north of the Indian County–St. Lucie County line.

Directions: From FL 60 in Vero Beach drive about 7 miles south on A1A to the park. Fort Pierce Inlet is another 5 miles south.

Address: 2200 Highway A1A, Vero Beach, FL

48. Indian River County Beaches
Salt – Surf

Description: Seven county beaches are open to swimmers and anglers. Parts of some beaches may be restricted for swimmers only, but there is plenty of room for surf anglers to find a place to fish.

Fishing Index: There are live "worm reefs" just offshore of the beaches in this county. Some of them are very close to shore and that creates good habitat for fish. Like all the surf zones along this part of Florida, late fall to early spring fishing for bluefish is very good. In spring and into early summer, pompano are a popular target. Surf fishing also yields snook, redfish, and occasionally tarpon and Spanish mackerel.

Directions: A1A parallels the beach. The county parks and other public parking areas are on this road.

Indian River County Beach Parks include:

Ambersands Beach Access—12566 N. A1A, Vero Beach
Goldensand Park—10350 N. A1A, Vero Beach
Seagrape Trail Beach Access—8302 N. A1A, Vero Beach
Tracking Station Park—800 46th Place, N. A1A, Vero Beach
Turtle Trail Beach Access—8102 N. A1A, Vero Beach
Wabasso Beach Park—1820 County Rd. 510 and A1A, Vero Beach

49. ATLANTIC OCEAN
Salt – Boat

Description: Offshore fishing along the east central coast offers anglers a chance to catch a wide variety of fish. This part of Florida has two populations of some species, such as dolphin and Spanish and king mackerel. One population migrates up and down the Atlantic coast in spring and fall. The other moves up from south Florida and the Keys in summer. The result is longer seasons for some of the most popular offshore species.

Fishing Index: Close to shore, boaters seek Spanish and king mackerel during

Getting to see a bottlenose dolphin up close is fun and fascinating, but these air-breathing mammals will slow down or stop the fishing action.

the spring and fall runs. Cobia, following the manta rays, also move close to shore most years in spring and fall. Farther out, dolphin fishing is very good spring through fall; sailfish fishing is best in fall and winter. Add to that the year-round presence of amberjack, wahoo, grouper, snapper, and cobia, and anglers can always count on at least one or two species for good action.

Fleet Locations:

PONCE DE LEON INLET
Description: Most of this fleet is based in the community of Ponce Inlet on the north side of the inlet. A few boats also operate from New Smyrna Beach.
For more information: Try a Google search of Daytona Beach or New Smyrna Beach Charter Fishing. There are numerous listings.

PORT CANAVERAL
Description: Anglers visiting the Orlando area are only 45 minutes from the fleet at Port Canaveral. It is a direct shot on the Bee Line Expressway to the port. Party and sport fishing boats are available.
For more information: Try a Google search of Port Canaveral Charter Fishing. There are numerous listings.

SEBASTIAN INLET
Description: A few boats operate from small marinas near the inlet.
For more information: Call Wabasso Tackle Shop at (772) 589-8518.

MONTH BY MONTH IN EAST CENTRAL FLORIDA
Note: Offshore is defined as greater than 2 miles from the coast. Coastal waters include open waters inside of 2 miles, including surf fishing, and all brackish water areas such as bays, the saltwater regions of rivers, and lagoons. Fresh water includes lakes, ponds, reservoirs, and rivers.

JANUARY

Offshore: Sailfish, wahoo, king mackerel, snapper, and grouper are the best bets, but be prepared for days with rougher-than-average seas. There may be some cobia and amberjack over the inshore reefs. Bottom fishing for grouper and snapper will be good.

Coastal: An excellent time to surf fish for bluefish and whiting. Pompano may be plentiful when the water is above 68 degrees. Sand fleas are the top bait. Also the prime time for big flounder and spotted seatrout. Fish for them in the inlets and deeper spots of the Halifax, Banana, and Indian rivers. For flounder, drop a big live shrimp or finger mullet to the bottom.

Freshwater: Striped and sunshine bass fishing is very good in the St. Johns River. Largemouth bass begin spawning in the lakes and rivers. Crappie action steadily improves this month. Shad anglers may see some fish toward mid-month.

FEBRUARY

Offshore: A repeat of the top sailfish, snapper, and grouper action seen in January. Anglers will also find good numbers of wahoo, amberjack, blackfin tuna, and cobia out near the edge of the Gulf Stream. Cold fronts sweeping through from the northwest make it too rough to fish some days.

Coastal: Bluefish, pompano, and whiting reward surf anglers this month. Use a 10- to 12-foot surf rod and expect to wade into the surf zone so your casts reach the trough that holds fish. Spotted seatrout action is very good with the bigger fish staying in deeper and warmer water near the flats. Try fishing for them later in the day. If the water on the flats is going to warm up and entice them to feed, this is when they'll show up, tides permitting.

Freshwater: This is one of the peak months for trophy largemouth bass. The best bait is live wild shiners. Normally, this is also one of the best American shad months on the upper St. Johns River. Add the excellent crappie fishing typical in February and this is one of the best months for freshwater fishing in the region.

MARCH

Offshore: Bottom fishing for snapper and grouper is reliable and rewarding in March. There should also be plenty of cobia around. Closer to shore, Spanish and king mackerel also move north and the action will get progressively better towards the end of the month.

Coastal: The big three—redfish, spotted seatrout, and snook—dominate the desires of anglers. Redfish and big trout action is in its prime. Snook action is good but will improve in the next two months. Schools of black drum will also be found on the grass flats. Around docks and the Sebastian Inlet jetties there will be sheepshead and jacks. Surf fishing falls off as the bluefish leave, but a king mackerel or two may pick up the bait, especially if it's a live baitfish.

Freshwater: The peak time for shad will come and go in this month. Check the local conditions and don't procrastinate if you hear the fish are biting. Crappie action will begin to slow down for anglers who can't find the cooler waters in lakes and rivers. Largemouth bass are past peak spawning time but they are still around and hungry.

April

Offshore: Dolphin is on anglers' minds, and this traditionally marks the beginning of the spring northward migration of the tasty fish. A wahoo, sailfish, or marlin may also liven up the day. Spanish and king mackerel continue to be very good. Small schools of cobia, following the manta rays, offer exciting sight fishing. An excellent way to find some blackfin tuna is to set out a chum slick behind the shrimp boats that anchor offshore during the day. Throw some chum in the water and if the tuna are present, you will see them. At that point, they are so worked up that they will hit just about anything you toss their way.

Coastal: Around the inside of inlets and in lagoons, the redfish, snook, and seatrout action is excellent. Surf anglers have a chance of catching the last of the spring migrating cobia and plenty of Spanish mackerel. There will also be flounder, sheepshead, and black drum in the inlets and around docks. Drifting live bait, weighted down so there is just enough to keep the bait a few feet off the bottom, is a proven technique in the inlets. The shrimp run, if there is one, can be very good this month. Trouble is, the run is very unpredictable and success hinges on watching and waiting just about every night.

Freshwater: Largemouth bass move into the post-spawn feeding pattern and that makes for good fishing, but it is the last good month until late fall. Panfish lovers turn out in force as the bluegills begin to spawn.

May

Offshore: Spring has better-than-average fishing because of the migratory species, dolphin and king mackerel, moving past the east central coast. This is also a month in which you could find sailfish, blue marlin, and wahoo offshore in the Gulf Stream. Grouper and snapper fishing falls off, but you can always catch a few over the reefs and wrecks.

Coastal: Snook fishing, especially around the inlets, is the best bet. Shark fishing also improves. The inlets and along the beaches are the most popular places to find them. Start your fishing early in the morning and late in the day or at night.

Freshwater: Bluegills and shellcrackers are on their beds and that translates into top action for both species. Largemouth bass and crappie action slows for summer unless you know how to fish the deeper spots in the lakes and rivers. Get the bait down to the fish and work it slowly. Heat makes the fish sluggish, even when eating.

JUNE

Offshore: Summer action is slower than in spring and fall, but you can still catch fish. Expect average fishing for a variety of species including cobia, wahoo, king mackerel, amberjack, sailfish, and dolphin. Blue marlin fishing is in its prime and a trip to the Gulf Stream may be productive. Bottom fishing for grouper and snapper always brings in some fish. The question is, how many will be legal size?

Coastal: Snook fishing is great but the season will be closed, so you can't keep the fish this month. That's how we ensure there will be new fish for tomorrow's generation to catch. Shark anglers usually do well with the small coastal species such as blacktip. If you catch some pigfish (known by some as grunts), use them for bait for the big spotted seatrout that are around but reluctant to bite.

Freshwater: Early and late—those are the times of day for the best chance at catching some largemouth bass. There is very good year-round angling for catfish in virtually every freshwater body in the region. They are easy to catch and a catfish fry with some hushpuppies and cole slaw is hard to beat for great eating.

JULY

Offshore: Fishing for mangrove and lane snapper is popular for offshore anglers. The best action is at night. Blue marlin action will still be better than average for the area. If you have the time and gas money, a trip farther offshore will produce some yellowfin tuna. Other offshore fish are there, but summer is the slowest time of the year.

Coastal: Thanks to the excellent habitat in the Indian River Lagoon, anglers can usually find some hungry redfish and seatrout. Fish early in the morning or late in the day. At the end of the day, watch for thunderstorms. Anyone can fish the surf this time of year. All you need is light tackle. The fish are in the first trough, which is always very close to shore. For pompano, use live sand fleas, which you can dig on the beach. If none are found, go to the grocery store and buy some clams. Snook will also be prowling the shoreline as will some tarpon, but use beefier tackle if targeting those silver kings.

Freshwater: The best bets are shellcrackers. If you are familiar with the places you fish, try a night trip for largemouth bass. The cooler evenings are likely times for bass to move into shallow waters to feed.

AUGUST

Offshore: A little of this and a little of that describes midsummer offshore fishing. The species swimming around include all the familiar names: cobia, dolphin, king mackerel, sailfish, wahoo, and others. Some days the fishing will be good and other times it will be tough. The best bets are night fishing for snapper and shark.

Coastal: Another month when experienced anglers can catch redfish in good numbers. If you lack experience but want to catch a lot of fish, try a trip with a guide. Snook and trout are caught in respectable numbers. In the surf, whiting and pompano are the most likely catches.

Freshwater: Limit your fishing to early in the morning or late in the day. The fish don't like the heat any more than you do. Actually, it's harder on them because the warmer the water, the less life-sustaining oxygen it holds. If you know of a deep hole, work that area carefully. It should have fish in it.

SEPTEMBER

Offshore: Anglers are ready for a change and September usually brings one. Baitfish, chased south by mackerel and cobia, run down the coast, signaling prime angling offshore all the way in to the beach. Water temperature apparently determines when the run begins. For those who want to venture out 50 miles or more, the yellowfin tuna action is a good bet.

Coastal: Surf and inlet anglers are also waiting for the bait to show up and stimulate the snook, tarpon, and seatrout action. Redfish provide the most reliable action until the feeding frenzy begins. Expect good fishing for mangrove snapper off bridges at night.

Freshwater: A slow month—still hot and humid—but better days are ahead. Not much change in activity or strategy since June.

OCTOBER

Offshore: The action for cobia, both mackerel species, and tarpon swings into high gear by the end of the month. A trolled or cast silver spoon is usually irresistible for the mackerel once you've found them. This month and next are the best for offshore tarpon fishing. There may not be greater numbers of fish, but the action is noticeably better.

Coastal: Prime month to catch the big three: snook, redfish, and seatrout. Fish around the inlets, on the deeper flats, and within 0.5 mile of shore. Freeline a live bait and hold on. Tarpon also move close in now. A few are always caught from the surf as are good numbers of snook.

Freshwater: The first signs of cooler weather bring largemouth bass anglers to the lakes and rivers and the bass back into the shallow water. Action is better but is not back to the peak experienced during spawning season. Sunshine and striped bass, if present, begin to bite again. So do crappie.

November

Offshore: Grouper and snapper action picks up as the fish move closer to the coast. King and Spanish mackerel and cobia are top choices this month as the fall run is in full swing. Sailfish activity begins to build toward the winter peak. Weather becomes a factor in making long offshore trips.

Coastal: Bluefish arrive and surf anglers dig out their big rods and reels. Snook, seatrout, tarpon, and redfish are in their fall prime. Flounder fishing begins to improve and pompano will begin to show up along the beaches to make the surf anglers happy.

Freshwater: Cool water stimulates the appetites of the three bass species. Largemouths start to feed in anticipation of the spawn. Crappie action can be very good if the water cools off faster than normal.

December

Offshore: This is one of the best times of year for grouper and sailfish. On warm days anglers can also find some amberjack, cobia, king mackerel, and blackfin tuna. Only the weather can spoil your plans.

Coastal: Bluefish and pompano from the surf and flounder in the inlets keep coastal anglers busy this month. Both are best bets. In the lagoons and saltwater rivers, sheepshead action is good around the numerous bridges and causeways that link the mainland to the beaches. There should be lots of flounder in the inlets.
Freshwater: Prime crappie season begins this month. In the St. Johns, striped bass fishing enters its prime season.

East Central Florida Fish Availability Chart

NOTE: Refer to the month-by-month table for additional information. Information in this chart represents the seasonal patterns observed over the past three years. For saltwater species, the arrival of the migrant species and the peak times for each species are heavily dependent on water temperature. Unusually warm or cold periods will affect the patterns described above. Bream is the local name for bluegills and shellcrackers. Specs is a local name for crappie. Speckled trout is a local name for spotted seatrout.

■ signifies a reasonable chance of catching this species in that month.

□ signifies the optimal months for catching the species.

Species	Jan	Feb	Mar	Apr	May	Jun	Jul	Aug	Sep	Oct	Nov	Dec
Redfish	■	■	□	□	□	□	□	□	□	□	□	■
Snook	■	■	■	■	□	□	■	■	□	□	□	■
Spotted Seatrout	□	□	□	□	□	■	■	■	□	□	□	■
Sheepshead	■	■	■	■	■	■	■	■	■	■	■	□
Mangrove Snapper	■	■	■	■	■	■	■	■	■	■	■	■
Gag Grouper	□	□	■	■	■	■	■	■	■	□	□	□
Bluefish	□	□	■	■	■	■	■	■	■	■	□	□
Flounder	□	□	■	■	■	■	■	■	■	■	■	□
Black Drum	■	■	■	■	■	■	■	■	■	■	■	■
Dolphin	■	■	■	□	□	□	■	■	■	■	■	■
Blackfin Tuna	■	■	■	■	■	■	■	■	■	■	■	■
Blue Marlin	■	■	■	□	□	□	□	■	■	■	■	■
Wahoo	■	■	■	■	■	□	□	■	■	■	■	■
Whiting	□	□	■	■	■	■	■	■	■	■	■	□
Amberjack	■	■	■	■	□	□	□	□	■	■	■	■
Sailfish	□	□	■	■	■	■	■	■	■	■	■	□
Cobia	■	■	■	□	□	■	■	■	■	□	□	■
Spanish Mackerel	■	■	□	□	□	■	■	■	■	□	□	■
King Mackerel	■	■	■	□	□	■	■	■	■	□	□	■
Crevalle Jack	■	■	■	■	■	■	■	■	■	■	■	■
Tarpon	■	■	■	■	■	■	■	■	□	□	□	■
Pompano	□	■	■	■	■	■	■	■	■	■	□	□
Shrimp	■	■	■	■	■							
Shark (all species)				■	■	□	□	□	■	■		
Largemouth Bass	□	□	□	□	■	■	■	■	■	■	■	■
Bluegills	■	■	■	□	□	□	■	■	■	■	■	■
Catfish	■	■	■	■	■	□	■	■	■	■	■	■
Shellcracker	■	■	■	■	□	□	□	■	■	■	■	■

Species	Jan	Feb	Mar	Apr	May	Jun	Jul	Aug	Sep	Oct	Nov	Dec
Sunshine Bass	☐	☐	■	■						■	■	☐
Striped Bass	☐	☐	■	■						■	■	☐
Crappie	☐	☐	☐	■	■						■	☐
American Shad	■		☐		☐		■		■			

West Central Regional Map

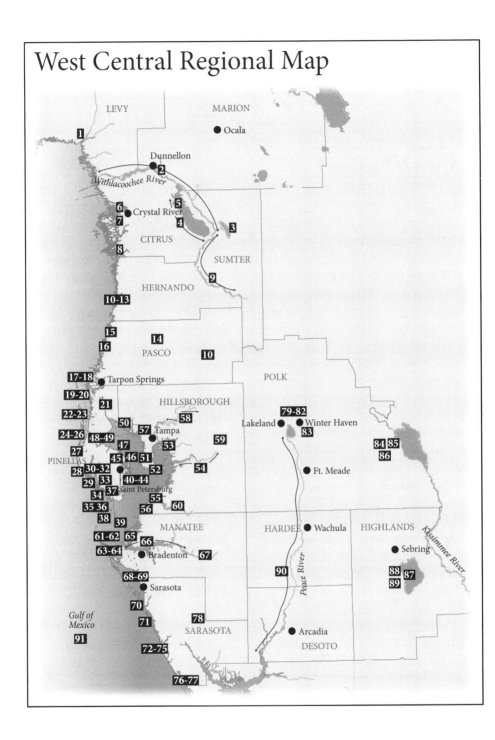

West Central Florida_____

Counties:
• Levy (southern portion) • Citrus • Marion (western portion)
• Hernando • Sumter • Pasco • Pinellas • Hillsborough • Polk
• Manatee • Hardee • Sarasota • DeSoto • Highlands

Saltwater Fishing

From the chance at a world-record tarpon to the hundreds of bass-filled lakes, great fishing is never more than a few miles away in west central Florida. Most of the coastline from Waccasassa Bay to Weeki Wachee is relatively undeveloped. Salt marshes blanket the shoreline and four rivers and several smaller tidal creeks provide enough fresh water to create miles of fish-friendly estuarine habitat and great places to fish. In the nearshore Gulf waters seagrasses flourish, creating perfect conditions for spotted seatrout, redfish, tarpon, and flounder. In fact, most of the biggest tarpon landed in Florida come from Homosassa Bay in late spring and early summer when the giant fish move onto the flats to feed.

A few miles south of Weekie Wachee the tendrils of development have reached out so that developed land dominates the landscape along almost every waterway and the shoreline of the Gulf of Mexico. When these areas were first developed, not much thought went into protecting the coastal waters from the polluted runoff coming from the land. Fortunately, most communities have come to realize that the beaches and coastal waters are vital economic engines, and they are working to clean up the pollution. The results in places like Old Tampa, Hillsborough, Tampa, and Boca Ciega bays, as well as in Clearwater Harbor and St. Joseph Sound, are evident as fishing is considered to be better now than it was in the 1980s and '90s.

Anglers can fish from the area's many bridges and seawalls, wade in the shallow waters, or launch a boat at a local ramp. The passes—Hurricane, Clearwater, John's, and North Channel—are good places to look for big snook and predatory fish in summer. Fishing is good when the tide is going in or coming out.

On the south side of Tampa Bay are the popular destinations of Bishop's Harbor, Terra Ceia Bay, and the flats around Snead Island. A bit further south takes you into Anna Maria Sound and then to Sarasota Bay. There are plenty of access points for boaters, several fishing piers, and numerous public access points throughout the region that allow surf anglers a convenient way to get on the beach.

Charter boats operate from almost every coastal community, especially those near the passes connecting to the Gulf of Mexico. A few big party boats specialize in trips to the Florida Middle Grounds 100 miles offshore. These are one- or two-night trips where anglers bottom fish for grouper, snapper, amberjack, and other species.

Freshwater Fishing

Hundreds of lakes dot this region and all contain fish. Over half of the lakes are accessible from public or private ramps or via waterways connecting one or more lakes. The bigger lakes attract most of the out-of-town anglers because outdoor magazines have popularized these over-sized fishing holes. But fishing can be very good in the smaller, lesser-known lakes too, including all those listed in this chapter. Stop at one of the local bait and tackle shops for tips on which lakes have the best action.

The region's rivers—particularly the Withlacoochee and Peace—are known for their scenic beauty and "old Florida" feel. The fishing is fine, but even devoted anglers may end up spending as much time watching wildlife as fishing.

Largemouth bass is the freshwater king in this region and a record fish is certainly lurking somewhere in the region. The water is too warm for striped bass, and while the FWC stocks hybrid (sunshine) bass, the fish seldom reach the size they do in the cooler waters to the north. Crappie are another popular target, especially during the colder months.

LEVY (SOUTHERN PORTION), MARION (WESTERN PORTION), CITRUS, AND SUMTER COUNTIES

1. WACCASASSA RIVER AND BAY
Salt – Boat – Ramp

Description: The bay is a great place to fish if you like to get away from the crowds. The area is among the most remote along the west central coast. Access is via a boat ramp at the end of FL 326. No services are available so bring everything you need or stop at the small store in Gulf Hammock at the intersection of US 19 & 98 and CR 326. Most anglers head downriver from the ramp to fish the brackish waters of the river or the open waters of the Gulf of Mexico. It's about a 6-mile trip to the Gulf. Most of the land along the coast is part of the Waccasassa Bay Preserve State Park.

Fishing Index: In the extensive salt marshes and numerous tidal creeks, redfish and spotted seatrout are the most sought-after species. The area is famous for its extensive oyster bars and reefs, which is one of the main reasons the area attracts

Levy (southern portion), Marion (western portion), Citrus and Sumter Counties

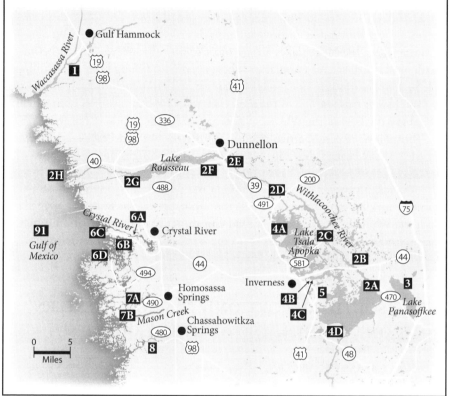

and holds so many fish. For this reason, top-water lures are a good choice, especially when fishing in shallow water. The area also produces some nice black drum. A hole at the mouth of the river is a frequent gathering spot for drum. Boaters unfamiliar with the area should exercise caution as there are many hard-bottom areas ready to do battle with your prop or lower unit. Chances are excellent that the hard bottom will win most every time.

Directions: From US 19 in Gulf Hammock, drive 3.7 miles on FL 326 to the boat ramp. The area can also be reached from departure points in Cedar Key and Bird Creek Park (2H) in Yankeetown.

For more information: Go to *www.floridastateparks.org* and click on the link to the park.

2. WITHLACOOCHEE RIVER
(LAKE PANASOFFKEE TO GULF OF MEXICO) ———————
Salt and Fresh – Boat and Bank – Ramp

Description: This 157-mile river begins in the Green Swamp and flows northwest to the city of Dunnellon, then turns and flows more or less due west to the Gulf. Cypress swamp flanks most portions of the river from the Green Swamp to Dunnellon making it one of the most scenic rivers in the state. Most of the fishing occurs downriver from where water from Outlet River connects Lake Panasoffkee to the Withlacoochee. A few miles west of this confluence, the Withlacoochee's waters mix with the waters of Lake Tsala Apopka via a swampy area that extends along most of the lake's poorly defined shoreline. Just east of Dunnellon, Blue Run joins the Withlacoochee, adding the clear water of Rainbow Springs to the river. The water boiling up from the spring is a nearly constant 70 to 72 degrees throughout the year. West of Dunellon, the river widens and is known as Lake Rosseau. The lake formed when this part of the river and the cypress swamp that flanked it were flooded by construction of a dam near the town of Inglis at the west end of the lake. The last section of the river, from the dam to the Gulf, is cut off from the rest of the river by a remnant section of the now-defunct Cross Florida Barge Canal. There is no direct boat access from the lake to the Gulf.

Fishing Index: Saltwater anglers will find some good places to fish for redfish and seatrout along the lower reaches of the river and the canal. The shallow flats along the coast are popular places to fish as well. Anglers also have a chance to hook up with some cobia around the channel markers seaward of the river mouth and a few legal-size grouper where the barge canal opens into the Gulf of Mexico.

Freshwater fishing for bass, crappie, and bluegill is best on Lake Rousseau, with February to May being the best months. Boaters must exercise extreme caution as the lake, except for a few naturally deep areas, has countless submerged snags. Idle speed is usually the best speed. The upside to this is that the huge amount of submerged structure makes really good fish habitat. Live shiners are a good choice for bait if you want to catch some big bass. Lures can be effective but, with so much submerged structure, hang-ups tend to run higher than average.

Upriver from Dunnellon, the river narrows and small boats, canoes, and kayaks are the preferred method for fishing the river. Detailed information about the 76-mile Withlacoochee River South Paddling Trail that begins in Dunnellon is available at *http://www.dep.state.fl.us/gwt/guide/designated_paddle/WithSouth_guide.pdf.* This includes information on walk-in sites to the middle reaches of the Withlacoochee

Lake Panasoffkee is noted for bass, shellcracker, and bluegill fishing. It has dense areas of eelgrass, a submerged aquatic plant throughout the extensive shallow waters of this lake.

Directions: The river forms the boundary between Citrus and Levy and Marion and Sumter counties. Yankeetown is the last community before the river empties into the Gulf of Mexico, and Dunnellon is the town at the eastern end of Lake Rousseau. In addition to the sites described below, there are several fish camps on lakes Rousseau and Panasoffkee.

For more information: Go to the FWC website, *http://myfwc.com/Recreation/ FW_forecasts_ncr.htm,* for a quarterly fishing forecast for Lake Rousseau. Also try Big Bass Village (352) 447-3474 (*www.bigbassvillage.com*) or Lake Rousseau RV Park/Fishing Resort (352) 795-6336 *(www.lakerousseaurvpark.com).*

Access Points:

2A. WYSONG PARK—*Boat and Bank – Ramp*
Description: A small dock adjacent to the single-lane ramp is used by local anglers. This is also the site of the Wysong-Coogler Dam and boat lock.
Directions: From Inverness drive about 10 miles east on FL 44. Turn right onto FL 470 and drive about 2.5 miles south to CR 307. Turn right on CR 307, drive one block, and then turn right onto CR 300. Drive 0.3 mile to the park entrance. From I-75 at the town of Lake Panasoffkee, drive north about 4 miles on FL 470 to CR 307. Turn left and follow directions above.
Address: 4790 NW 46th Rd., Lake Panasoffkee, FL

2B. RUTLAND PARK—*Boat – Ramp*
Description: The two-lane ramp at this Sumter County park is on the north side of the river. The ramp connects to the river via a short canal.
Directions: From the I-75 exit for FL 44, drive 8 miles and look for the park on the lefthand side of the road.
Address: 6805 W. SR 44, Lake Panasoffkee, FL

2C. TURNER CAMP—*Boat and Bank – Ramp*
Directions: From US 41 in Inverness, drive 7.1 miles northwest on CR 581 (E. Turner Camp Rd.) to the end of the road and the ramp.
Address: 9460 E. Turner Camp Rd., Inverness, FL

2D. Spruce Drive Ramp—*Bank and Boat – Ramp*

Description: This single-lane ramp is maintained by Citrus County and is along the south shore of the river.

Directions: From US 41 and FL 200, drive north on FL 200 6.9 miles. Turn left onto E. Spruce Dr. and drive 0.3 mile to the ramp on your right.

Address: 4863 E. Spruce Dr., Dunnellon, FL

2E. Dunnellon—*Boat – Ramp*

Directions: From the intersection of US 41 and FL 40 in Dunnellon, drive 0.3 mile south on US 41 to the entrance to the ramp on your right.

2F. Goldendale Ramp—*Boat – Ramp*

Directions: From US 41 in Dunnellon just south of the US 41 bridge over the river, turn west onto CR 488 (W. Dunnellon Rd.). Drive 2.3 miles west on CR 488 to N. Goldendale Ave. Turn right and go 0.3 mile to the Citrus County ramp at the eastern end of Lake Rousseau.

Address: 12199 N. Goldendale Ave., Dunnellon, FL

2G. Inglis Dam Recreation Area—*Bank and Boat – Ramp*

Description: This facility is operated by the Florida Office of Greenways Management. There are two ramps, one for access to the lake and one for access to the Gulf.

Directions: From the intersection of FL 40 and US 19 in Inglis, drive south on US 19 for 3.4 miles to the intersection with W. Riverwood Dr. Turn left and follow the road about 2.0 miles. The entrance to the ramps is on your left.

2H. Bird Creek Park—*Boat and Bank – Ramp*

Description: The Levy County park ramp provides access to the marsh-fringed shoreline along the Gulf of Mexico, Waccasassa Bay, and the mouth of the Cross Florida Barge Canal.

Directions: From US 19 turn west onto FL 40 and go about 6 miles to the end of the road.

Address: 8000 Highway 40, West Yankeetown, FL

3. Lake Panasoffkee
Fresh – Boat and Bank – Ramp

Description: Water levels in this spring-fed lake fluctuate in response to changes in the underlying aquifer. The developed part of the lake, including several fish camps, is along the southwest shoreline. Extensive marshes fringe the remainder of the lake. Lake Panasoffkee connects to the Withlacoochee River via the Outlet River.

Fishing Index: Panasoffkee, like many Florida lakes, is a good place to catch bass and especially panfish. The lake has a reputation as a top shellcracker (redear sunfish) lake because of the abundant supply of apple snails and freshwater clams that are the preferred food of this panfish. Crappie is another favorite. Look for them in Coleman Landing Channel and along the western side of the lake where the water is deeper. Bank fishing is allowed at Marsh Bend Park on the Outlet River.

Directions: To reach the fish camps, exit I-75 and drive a couple of miles north on FL 470. The public ramp at Marsh Bend "Outlet" Park is on FL 470 where it crosses the Outlet River, about 4.9 miles north of I-75.

Address: 3100 CR 413, Lake Panasoffkee, FL

For more information: Call the Pana Vista Lodge at (352) 793-2061 or Tracy's Point Fishing Lodge (352) 793- 8060.

4. LAKE TSALA APOPKA
Fresh – Boat, Bank, and Pier – Ramp

Description: Lake Tsala Apopka is a unique lake. It is more like a collection of ponds surrounded and partially filled by marshes. The lake has three distinct regions referred to as pools. As of March 2010, the FWC says the Floral City pool at the southwest end of the lake has the best bass fishing. But the hot action does change over time, so don't overlook the Hernando pool located at the northwest end of the lake and the Inverness pool, located in the central part of Tsala Apopka. Local anglers have an advantage over visitors since they know the hot spots, but getting that information out of them may be difficult. If nothing else look for yellow buoys as they indicate the location of fish attractors.

Fishing Index: The lake is a good place to fish for largemouth bass and bream. Move around and try different areas if the fish are not biting. Fluctuating lake levels are a fact of life on this lake and it does affect fishing and navigation in the area. Boaters are advised to exercise caution and travel about slowly if unfamiliar with the lake's waters.

Directions: There are four boat ramps and several private fish camps on the lake. The ramps are all accessible from US 41. The City of Inverness has several lakefront parks that offer bank and pier fishing.

For more information: Visit the website of the City of Inverness at *www. inverness-fl.gov*. For a quarterly fishing forecast for Lake Tsala Apopka, go to the FWC website, *http://myfwc.com/Recreation/FW_forecasts_ncr.htm*.

Access Points:
4A. HERNANDO BEACH—*Boat and Pier – Ramp*
Description: A Citrus County facility with picnicking, a playground, and two ramps. The ramp provides boaters with access to the Hernando pool.
Directions: From the intersection of US 41 and CR 486 (Norvill-Bryant Highway) in Hernando, drive 0.2 mile north on US 41 to E. Lake Place. Turn right and go 0.1 mile to the ramp.
Address: 3650 E. Lake Place, Hernando, FL

4B. FL 44 RAMP—*Boat – Ramp*
Directions: From US 41 in Inverness, drive 0.5 mile east on FL 44 to the ramp and access to the Inverness pool.
Address: 1025 Highway 44, Inverness, FL

4C. EDEN PARK—*Boat and Pier – Ramp*
Description: A Citrus County park with a playground and picnic facilities. The ramp provides boaters with access to the Inverness pool.
Directions: From the intersection with FL 44 south of Inverness, go south on US 41 about 0.8 mile. Turn east on Eden Drive and go 0.4 mile to Park Lake Terrace. Turn left and go 0.1 mile to the park.
Address: 614 Park Lake Terrace, Inverness, FL

4D. DUVAL ISLAND—*Boat – Ramp*
Directions: From US 41 in Floral City, drive 0.75 mile southeast on FL 48 to Duval Island Dr. Turn left and follow the road 0.1 mile to the ramp. The ramp provides boaters with access to the Floral City pool.
Address: 7790 S. Duvall Island Dr., Floral City, FL

5. FORT COOPER STATE PARK
Fresh – Bank and Canoe – $

Description: The park is named after Major Mark Anthony Cooper, who was in charge of protecting the sick and wounded soldiers who fought in the Second

Seminole War. The park is also a well-known site for bird watching. No private boats are allowed, but there are canoes available to rent in the park.

Fishing Index: Fish in the clear, spring-fed waters of Lake Holathlikaha for largemouth bass and bream.

Directions: From the intersection with FL 44 south of Inverness, drive 0.8 mile south on US 41. Turn left onto Eden Dr. Go 0.1 mile to the intersection with Old Floral Rd. and turn right. Drive 1.0 mile to the park enttrance on your right.

Address: 3100 S. Old Floral City Rd., Inverness, FL

For more information: Call the park office at (352) 726-0315 or go to www.floridastateparks.org.

6. CRYSTAL RIVER AND BAY
Salt and Fresh – Boat, Bank, and Pier – Ramp

Description: This seven-mile river begins in King's Bay where a series of springs send millions of gallons of water down the river and into the Gulf of Mexico. The Crystal River National Wildlife Refuge was established in 1983 to protect manatees, an endangered species that takes refuge in the river during the winter. Special speed zones and boating closures within parts of the bay are enforced in winter, the prime time for manatees to be in the area. Please obey the posted regulations.

Fishing Index: In the clear, spring-fed waters of the river, you can fish for bass, panfish, and catfish. Redfish and spotted seatrout often move into King's Bay, headwaters of the Crystal River, during the coldest months of winter. Crystal Bay, where the river empties into the Gulf, is part of a vast coastal mangrove system renowned as an excellent place to catch redfish, sea trout, and flounder. Cobia, normally an offshore fish, can move in close to shore in the spring and summer. When in the area, try your luck fishing around the rock jetties at the mouth of the Crystal River.

For more information: Call Citrus County Parks and Recreation Department at (352) 527-7540.

Access Points:
6A. CRYSTAL RIVER PRESERVE STATE PARK — *Bank*

Description: Anglers can walk from an access road to a canal and fish along the bank for redfish, trout, and flounder.

Directions: From the intersection of US 19 and FL 44 in Crystal River, drive north 2.3 miles on US 19 to the intersection with State Park Dr. Turn left and drive 0.8 mile to Sailboat Ave. Turn left onto Sailboat and drive 0.4 mile. Turn left into the driveway that leads to the canal.

Address: 3266 N. Sailboat Ave., Crystal River, FL

For more information: Call the park office at (352) 563-0450 or go to *www.floridastateparks.org.*

6B. FORT ISLAND TRAIL PARK—*Boat and Pier – Ramp*

Description: This Citrus County park is on the Crystal River and provides access to the Gulf of Mexico via the Salt River. Facilities are barrier free.

Directions: From the intersection of US 19 and FL 44 in Crystal River, drive south 0.5 mile on US 19 to W. Fort Island Trail. Turn west and go about 5 miles to the park entrance on your right.

Address: 12073 W. Fort Island Trail, Crystal River, FL

6C. FORT ISLAND GULF BEACH—*Boat and Pier – Ramp*

Description: This beachfront Citrus County park is also a popular place to picnic and swim.

Directions: From the intersection of US 19 and FL 44 in Crystal River, drive south 0.5 miles on US 19 to W. Fort Island Trail. Turn west and go about 9 miles to the site at road's end.

Address: 16000 W. Fort Island Trail, Crystal River, FL

6D. OZELLO COMMUNITY PARK—*Boat – Ramp*

Description: A remote park at the south end of Crystal Bay

Directions: From the intersection of US 19 and CR 494 south of Crystal River, take CR 494 (Ozello Trail) west approximately 9.3 miles to the end of the road. Turn right onto Sand Dollar Lane, drive 0.1 mile to Pirate Point. Turn left onto Pirate Point and the park will be ahead.

7. HOMOSASSA RIVER AND BAY
Salt and Fresh – Boat – Ramp

Description: This short river begins as a spring near US 19. The Homosassa Springs Wildlife State Park is nearby and an outstanding place to see manatees from the "underwater" walkway in the park. The river meanders toward the coast along miles of winding waterways and islands. Once away from the developed area, there are few signs of civilization. Several commercial marinas and motels are along the river close to the spring.

Fishing Index: This is one of the world's hot spots for tarpon. The big fish, in excess of 150 pounds, reach their peak abundance in May and June. The area attracts some of the top fishing guides in Florida who, along with their anglers, are looking to break the world record for tarpon on the fly. To do that you will have to bring in a fish weighing in excess of 200 pounds. This is the only place where you can fish for these big tarpon in shallow, crystal-clear water. First-time anglers wanting to catch a big tarpon are advised to hire a guide because it takes local knowledge to find—and land—the fish.

There is life after tarpon time in the Homosassa. The river is fresh water and harbors a good population of bass and panfish. And thanks to the high mineral content of the water, saltwater species such as sheepshead and snook may also take your bait.

In the waters of Homosassa Bay and the Gulf, anglers will find year-round redfish and seatrout action. A few miles offshore there are cobia, Spanish and king mackerel, sharks, and grouper. Spanish mackerel make a strong run along the coast in the spring. The schools, feeding on shrimp and other bottom-dwelling organisms, create a highly noticeable patch of cloudy water called a "mud."

Access Points:

7A. MacRae's Boat Ramp—*Boat – Ramp*

Description: This ramp is part of a commercial marina, bait shop, and motel, but the ramp is free and open to the public. From here you will have direct access to the Homosassa River. There are no public ramps along the river.
Directions: From the intersection of US 41 and Yulee Dr. in Homosassa Springs, take Yulee Dr. about 2.5 miles to the center of Homosassa. The road has numerous twists and turns. Turn right onto S. Cherokee Way and follow the road 0.2 miles to the end of the road and the ramp.
Address: 5300 S. Cherokee Way, Homosassa, FL

7B. Mason Creek Boat Ramp—*Boat – Ramp*

Description: This ramp provides access to Mason Creek, which flows into Homosassa Bay south of the Homosassa River. Use it to access the coastal waters.
Directions: From the intersection of US 41 and Yulee Dr. in Homosassa Springs, take Yulee Dr. about 2.5 miles to the center of Homosassa. The road has numerous twists and turns. Turn left onto S. Mason Creek Rd. and follow it to the end of the road and the ramp, about 2.0 miles
Address: 6891 S. Mason Creek Rd., Homosassa, FL

8. CHASSAHOWITZKA RIVER
Salt – Boat – Ramp – $

Description: Most of the coastal waters south of the Homosassa River make up the Chassahowitzka National Wildlife Refuge. A large part of the refuge is a manatee sanctuary and no boats are allowed in the area from October 15 to February 15.

Fishing Index: A great place to catch fish but dangerous for boating. Many local anglers don't fish the area because of the shallow water and rocky bottom of the Chassahowitzka. But several guides regularly fish the area and know how to keep from running aground. Some of them use a specially designed flat-bottomed, tunnel-drive boat so they can get to places few people fish and where they usually have good luck.

The area has very good to excellent angling for redfish and spotted seatrout. Sheepshead, flounder, and mangrove snapper are also common catches. Along the outer edges of marshes, cobia are taken from late spring through summer. Many tarpon anglers from Homosassa fish the flats along the outer edge of the refuge. Some very big fish are caught in this area.

Directions: The only public ramp is located at the Chassahowitzka River Campground and Recreation Area operated by Citrus County. There is a small bait store on-site. At the junction of US 19 and US 98, drive 1.8 miles west on W. Miss Maggie Dr. (CR 480) to the campground and ramp.

Address: 8600 W. Miss Maggie Dr., Homosassa, FL

For more information: Call the campground office at (352) 382-2200.

HERNANDO AND PASCO COUNTIES

9. WITHLACOOCHEE RIVER (LAKE PANASOFFKEE TO GREEN SWAMP)
Fresh – Boat/Canoe, Bank, and Pier – Ramp

Description: This 157-mile river begins in the Green Swamp and flows northwest to the city of Dunnellon, then turns and flows more or less due west to the Gulf. The river is surrounded by swampland from the Green Swamp to Dunnellon, making it one of the most scenic rivers in the state. This section of the river is narrow, making it an ideal place to fish from a canoe, kayak, or jon boat. Fishing success along the upper part of the river depends on water levels. Generally the river is difficult to fish when water levels are low.

Fishing Index: Bass, redbreasts (stumpknockers), bluegills, and warmouths are the most commonly caught species. Fishing success is variable.

Access Points:

9A. WITHLACOOCHEE RIVER PARK—*Canoe, Bank, and Pier – Canoe launch*
Description: A Pasco County park with canoe dock, primitive camping, nature trails, and picnic area. There is a small fishing pier next to the canoe launch.
Directions: From the intersection of US 301 and Clinton Ave. south of Dade City, drive east on Clinton 1.4 miles. The road changes names to Enterprise Rd. at the intersection with Old Lakeland Hwy. (FL.35). Continue on Enterprise for 1.9 miles to Auton Rd. Turn left and drive 1.4 miles to Withlacoochee Blvd. Turn right and follow the road to the park, about 0.6 mile.
Address: 12449 Withlacoochee Blvd., Dade City, FL
For more information: Call the park office at (352) 567-0264.

9B. SILVER LAKE—*Boat and Bank– Ramp – $*
Description: Part of the Withlacoochee State Forest. Camping.
Directions: From I-75, take the US 98 Brooksville exit and drive 1 mile east to Croom Rital Rd. Turn left and go about 3.5 miles to the lake.

9C. NOBLETON WAYSIDE PARK—*Boat and Bank – Ramp*
Description: A Hernando County park with picnic facilities.
Directions: From the intersection with US 98 in Brooksville drive 6.3 miles north on US 41 to CR 476 (Lake Lindsey Rd). Turn right and go about 4.7 miles to Lamkin Dr. on your left. Turn left on Lamkin Dr. The ramp is ahead about 200 feet.
Address: 29061 Lamkin Dr., Nobleton, FL

10.   BAYPORT PARK
Salt – Boat and Pier – Ramp

Description: A Hernando County park with a lighted pier, picnicking, and ramp with direct access to the Gulf of Mexico.

Fishing Index: Fish for spotted seatrout and redfish along the coast or head farther offshore for cobia, grouper, snapper, and king mackerel.

Directions: From the intersection of US 19 and FL 550 (Cortez Blvd.) in Weeki Wachee, take FL 550 west about 5.8 miles to the park at road's end.

Address: 4140 Cortez Blvd., Spring Hill, FL

11. ROGERS PARK
Salt and Fresh – Boat and Bank – Ramp – $

Description: This Hernando County park on the Weeki Wachee River has a freshwater beach, picnicking, and a ramp with access to the Gulf of Mexico.

Fishing Index: Fish for sheepshead, redfish, spotted seatrout, and offshore species. Boaters can also go upriver to fish for largemouth bass.

Directions: From the intersection of US 19 and FL 550 (Cortez Blvd.) in Weeki Wachee, take FL 550 west about 3.2 miles to FL 597 (Shoal Line Blvd.). Turn left and go about 1.5 miles to the park.

Address: 7244 Shoal Line Blvd, Spring Hill, FL

12. JENKINS CREEK PARK AND LINDA PEDERSEN PARK AT JENKINS CREEK
Salt – Boat and Pier – Ramp

Description: At these two adjacent Hernando County parks, there are two lighted piers (one of which is barrier free), picnicking, and a ramp for canoes, kayaks, and boats 16 feet and under.

Fishing Index: Fish the tidal waters for redfish, sheepshead, spotted seatrout, and some snook. Watch out for submerged rocks when fishing close to shore.

Directions: From the intersection of US 19 and FL 550 (Cortez Blvd.) in Weeki Wachee, take FL 550 west about 3.2 miles to FL 597 (Shoal Line Rd.). Turn left and go about 2 miles to the park.

Address: Linda Pederson Park at Jenkins Creek—6300 Shoal Line Blvd. (CR 595), Spring Hill, FL
Jenkins Creek Park—6401 Shoal Line Blvd., Spring Hill, FL

13. HERNANDO BEACH BOAT RAMP
Salt – Boat – Ramp

Fishing Index: The ramp at this Hernando County facility provides direct access to the Gulf of Mexico. Fish for grouper, snapper, king and Spanish mackerel, and other offshore species. The marsh-lined, low-energy coast offers numerous places to find redfish and spotted seatrout. Watch out for submerged rocks when fishing close to shore.

Directions: From the intersection of US 19 and FL 550 (Cortez Blvd.) in Weeki Wachee, take FL 550 west about 3.2 miles to FL 597 (Shoal Line Rd.). Turn left and go about 3.2 miles to Hernando Beach. Turn right onto Calienta St. The ramp is on the left.

14. CREWS LAKE
Fresh – Boat, Bank, Pier – Ramp

Description: A Pasco County park with nature and bike trails, picnicking, and tent camping. Boats are limited to motors of 10 horsepower or less. The ramp may not be usable during periods of low water.

Fishing Index: Fair fishing for largemouth bass and bluegills.

Directions: From US 41 in Growers Corner, drive 2.3 miles west on FL 52 or exit Suncoast Parkway at FL 52 and drive east 0.6 mile to Shady Hills Rd. Drive north on Shady Hills Rd. for 2.9 miles to the intersection with Lenway Rd. Turn right onto Lenway and drive 0.3 mile to the intersection with Crews Lake Drive. Turn right and follow this road into the park, about 0.5 mile.

Address: 16739 Crews Lake Dr., Shady Hills, FL

For more information: Call Park Office at (727) 861-3038.

15. ROBERT J. STRICKLAND MEMORIAL PARK
Salt – Boat and Bank – Ramp – $

Description: This Pasco County park is a good place to launch your boat for a day of nearshore or offshore fishing.

Fishing Index: Fish in close for seatrout, redfish, sheepshead, and flounder. Farther offshore you will find grouper, cobia, and permit over the wrecks and hard-bottom areas.

Directions: From the intersection of US 19 and Clark St. in Hudson, drive west on Clark 0.9 miles to the park.

Address: 6345 Clark St., Hudson, FL

16. ROBERT K. REES MEMORIAL PARK
Salt – Canoe and Surf –Canoe Launch

Description: This Pasco County park occupies a small spit of land that extends into the Gulf of Mexico. There is also a swimming beach and picnic area.

Fishing Index: Fish the Gulf-front beach area for redfish and Spanish mackerel and wade the shoreline in the backwaters for seatrout and redfish.

Directions: From the intersection of US 19 and Green Key Rd. in New Port Ritchey, drive west on Green Key 1.4 miles to the park.

Address: 4835 Green Key Rd., New Port Richey, FL

17. ANCLOTE GULF PARK
Salt – Pier

Description: A Gulf-front Pasco County park located where the cooling canal from the Progress energy power plant opens into the Gulf.

Fishing Index: Fish from the pier for seatrout, redfish, snook, tarpon pompano, and shark. When the water is cold, fish tend to congregate in the canal taking advantage of the warm water being discharged from the power plant, making this a hot spot for anglers.

Directions: From the intersection of Alternate US 19 and Anclote Blvd. in Holiday, drive west on Anclote Blvd. approximately 2.6 miles to where the road bends to the north and becomes Baillies Bluff Rd. The park entrance is approximately 1.2 miles farther on the left.

Address: 2305 Baillies Bluff Rd., Holiday, FL

For more information: Call the Park office at (727) 942-4030.

18. ANCLOTE RIVER PARK
Salt – Boat and Bank – Ramp – $

Description: This Pasco County park is located at the mouth of the Anclote River and the south entrance to the canal leading to the power plant. Just across the river is the city of Tarpon Springs. A center of Greek culture, the town also boasts the state's only commercial sponge-diving industry, a tradition started by the Greeks when they came to Tarpon Springs. The town features numerous ethnic restaurants and historical exhibits.

Fishing Index: Fish from the beach for seatrout, redfish, and snook. The site is a convenient place to launch a boat and head to the protected waters between the mainland and Anclote Key to fish for snook, redfish, and trout or offshore for a day of grouper or permit fishing.

Directions: From the intersection of Alternate US 19 and Anclote Blvd. in Holiday, drive west on Anclote approximately 2.6 miles. The park entrance is on the left where the road bends to the north and becomes Baillies Bluff Rd.

Address: 1119 Baillies Bluff Rd., Holiday, FL

For more information: Call the Park office at (727) 938-2598.

PINELLAS AND HILLSBOROUGH COUNTIES

These two counties boast well over 100 public launching ramps, bridges, waterfront parks, and beaches open to anglers. Although densely populated, there are plenty of good places to fish. The counties, with help from the state and federal governments, have worked diligently to clean up the pollution in Tampa Bay and surrounding waters. Local leaders recognize the economic value of a healthy and productive estuarine system and the recreational fishing industry. Today seagrasses have returned to some areas, and the fishing success remains good despite the high number of people living near the water and the growing number of anglers.

19. FRED HOWARD PARK
Salt – Wade

Description: The one-mile causeway to this 155-acre Pinellas County park leads to a popular swimming beach that also is a great place to watch the sun set over the Gulf of Mexico. The park is off the main roads but is worth the effort to find.

Fishing Index: Anglers who like to wade-fish will find the shallow waters along the causeway a good place to fish for snook, trout, and redfish.

Directions: From the intersection of US 19 and Klosterman Rd. south of Tarpon Springs, drive west on Klosterman for 2.0 miles to Carlton Rd. Turn right and drive north for 0.5 mile to Curlew Place. Turn left and drive 0.4 mile

Pinellas and Hillsborough Counties

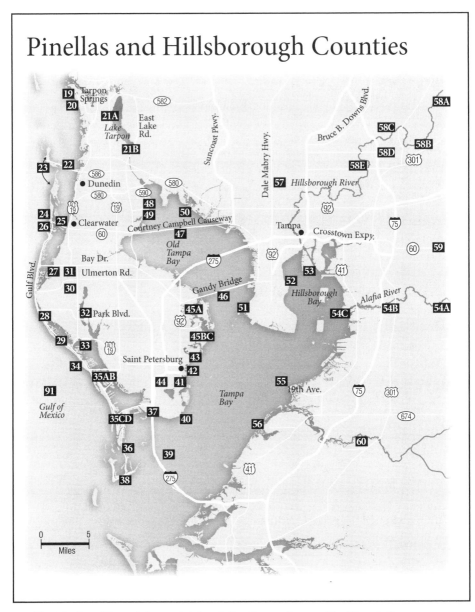

to Florida Ave. Turn right and drive 1.5 miles to Sunset Dr. Turn left onto Sunset and follow the road 0.25 miles until it ends at the park.
Address: 1700 Sunset Dr., Tarpon Springs, FL

For more information: Call the park office at (727) 943-4081.

20. SUNSET BEACH PARK
Salt – Wade

Description: This City of Tarpon Springs park is off the main roads but is worth the effort to find. Fortunately, Sunset Beach and Fred Howard Park are close to each other. Find one and you can find the other.

Fishing Index: This is a good place to wade-fish for spotted seatrout, especially during the late winter and early spring. Look for these fish over the seagrass flats along the causeway.

Directions: From the intersection of US 19 and Klosterman Rd. south of Tarpon Springs, drive west on Klosterman for 2 miles to Carlton Rd. Turn right and drive north for 0.5 mile to Curlew Place. Turn left and drive 0.4 mile to Florida Ave. Turn right and drive 1.0 mile to Gulf Rd. Turn left onto Gulf and follow the road until it ends at the park.

Address: 1800 Gulf Rd., Tarpon Springs, FL

21. LAKE TARPON
Fresh – Boat, Bank, and Pier – Ramp

Description: One of the few freshwater fishing sites in the county. The lake is 5 miles long and up to 1 mile wide.

Fishing Index: The 2,500-acre lake produces plenty of two- to four-pound largemouth bass. The FWC rates Lake Tarpon as one of its Top Spots for bass. There is also good year-round fishing for redear sunfish (shellcracker) and black crappie (specs). The FWC reports that most bass caught are in the 12- to 16-inch range. Fish the shoreline where there is bulrush or in the open water areas where there are ledges and eelgrass beds.

For more information: Call the Anderson Park office at (727) 943-4085 or Chesnut Park office at (727) 669-1951.

Access Points:
21A. A. L. ANDERSON PARK—*Boat and Bank – Ramp – $*
Directions: The entrance to this Pinellas County park is on US 19 about 0.9 miles south of the intersection with FL 582 (Tarpon Ave.) in Tarpon Springs.
Address: 39699 US Highway 19 N., Tarpon Springs, FL

A good-size boat for fishing the Gulf coast nearshore waters

21B. John Chesnut Sr Park—*Boat, Bank, and Pier – Ramp – $*
Directions: From US 19 and Curlew Rd (FL 586), drive east on Curlew Rd. for 1.8 miles to the intersection with McMullen Booth Rd. Turn left and drive north on McMullen Booth Rd. for 1.5 miles. The road joins with and becomes East Lake Rd. Continue north for an additional 1.3 miles to the park entrance on your left.
Address: 2200 East Lake Rd., Palm Harbor, FL

22. Dunedin Beach Causeway
Salt – Bank and Wade

Description: Causeway Blvd., the road to Honeymoon Island, is a popular place to wade-fish or cast a line around the bridge pilings from a boat or the seawalls around the bridges

Fishing Index: Fish by day for trout, redfish, sheepshead, and snook. Also, fishing around the bridges for snook at night is popular during the summer as is nighttime angling for tarpon and big reds.

Directions: The Causeway begins along CR 586 (Curlew Rd.) 3.2 miles from the intersection with US 19.

23. HONEYMOON ISLAND AND CALADESI ISLAND STATE PARKS
Salt – Surf and Wade – $

Description: These two parks are on undeveloped barrier islands near the city of Dunedin. Honeymoon Island has a bridge and road to it but Caladesi doesn't. It is accessible by private boat or scheduled ferry from Honeymoon Island State Park. There is a marina with electric and water hook-ups for overnight boaters. Reservations can be made through *www.reserveamerica.com.*

Fishing Index: Surf fishing is popular on both islands. Anglers report good catches of spotted seatrout, snook, redfish, and Spanish mackerel. Try wade-fishing the flats on the inside of the islands in summer for redfish, jacks, and small cobia.

Directions: Honeymoon Island State Park is at the western end of CR 586 in Dunedin. From US 19, turn west onto CR 586 (Curlew Rd.) and go 5.2 miles to the park. To reach Caladesi Island State Park, take the ferry from Honeymoon's dock.

Address: 1 Causeway Blvd., Dunedin, FL

For more information: Call Honeymoon Island State Park office at (727) 469-5942 or Caladesi Island State Park office at (727) 469-5918.

24. BIG PIER 60
Salt – Pier – $

Description: This 1,080-foot pier is operated by the City of Clearwater and was rebuilt in 1994. It provides anglers with access to the Gulf of Mexico and is open round the clock. There is a bait shop and snack bar on-site.

Fishing Index: The pier regulars come here to fish for snook. The pier's many lights attract baitfish at night and that brings plenty of snook. Some Spanish mackerel, redfish, and tarpon are taken seasonally. Winter fishing is for silver trout. Flounder are caught throughout the year except during the coldest months.

Directions: From the intersection with US 19 in Clearwater, take FL 60 (Gulf to Bay Blvd.) 6.2 miles west to the end of the road at Gulf Blvd. and the pier.

Address: 1 Causeway Blvd., Clearwater, FL

For more information: Call the pier office at (727) 462-6466 or go to *www. pier60fishing.com.*

25. MEMORIAL CAUSEWAY ───────────────
Salt – Bank and Wade

Description: Gulf to Bay Boulevard, where it crosses Clearwater Harbor, is called Memorial Causeway. Anglers can fish off the seawall of the new causeway or wade the shallow flats on either side of the roadway.

Fishing Index: Fish for spotted seatrout on the grassflats on the north side of the causeway and for snook, trout, and redfish off the south side.

Directions: The causeway (FL 60) is the major road leading to Clearwater Beach. From the intersection with US 19 in Clearwater, take FL 60 (Gulf to Bay Blvd.) 4.5 miles west to the causeway.

26. SAND KEY PARK ──────────────────
Salt – Surf and Bridge – $

Description: This 90-acre county park is heavily used by beachgoers. Anglers can park in one of the metered parking places and walk to the beach to fish in the Gulf or along Clearwater Pass. Or fish from the walkway on the bridge near the park.

Fishing Index: The pass is a favorite hangout for snook and redfish. Use live bait for your best chance at catching the big fish.

Directions: From the intersection with US 19 in Clearwater, take FL 60 (Gulf to Bay Blvd.) 6.2 miles west to the end of the road at Gulf Blvd. Turn left and drive 1.8 miles to the park entrance on your right.

Address: 1060 Gulf Blvd., Clearwater, FL

For more information: Call the park office at (727) 588-4852.

27. BELLEAIR BOAT RAMP PARK ──────────
Salt – Boat, Bank, and Pier – Ramp – $

Description: A Pinellas County facility, the site was refurbished in 2010. There are 10 launching lanes and 108 boat-trailer parking spaces.

Fishing Index: Fish from the pier or along the seawalls for snook, redfish, mangrove snapper, and spotted seatrout. Boaters can access Clearwater Harbor and the Gulf of Mexico via Clearwater Pass. The protected waters of the Harbor offer excellent fishing for snook, redfish, spotted seatrout, and flounder.

Directions: The ramp is on the mainland side of the Belleair Causeway, which is called West Bay Drive. From the intersection of East Bay Drive and US 19, head 5.7 miles west on East Bay Drive to the ramp. East Bay Drive changes to West Bay Drive at the intersection with Alternate US 19.

Address: 3900 W. Bay Dr., Belleair Bluffs, FL

For more information: Call the park office at (727) 588-4847.

28. PARK BOULEVARD BOAT RAMP PARK ───────────
Salt – Boat and Pier – Ramp – $

Description: A very popular Pinellas County facility with six launching lanes. The site is also known as War Veterans Memorial Park.

Fishing Index: Located in an area known as "The Narrows," this ramp gives boaters access to Clearwater Harbor to the north and Boca Ciega Bay to the south. Both areas have many good places to fish for snook, redfish, spotted seatrout, and flounder.

Directions: The ramp is located where Park Blvd. North merges with Gulf Blvd. in Indian Shores. From the intersection of Alternate US 19 and Park Blvd., drive west for 3.3 miles to Gulf Blvd. Drive south on Gulf Blvd. for 0.2 mile to the entrance to the ramp on your left.

Address: 18651 Gulf Blvd., Indian Shores, FL

For more information: Call the park office at (727) 549-6165.

29. DUBAI LONG PIER ─────────────────────
Salt – Pier – $

Description: This 1,021-foot pier was formerly known as the Redington Fishing Pier. It was renamed by the owner to draw attention to his ongoing political feud with the City of Redington Shores. The bait shop has cut and live bait and has rod rentals available.

Fishing Index: Anglers catch a mixed bag including whiting, flounder, sheepshead, tarpon, cobia, Spanish mackerel, and redfish. Snook fishing, practiced at night by the local veteran anglers, is popular.

Directions: From the intersection of Alt. US 19 and Tom Stuart Causeway (CR 666) turn onto the causeway and go 1.3 miles to Gulf Blvd. Turn right and drive 2.3 miles north on Gulf Blvd. to the pier in Redington Shores.

Address: 17490 Gulf Blvd., Redington Shores, FL

For more information: Call the pier office at (727) 391-9398.

30. WALSINGHAM PARK
Fresh – Boat and Bank – Ramp – $

Description: A 354-acre Pinellas County park with the 100-acre Walsingham reservoir dominating the park. Picnicking, a multi-purpose trail, and quiet parkland make this a favorite destination for local residents.

Fishing Index: Fishing is allowed, but internal combustion engines are not allowed in the reservoir. This is a good place to canoe-or kayak-fish for bass, bream, and catfish.

Directions: From the intersection of Alternate US 19 and CR 688 (Ulmerton Rd.) in Largo, take Ulmerton Rd. west for 2 miles. Turn left onto Walsingham Rd. and go 0.6 mile to the entrance on your right.

Address: 12620 102nd Ave. N., Largo, FL

For more information: Call the park office at (727) 549-6142.

31. JOHN S. TAYLOR PARK
Fresh – Boat and Bank – Ramp

Description: A 156-acre Pinellas County park with picnicking, a recreation trail, and play area. This community park is a good place to take the kids fishing.

Fishing Index: The 53-acre Taylor Lake is a good place to fish for bass, bream, and catfish.

Directions: From the intersection of Alternate US 19 and CR 688 (Ulmerton Rd.) In Largo, take Alternate US 19 north for 1 mile. Turn left onto 8th Ave SW and follow it to the park entrance on your left.

Address: 1100 8th Ave. S.W., Largo, FL

For more information: Call the park office at (727) 588-4847.

32. LAKE SEMINOLE PARK
Fresh – Boat and Bank – Ramp – $

Description: A 255-acre Pinellas County park with picnicking, a recreation trail, and play area. A good place to take the kids fishing.

Fishing Index: Fair year-round fishing for bass, bream, and catfish.

Directions: From the intersection of US 19 and CR 694 (Park Blvd.), take Park Blvd. 5.6 miles west to the park entrance on your right.

Address: 10015 Park Blvd., Seminole, FL

For more information: Call the park office at (727) 549-6156.

33. WAR VETERANS' MEMORIAL PARK
Salt – Boat – Ramp – $

Description: The 6-lane ramp at this Pinellas County park offers easy access to Boca Ciega Bay and the Gulf of Mexico via Johns Pass. There is also a canoe launch at the southern end of the park.

Fishing Index: Boca Ciega Bay has numerous grassflats that provide excellent fishing for spotted seatrout and redfish.
Directions: From the intersection of US 19 and Alt US 19 (5th Ave.), follow Alt US 19 west for 2 miles. Alt US 19 bears right onto Tyrone Blvd. Drive northwest for 3.7 miles to where the road crosses Long Bayou. The road becomes Bay Pines Blvd and the entrance to the park is an additional 0.6 mile on your left. It is adjacent to the Bay Pines Veterans Hospital grounds.

Address: 9600 Bay Pines Blvd., St. Petersburg, FL

For more information: Call the park office at (727) 549-6165.

34. JOHNS PASS ———————————————
Salt – Bank and Surf

Description: One of the major inlets along this part of the coast. A large offshore fishing fleet is based here. The new bridge over the pass opened in 2010 so access to parking changed. Most parking is related to nearby commercial facilities, so make sure you are parked legally.

Fishing Index: Fish from the jetties on the north and south sides of the pass for mackerel and sheepshead in the winter and spring and snook and redfish in the summer and fall. Some big redfish and tarpon cruise the shoreline near the pass.

Directions: From Treasure Island Causeway, go north on Gulf Blvd. 1.2 miles to the bridge.

For more information: Call Don's Dock and talk to third-generation owner Don Beggs III at (727) 391-3223.

35. ST. PETERSBURG BEACH PIERS ———————
Salt –Boat and Pier– Ramp

Description: There are four small piers owned by the City of St. Petersburg Beach that provide access to portions of Boca Ciega Bay. McKinney (Blind Pass Park) and Egan Park piers are at the north end of town and located in city parks. Only Eagan Park has a ramp. Seventh Ave. Pier and Merry Pier, operated by a concessionaire, are at the south end of the city. Of the 4, Merry Pier is best known.

Fishing Index: A wide variety of fish can be caught from these piers, including sheepshead, snook, redfish, and Spanish mackerel when they are around. The ramp at Eagan Park provides direct access to Boca Ciega Bay.

Access Points:
35 A & B. BLIND PASS PARK AND EAGAN PARK—*Boat and Pier – Ramp*
Directions: Blind Pass Park and Eagan Park are on Blind Pass Rd. From the intersection of Gulf Blvd. and Blind Pass Rd., drive south on Blind Pass Rd. 0.3 mile to Blind Pass Park on your right and 0.4 mile to Eagan Park on your left.
Address: Eagan Park – 9101 Blind Pass Rd., St. Petersburg Beach, FL
Blind Pass Park – 93rd Ave. and Gulf Blvd., St. Petersburg Beach, FL

35 C & D – Seventh Avenue Pier and Merry Pier—*Pier*
Directions: These piers are accessed from Pass-a-Grille Way one block east of Gulf Way in St. Petersburg Beach. Seventh Ave. and Merry piers are at the intersections of 7th and 8th avenues, respectively.
Address: Merry Pier – 801 Pass-a-Grille Way, St. Petersburg Beach, FL
Seventh Avenue Pier – Pass-a-Grille Way, St. Petersburg Beach, FL
For more information: Call the bait shop at Merry Pier at (727) 360-6606

36. PINELLAS BAYWAY
Salt – Boat and Bank

Description: This toll road connects the southern tip of St. Petersburg to the south end of St. Petersburg Beach and Fort Desoto Park. It crosses the lower part of Boca Ciega Bay. Fish from the three bridges or the seawalls at the foot of each bridge, or wade the flats along the causeways.

Fishing Index: Fish for sheepshead and snook around the pilings and spotted seatrout and redfish on the flats.

Directions: Exit I-75 at the first exit after crossing the Sunshine Causeway if heading north or the last exit before the bridge if going south. Follow the big overhead signs to St. Petersburg Beach and Fort Desoto Park. This is a toll road.

37. MAXIMO PARK
Salt – Boat – Ramp

Description: A City of St. Petersburg park that is a popular place to launch your boat if you want to fish around the Sunshine Skyway Bridge pilings or head into the lower part of Boca Ciega Bay.

Fishing Index: Fish the flats around the ramp and in Boca Ciega Bay for spotted seatrout and redfish. Fish around the docks for snook, especially lighted docks after dark.
Directions: Exit I-275 in St. Petersburg at Exit 3, Pinellas Point Dr. Follow the signs to 34th St. and go south to the park.

Address: Pinellas Point Dr. & 34th St. S., St. Petersburg, FL

A preferred way to release a fish is to place it in the water and gently hold it until it can swim away under its own power.

38. FORT DESOTO PARK
Salt – Boat, Bank and Pier – Ramp – $

Description: This Pinellas County park is on five connected islands at the mouth of Tampa Bay. The park has a 238-acre site campground, miles of recreational trails, 2 fishing piers, more than 7 miles of beach, and historic Fort DeSoto. The boat ramps afford quick and easy access to the lower parts of Tampa Bay and Boca Ciega Bay and the Gulf of Mexico.

Fishing Index: The 500-foot Bay pier and the 1,000-foot Gulf pier are good places to fish for Spanish mackerel during the spring and fall runs. At other times of the year, sheepshead and snook are the targets. Both have food and bait concessions. Boaters can fish the flats of Mullet Key Bayou for spotted seatrout and redfish. Note that there are large areas where boats must travel at slow speeds. Pay attention to and obey the signs.

Directions: The Pinellas Bayway goes to the park. From the I-275 exit for the Bayway, at the north end of the Sunshine Skyway, drive approximately 6.4 miles to the park entrance.

Address: 3500 Pinellas Bayway S., Tierra Verde, FL

For more information: Call the park office at (727) 893-9185.

39.   SKYWAY FISHING PIER STATE PARK ⸻

Salt – Boat and Bridge – $

Description: How about a state park that is dedicated to anglers! This one-of-a-kind Florida state park consists of the portions of the old Sunshine Skyway Bridge that once spanned the entrance to Tampa Bay. It is now the world's longest fishing pier.

    With access points at the north and south ends, anglers can drive their cars or campers on the pier, park, and drop a line in the water a few feet from their vehicles. The pier is open 24 hours and is lighted at night. Bait, tackle, and snacks are available at both access points. Use heavy-duty tackle to keep the fish from getting under the bridge and cutting your line on the barnacle-encrusted pilings. A bridge net will be very handy when it comes time to bring a big fish out of the water. From a boat, anglers can also fish around the hundreds of pilings that support the fishing pier.

Fishing Index: There is a wide diversity of fish caught around these piers. At night, fish for snook and sharks. In the day, anglers can catch either of these species plus cobia, tarpon, grouper, sheepshead, Spanish mackerel, and mangrove snapper.

Directions: The access points are exits off I-275 at either end of the main span of the Sunshine Skyway (I-275) Bridge.

For more information: Call the park office at (727) 865-0668 or go to *www. floridastateparks.org.*

Sites 40 to 53 provide access to Tampa Bay

40.   BAY VISTA PARK ⸻

Salt – Boat – Ramp

Description: The 2-lane ramp provides good access to the lower half of Tampa Bay. It is closed at night.

Fishing Index: Boaters can head any direction between east and south and intersect the buoys that mark the main shipping channel. Fish around them for cobia. The fish could be there any month, but May through September are best. From here you can also fish the shallow waters along the St. Petersburg shoreline for snook, trout, and redfish.

Directions: Exit I-275 at Pinellas Point Dr. and drive east about 2.4 miles to road's end at 4th St. The ramp is on the right.

Address: 500 Pinellas Point Dr. S., St. Petersburg, FL

For more information: Call the City of St. Petersburg Parks and Recreation Department at (727) 893-7335

41. GRANDVIEW PARK
Salt – Boat – Ramp

Description: The 2-lane ramp provides access to the lower half of Tampa Bay via Big Bayou. It is open 24 hours.

Fishing Index: Boaters can head any direction between east and south and intersect the buoys that mark the main shipping channel. Fish around them for cobia. The fish could be there any month, but May through September is best. From here you can also fish the shallow waters along the St. Petersburg shoreline for snook, trout, and redfish.

Directions: Exit I-275 at 22nd Ave and drive east about 2.4 miles to the intersection with 6th St. S. Turn right and drive south for 1.0 mile to the intersection with 39th Ave. S. The ramp is on your left.

Address: 3700 6th St. S., St. Petersburg, FL

For more information: Call the City of St. Petersburg Parks and Recreation Department at (727) 893-7335.

42. DEMENS LANDING PARK
Salt – Boat – Ramp

Description: The 2-lane ramp provides access to the lower half of Tampa Bay. It is immediately south of the St. Petersburg Municipal Pier and is open 24 hours.
Fishing Index: Boaters can head any direction between east and south and intersect the buoys that mark the main shipping channel, or head north to the shallow waters of Upper Tamp Bay. From here you can also fish the shallow waters along the St. Petersburg shoreline for snook, trout, and redfish.

Directions: Exit I-75 at Exit 22 and join I-175 East to Tropicana Field for 1.4 miles until I-175 ends and becomes 5th Ave. S. Continue on 5th Ave. S. for 0.6 mile. The road curves northward and becomes Bay Shore Dr. SE. Follow Bay Shore for 0.3 mile to the park entrance on your right.

Address: 690 1st Ave. SE, St. Petersburg, FL

43. St. Petersburg Municipal Pier ————————
Salt – Pier

Description: This pier is open to vehicular traffic and big enough at the end for a small shopping area and restaurant. At 0.7-mile long, it is the longest pier into Tampa Bay. It is a popular place for tourists to enjoy the sights. Fishing is from the approach to the bridge to the pier and off the catwalk along the east end of the pier.

Fishing Index: Although it may not look like a good place to fish, the pier has 3,000 pilings, and that translates into plenty of habitat for sheepshead and snook. The best sheepshead fishing is from February through April. Whiting, mangrove snapper, and flounder are also taken from the pier. With some stout tackle, try casting your line under the pier and among the pilings. That's where you may find the bigger fish, but you have to be quick to turn their heads and get them out before they duck behind a piling and cut you off.

Directions: The pier is in downtown St. Petersburg at the end of Second Ave. NE. Exit I-275 at "The Pier" exit and follow the signs.

For more information: Call The Pier Bait House at (727) 821-3750.

44. Freshwater Fishing in City of St. Petersburg ———

Description: The following list comes from the City of St. Petersburg's website *(http://www.stpete.org/parks/fishing.asp).* It describes places where you can bank fish. These are good places to take a child and introduce them to fishing. The lakes are periodically stocked with bass, bream, catfish, and nile perch.

These lakes are open for fishing year-round:

> **Bartlett Lake** - 22nd Ave. & Fifth St. S.
> **Fossil Park Lake** -70th Ave. & Seventh St. N.
> **Walter Fuller Lake** - 26th Ave. & 78th St. N.
> **Lake Maggiore** - 38th Ave. and Dr. Martin Luther King Jr., St. S.
> **Lake Eli (Little Lake Maggiore)** - 25th St. & Lamparilla Way S.

The following lakes are open for shoreline fishing from Memorial Day to Labor Day:

> **Booker Creek Park** - 13th Ave. & 22nd St. N.
> **Childs Park Lake** -11th Ave. & 42nd St. S.
> **Crescent Lake Park** - 22nd Ave. & Fifth St. N.
> **Eagle Crest Lake** - Sixth Ave. & 66th St. N.
> **Euclid Lake** - 25th Ave. & 17th St. N.
> **Moon Lake** - 13th Ave. & 42nd St. N.
> **Kelley Lake** - 40th Ave. & 20th St. N.
> **Lake Jude** - Sixth Ave. & 55th St. N.
> **Lake Vista Park** - 62nd Ave. & 14th St. S.
> **Lynch Lake** - 70th Ave. & 18th St. N.
> **Mastry Lake** - 64th Ave. & 14th St. N.
> **Mirror Lake** - Second Ave. & Mirror Lake Dr. N.
> **Ruby Lake** - 26th Ave. & 35th St.
> **Sheffield Lake** - 24th Ave. & 49th St. N.
> **Sirmons Lake** - 33rd Ave. & 41st St. N.
> **Teresa Gardens Lake** - 32nd Ave. & 71st St. N.
> **Viking Lake** - 75th Ave. & 14th St. N.

45. WEEDON ISLAND PRESERVE ———
Salt – Boat, Bank, Wade, and Pier

Description: This 3,100-acre county-operated preserve is a great place to wade-fish the quiet, seagrass-rich waters. You can drive to the site but many anglers arrive by boat. Thirty-five percent of the waters in the preserve are closed to gasoline-powered motors. In these areas, which are well marked, use a trolling motor or pushpole to get close to the fish. There is also a small fishing pier just off the road that separates Riviera Bay from Bayou Grande. The preserve does not have a boat ramp.

Fishing Index: Wade fish for redfish, snook, and spotted seatrout. The outgoing tide is the preferred time to fish.

Directions: From the intersection of Gandy Blvd. and San Martin Blvd. 2.1 miles west of the Gandy Blvd. exit from I-75, turn south onto San Martin Blvd. and drive 1.0 miles to the intersection with Weedon Dr. Turn left onto this road and follow it 1.7 miles to the fishing pier.

Address: 1800 Weedon Dr. NE., St. Petersburg, FL

For more information: Call the preserve office at (727) 453-6500. The location of the nearby boat ramps that provide access to the preserve and surrounding waters is provided below or by visiting *http://mapguide.stpete.org/stpetegoogle/ default_boatramps.htm.*

Access Points:
45A. SUNLIT COVE PARK—*Ramp*
Description: A single-lane ramp maintained by the City of St. Petersburg. It is the closest ramp to Weedon Island.
Directions: From the intersection of Gandy Blvd. and 4th St. N. in St. Petersburg, drive south on the 4th St. for 0.7 mile to the intersection with 89th Ave. N. Turn left onto 89th Ave. N. and drive 0.3 mile to Bay St. Turn right onto Bay St. and drive 0.3 mile to the park.
Address: 234 Sunlit Cove Dr., St. Petersburg, FL

45B. CRISP PARK— *Ramp*
Description: A dual-lane ramp maintained by the City of St. Petersburg.
Directions: Exit I-275 at 38th Ave. N. and drive east for 2.2 miles to Poplar St. NE. Note that 38th Ave. curves and becomes 40th Ave. 0.4 mile before Poplar St. Turn right onto Poplar and drive south for 0.3 mile to the park on your right.

Address: 3527 Poplar St. NE., St. Petersburg, FL

45C. Coffee Pot Park — *Ramp*
Description: A single-lane ramp maintained by the City of St. Petersburg.
Directions: Exit I-275 at 38th Ave. N. and drive east for 1.8 miles to First St. NE. Turn right onto First St. NE and drive 0.5 mile to 31st Ave. N. and the park entrance on your left.
Address: 3100 First St. N., St. Petersburg, FL

46. Gandy Bridge
Salt – Boat, Bank, and Bridge – Ramp

Description: This is the southernmost bridge over Old Tampa Bay. There are fishing catwalks on the east and west sides of the bridge.

Fishing Index: Fish the catwalks for a wide assortment of fish, including snook and cobia during summer, Spanish mackerel in the spring and fall, and year-round sheepshead action. Anglers fishing from boats can get in on some top-notch tarpon action at night during the summer.

Directions: From the Pinellas County side, exit I-275 at the Gandy Bridge exit. From the Tampa side exit the Crosstown Expressway at Gandy Blvd. Drive west for 1.8 miles to the entrance road to the ramp at Gandy Park on your left.

For more information: Call Gandy Bait and Tackle on the Tampa side at (813) 839-5551.

47. Courtney Campbell Causeway
Salt – Boat, Bank, and Wade – Ramp

Description: The northernmost of the three bridges over Old Tampa Bay. Anglers can fish from shore, wade into the grassflats, or fish around the two bridges on the causeway. Watch for marked pull-off areas for vehicles.

Fishing Index: Spotted seatrout are on the flats near either end of the causeway. Snook and redfish are popular targets around the bridges.

Directions: From the Pinellas County side, turn onto FL 60 (Gulf to Bay Blvd.)

and go east until you reach the causeway. From Tampa, exit I-275 at the airport exit and follow the signs to the causeway. The ramp is on the Hillsborough County side of the causeway, approximately 2.75 miles west of the Shriner's Hospital.

For more information: Call Buddie's Bait and Tackle on the causeway at (813) 287-1026.

48. PHILIPPE PARK
Salt – Boat and Bank – Ramp – $

Description: A Pinellas County park. The day-use facility offers picnicking and a playground. The ramp provides access to Safety Harbor and upper Old Tampa Bay.

Fishing Index: Fish in Safety Harbor for seatrout, redfish, and snook.

Directions: From the intersection of CR 580 and CR 590 (Philippe Pkwy.), take CR 590 south 1.3 miles to the entrance to the park on your left.

Address: 2525 Philippe Pkwy., Safety Harbor, FL

For more information: Call the park office at (727) 669-1947.

49. SAFETY HARBOR MARINA AND PIER
Salt – Boat and Pier – Ramp

Description: Owned by the City of Safety Harbor. Fish from the pier for sheepshead and snook. The ramp provides convenient access to Upper Tampa Bay.

Directions: From the west end of the Courtney Campbell Causeway, turn onto Bayshore Blvd. and drive north for 2.5 miles to the pier and ramp. It is adjacent to the Safety Harbor Resort and Spa.

Address: 131 South Bayshore Blvd., Safety Harbor, FL

50. UPPER TAMPA BAY PARK
Salt – Canoe/Kayak – Canoe/Kayak Launch

Description: This county park and preserve is for anglers who like to fish in the small, quiet tidal creeks along this part of Old Tampa Bay. A great place to fish from a canoe or kayak.

Fishing Index: Anglers catch redfish, spotted seatrout, snook, cobia, black drum, and sheepshead in Double Branch Creek.

Directions: FL 580 (Hillsborough Ave. on the Hillsborough County side) skirts the north end of Old Tampa Bay. From the intersection with Memorial Highway (FL 576), take Hillsborough Ave. 4.0 miles northwest to Double Branch Rd. Turn left onto Double Branch Rd. and go 0.5 mile to the park entrance.

Address: 8001 Double Branch Rd., Tampa FL

For more information: Call the park office at (813) 855-1765.

51. PICNIC ISLAND BEACH PARK
Salt – Boat, Wade, and Pier – Ramp

Description: From this City of Tampa park you can access Old Tampa Bay or Tampa Bay by boat, fish from the pier, or wade the shoreline.

Fishing Index: Fish around the mangroves for snook and redfish and on the grass flats for seatrout.

Directions: From the intersection of Gandy Blvd. and CR 587 (S.W. Shore Blvd.), take CR 587 south for 1.9 miles to the intersection with W. Commerce St. Turn right onto Commerce and go 1.2 miles to the intersection with Picnic Island Blvd. Turn right and follow the road to the park and the ramp.

Address: 7409 Picnic Island Blvd., Tampa, FL

52. BALLAST POINT PARK

Salt – Boat, Bank, and Pier – Ramp

Description: A City of Tampa park with a 960-foot fishing pier extending into Hillsborough Bay and a boat ramp. You can also fish along the nearby Bayshore Blvd. seawall.

Fishing Index: Anglers can catch snook, redfish, sheepshead, and plenty of saltwater catfish.

Directions: From the intersection of Gandy Blvd. and Dale Mabry Hwy. (US 92) in Tampa, take Gandy Blvd. east 1.1 miles until it dead-ends at Bayshore Blvd. Turn right and go south on Bayshore Blvd. 0.6 mile to Interbay Blvd. Turn left on Interbay Blvd. and go 0.3 mile to the park.

Address: 5300 Interbay Blvd., Tampa, FL

53. DAVIS ISLAND

Salt – Boat and Bank – Ramp

Description: Two ramps at this city park provide good access to Hillsborough Bay.

Fishing Index: Anglers fishing from the shoreline catch snook, redfish, jacks, and, in summer, tarpon.

Directions: From the Crosstown Expressway (FL 618) in downtown Tampa, take the Davis Island exit (South Hyde Park Drive) and follow the signs to Davis Island Blvd. Follow the road around the island to the south end, about 3.4 miles. Go past the airport and look for the ramp on the right.

Address: 864 Severn Ave., Tampa, FL

54. ALAFIA RIVER

Salt and Fresh – Boat, Bank, and Pier – Ramp

Description: This river is popular with anglers and, as you move upstream, with canoeists and kayakers. The upper portions of the river are also a good place to find fossilized shark teeth on the shallow bars in the river.

54A. LITHIA SPRINGS PARK—*Canoe/Kayak – Canoe/Kayak Launch – $*

Description: The park is locally known for the year-round 72-degree spring, which is a popular place to cool off in the summer. Camping is also available.
Directions: From the intersection of FL 60 (Brandon Blvd.) and Lithia-Pinecrest Rd. in Brandon, turn onto Lithia-Pinecrest Rd. and drive south for 6.9 miles to the intersection with Lithia Springs Rd. Turn right onto Lithia Springs Rd. and drive 1.4 miles to the park.
Address: 3932 Lithia Springs Rd., Lithia, FL
For more information: Call the park office at (813) 744-5572.

54B. RIVERVIEW BOAT RAMP—*Boat, Bank, and Pier – Ramp – $*

Description: From this Hillsborough County park anglers can head upstream to fish for bass and panfish or downstream to fish in search of snook and redfish.
Directions: From the intersection of US 301 and Balm Riverview Rd. in Riverview, turn onto Balm Riverview Rd. and drive 0.1 mile to the intersection with Park Dr. Turn left onto Park Dr. and go 0.2 mile to the park entrance on your left.
Address: 1110 Park Dr., Riverview, FL

54C. WILLIAMS RAMP AND PIER—*Boat and Pier – Ramp*

Description: A county-maintained facility at the mouth of the Alafia River along the eastern shore of Hillsborough Bay. Boaters have easy access to the seagrass flats along the eastern shore of Hillsborough and Tampa bays. The pier extends into the Alafia River.
Fishing Index: The pier is a popular place for land-bound anglers to catch redfish, sheepshead, and snook. From the ramp, boaters can head south to the area around the Big Bend power plant. This is a favorite place for anglers to fish in the winter. Warm water discharged from the power plant attracts a variety of fish, including snook, trout, and cobia.
Directions: From the I-75 and Riverview Dr. exit, take Riverview Dr. west for 2.3 miles to US 41. Cross US 41 and look for the entrance road on your left.
Address: 8749 US 41, Riverview, FL
For more information: Call Fisherman's One Stop at (813) 677-5659.

55. E.G. SIMMONS PARK
Salt – Bank, Pier, and Boat – Ramp

Description: This Hillsborough County park along the eastern shore of Tampa Bay is a good place to take the family. There is a campground, picnic area,

A gold or silver spoon makes a reliable bait for redfish.

swimming beach, and several docks for land-bound anglers. Boaters have quick access to Tampa Bay.

Fishing Index: Fish from land or boat for redfish, spotted seatrout, flounder, and snook.

Directions: From the intersection of US 41 and FL 674, drive north on US 41 for 1.5 miles and turn left onto 19th Ave. Drive 2.0 miles west to the park.

Address: 2401 19th Ave. N.W., Ruskin, FL

For more information: Call the park office at (813) 671-7655.

56.   COCKROACH BAY
Salt – Boat – Ramp

Description: This mangrove-fringed bay along the southeast shore of Tampa Bay is one of the less developed stretches of the region and a popular destination for anglers. The Cockroach Bay Aquatic Preserve includes the waters of Cockroach Bay and the Little Manatee River up to US 301.

Fishing Index: Seagrass flats along this part of the bay offer good fishing for spotted seatrout, flounder, and redfish. When the weather is cold, fish the deeper waters around the flats. That's where the fish wait for the water to warm up enough to move back on the flats and feed.

Directions: From the intersection of US 41 and FL 674 in Ruskin, drive south on US 41 for 3 miles to the intersection with Cockroach Bay Rd. Turn right and go 3 miles to the ramp at road's end.

Address: 5299 Cockroach Bay Rd., Ruskin, FL

Other boat ramps in the Preserve and on the Little Manatee River in Ruskin include: Ruskin Commongood Park—1106 1st Ave. N.W., Ruskin, FL
Domino Ramp—2200 8th St. S.W., Ruskin, FL
Wildcat Creek Park—110 Stephens Rd., Ruskin, FL

57. AL LOPEZ PARK
Fresh – Bank and Pier

Description: One of the FWC's Southwest Urban Fishery Project ponds. These ponds are located in urban areas and provide freshwater fishing opportunities for city dwellers and visitors. This park is a few blocks from Raymond James Stadium, home of the Tampa Bay Buccaneers. For something different, try a morning fishing trip followed by a tailgate party and football game and maybe some more angling after the game while the traffic thins out.

Fishing Index: The 10-acre pond here is intensively managed to produce good fishing for catfish, bluegills, and largemouth bass. The bass fishing is strictly catch and release. This is a barrier-free fishing site.

Directions: From the intersection of Hillsborough Ave. (US 92) and Dale Mabry Hwy., drive east on Hillsborough Ave. 0.2 miles to the intersection with Himes Ave. Turn south onto Himes Ave. and drive south 0.4 miles to the park entrance on your right.

Address: 4810 N. Himes Ave., Tampa, FL

Other Hillsborough County Urban fishery ponds in Tampa include:
Bobby Hicks Park Pond—4201 W. Mango Ave.
Dover District Park Lake—2320 N. Gallagher Rd., Dover, FL 33527
Gadsden Park Pond—6901 S. MacDill Ave.
Steven Wortham Park Lake—12108 Rhodine Rd., Riverview, FL
To see a brochure describing these sites go to *http://www.fwc.state.fl.us/docs/ Freshwater/FMA_TampaUrbanPond_Map.pdf*

58. HILLSBOROUGH RIVER

Fresh – Boat/Canoe, Bank, and Dock – Ramp

Description: The first four sites are part of the Hillsborough River Wilderness Park, a multisite county park that provides access to the Hillsborough River. The last site, Rotary Riverfront Park, is a City of Temple Terrace park.

Fishing Index: This river has an abundance of submerged logs, branches, and other structures plus varying amounts of floating and rooted aquatic vegetation that attract and hold plenty of largemouth bass and bream.

Access Points:

58A. DEAD RIVER PARK—*Canoe and Bank– Canoe Launch*

Description: A park with a primitive trail, youth group camp, and picnicking. Fishing is best done from a canoe.

Directions: Exit I-75 onto Fowler Ave. and drive east 1.2 miles to US 301. Take US 301 north 7.9 miles to Dead River Rd. Turn left and drive about 2.5 miles to the park. The road makes several turns.

Address: 15098 Dead River Rd., Tampa, FL

For more information: Call the park office at (813) 987-6210.

58B. JOHN SARGEANT SR. MEMORIAL PARK— *Boat, Bank, and Dock – Ramp*

Description: The park has a boardwalk, picnicking, and a ramp for small boats. Fishing is allowed on the dock at the end of the boardwalk trail.

Directions: Exit I-75 onto Fowler Ave. and drive east 1.2 miles to US 301. Take US 301 north 3.4 miles to the park entrance on your left.

Address: 12856 Highway 301, Thonotosassa, FL

For more information: Call the park office at (813) 987-6208.

58C. MORRIS BRIDGE PARK—*Boat and Bank– Ramp – $*

Description: The park has nature trails, picnicking, and a ramp for small boats. Anglers can fish from portions of the boardwalk along the river.

Directions: Exit I-75 at Fletcher Ave. and Morris Bridge Rd. and take Morris Bridge Rd. (CR 579) north 3.7 miles to the park.

Address: 13820 Morris Bridge Rd., Thonotosassa, FL

For more information: Call the park office at (813) 987-6209.

58D. TROUT CREEK PARK— *Canoe and Bank– Canoe Launch*

Description: On a small tributary of the Hillsborough River, this park has a boardwalk and picnicking. Anglers can fish from the boardwalk or from the banks of the small man-made ponds.

Directions: Exit I-75 at Fletcher Ave. and Morris Bridge Rd., and take Morris Bridge Rd. (CR 579) north about 0.5 mile to Trout Creek. Turn left onto Trout Creek and drive 1.2 miles to the park entrance on your right.
Address: 12550 Morris Bridge Rd., Thonotosassa, FL
For more information: Call the park office at (813) 987-6200.

58E. ROTARY RIVERFRONT PARK—*Boat and Bank – Ramp*
Description: A City of Temple Terrace Park with restrooms and picnic facilities.
Directions: The park is on the north side of Fowler Ave. 1.5 miles east of I-75.

59. MEDARD PARK
Fresh – Boat, Bank, and Pier – Ramp – $

Description: The park has a 770-acre reservoir and is a popular destination for anglers. There is also camping, several miles of bridal paths, a swimming beach, and picnicking. A 730-foot fishing pier/footbridge is barrier free. Boats can operate only at idle speed in the reservoir.

Fishing Index: The reservoir is a good place to fish for sunshine bass, which are stocked by the FWC. Anglers also have good luck catching crappie, bluegills, and catfish. Largemouth bass fishing is fair to good. The reservoir has special regulations for largemouth bass. Check the current regulations at the park.

Directions: Exit I-75 at FL 60 (Brandon Blvd.) and travel east 9.8 miles to South Turkey Creek Rd. Turn south and drive 1.0 mile to the park entrance on your left.

Address: 5737 Turkey Creek Rd., Plant City, FL

For more information: Call the park office at (813) 757-3802.

60. LITTLE MANATEE RIVER STATE PARK
Fresh – Canoe and Bank – $

Description: About 4.5 miles of this 40-mile river flows through this state park. There are nature trails, a campground and picnicking. Canoes can be rented at the ranger station for a very reasonable fee.

Fishing Index: Fish for largemouth bass and bream year-round. During winter cold spells, some snook and redfish migrate upriver and mingle with the freshwater species. Snook, from the salt waters of Tampa Bay, are year-round inhabitants of the lower freshwater regions of the river.

Directions: Exit I-75 at the Moccasin Wallow Rd. exit, the first exit north of the I-275 exit. Drive east on Moccasin Wallow Rd. 4.9 miles to US 301. Turn left and drive north on US 301 for 5.6 miles to Lighfoot Rd. Turn left on the Lightfoot Rd. and drive 0.2 miles to the park entrance on your right.

Address: 215 Lightfoot Rd., Wimauma, FL

For more information: Call the park office at (813) 671-5005.

Manatee and Sarasota Counties

61. Rod and Reel Pier and Anna Maria City Pier ———
Salt –Pier

Description: These two piers are only 0.5 mile apart at the northern tip of Anna Maria Island. Both have bait shops. Rod and Reel Pier, 250 feet long, is privately owned. The city pier, a 750-footer, has a restaurant and bait shop at the end of the pier.

Fishing Index: Fish either pier for sheepshead, black drum, redfish, snook, and seasonally for Spanish mackerel. The piers are also known for the occasional large sharks that are caught, usually at night.

The Anna Maria City Pier

Manatee and Sarasota Counties

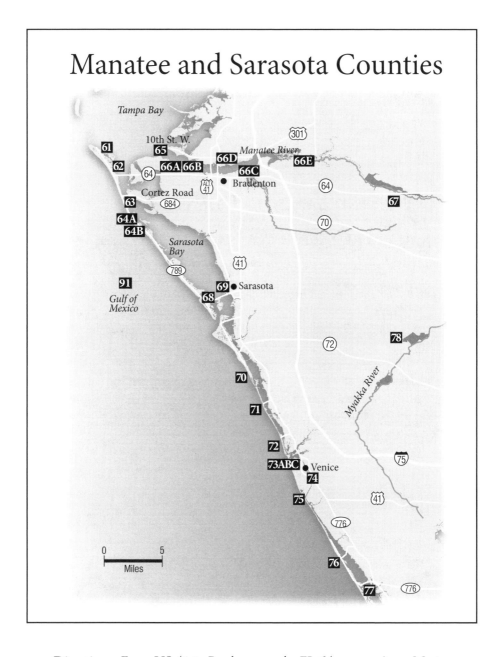

Directions: From US 41 in Bradenton, take FL 64 west to Anna Maria Island. The road dead-ends at Gulf Blvd. (FL 789). Turn right on Gulf Blvd. and drive north 2.9 miles to Pine Ave. and turn right. The city pier is at the end of Pine Ave. To reach Rod and Reel Pier, turn left off of Pine Ave. onto S. Bay Blvd. and drive 0.6 mile to Alamanda Rd. Turn right. The pier is at the end of the road.

Address: Rod and Reel Pier – 875 North Shore Dr., Anna Maria, FL
Anna Marina City Pier – 100 South Bay Blvd., Anna Maria, FL

For more information: Call the bait shop at Rod and Reel Pier at (941) 778-1885.

62. KINGFISH BOAT RAMP
Salt – Boat and Bank – Ramp

Description: From this ramp anglers have access to lower Tampa and upper Sarasota bays.

Fishing Index: Fish for redfish and snook from the banks around the ramp. From a boat, fish around the FL 64 bridge (Palma Sola Causeway) for snook and sheepshead or on the nearby grass flats for spotted seatrout.

Directions: The ramp is on Manatee Ave. (FL 64) 0.3 mile east of East Bay Dr. on Anna Maria Island. It is 8.1 miles east of the intersection of FL 64 and US 41 in Bradenton.

Address: 752 Manatee Ave., Holmes Beach, FL

For more information: Call Manatee County Parks and Recreation Department at (941) 742-5923.

63. BRADENTON BEACH PIER
Salt – Pier

Description: This city pier, in the upper part of Sarasota Bay, was created from the old bridge that connected Anna Maria Island to the mainland. It was rebuilt in 2007 and features a restaurant and bait shop on the pier.

Fishing Index: Fish off the pier for snook, flounder, and spotted seatrout.

Directions: From the intersection of US 41 and FL 684 (Cortez Rd.), take FL 684 west, cross the Cortez Bridge, and go until the road dead-ends at Gulf Drive. Turn south on Gulf Dr. and go 0.2 mile to a roundabout. Exit the roundabout going east on Bridge St. The pier is at the end of the road, 0.1 miles from Gulf Dr.

Address: 200 Bridge St., Bradenton Beach, FL

For more information: Call the pier bait shop at (941) 779-1706.

64. LONGBOAT PASS AND VICINITY
Salt – Boat, Bank, and Surf – Ramp

Description: A popular destination for anglers that is heavily used on the weekends. For a better fishing experience, anglers should fish the pass during the weekdays.

Fishing Index: Many anglers prefer the outgoing tide, but any time the water is moving the fish are likely to be biting. Snook, redfish, flounder, and Spanish mackerel are among the more popular species caught in the pass.

Access Points:
64A. COQUINA BAYSIDE LANDINGS NORTH —*Bank and Boat – Ramp*
Description: Fish from the beach or around the embankments beneath the bridge on the north side. The ramp provides convenient access to Longboat Pass, where anglers can fish around the bridge pilings.
Directions: From the intersection of FL 64 (Manatee Ave.) and Gulf Dr. on Anna Maria Key, take Gulf Dr. south 1.5 miles to the ramp on your left.
Address: 2000 Gulf Dr., South Bradenton Beach, FL

64B. BEER CAN ISLAND—*Bank and Surf*
Description: At the northern tip of Longboat Key on the south side of Longboat Pass. It is a good place to fish the pass from the shoreline or in the surf. It is also known as Greer Island Beach Park. Parking is limited to along Gulf Dr. Many who use the site arrive by boat.
Directions: The site is on Gulf Dr. about 1.9 miles south of Gulf Dr.'s intersection with Manatee Ave. (FL 64) and 10.6 miles north of St. Armand's Key.

65. SNEAD ISLAND
Salt – Canoe/Kayak and Wake – Canoe/Kayak Launch

Description: The island guards the north shore of the mouth of the Manatee River. While there are many homes on the island, the western tip is Manatee County's Emerson Point Conservation Preserve, a 365-acre county-managed preserve.
Fishing Index: The flats along the north side of the island are excellent wade- and kayak-fishing waters.

Directions: To reach the preserve from the intersection of 10th St. West and US

41 in Palmetto, drive west on 10th St. Follow this road about 3.0 miles to the bridge to Snead Island. Just over the bridge turn right onto Tarpon Rd. Drive 0.25 miles and take the first left onto 17th St. West and drive 2.3 miles to road's end and the launch.

Address: 58011 7th St. West, Palmetto, FL

For more information: Call Tropic Isles Marina near the Snead Island Bridge at (941) 721-6885 or go to the preserve website at *www.mymanatee.org/ conservation.html.*

66. MANATEE RIVER
Salt and Fresh – Boat, Bank, and Pier – Ramp

Description: From its headwaters in northeastern Manatee County, the river flows west to the lower part of Tampa Bay with only one interruption along its 60-mile run. Halfway down is a dam that impedes the river's flow and creates Lake Manatee, the freshwater supply for Manatee and Sarasota counties. The river is narrow and winding above the lake and also downstream until it reaches Fort Hammer, where the river opens up and comes under tidal influence. The river is navigable by boat up to Fort Hammer. Beyond that, small boats may continue up to the Lake Manatee dam.

Fishing Index: Saltwater anglers will find plenty of places along the river to fish for redfish, snook, mangrove snapper, sheepshead, and spotted seatrout. When cold winter weather arrives, redfish and snook swim upriver, often moving into freshwater areas. Bass fishing is very good from Fort Hammer to the Lake Manatee dam and in Lake Manatee.

Access Points:
66A. WARNER'S BAYOU RAMP (59TH ST. RAMP)— *Boat – Ramp*
Description: A Manatee County–maintained facility that provides access to the lower Manatee River, the flats around Snead Island at the mouth of the river, and Terra Ceia Bay.
Directions: From US 41 and FL 64 (Manatee Ave.) in Bradenton, drive 3.5 miles west on FL 64 to 59th St. Turn right onto 59th St. and drive 1.0 mile to Riverview Blvd. Turn right and the ramp will be on your left.
Address: 5800 Riverview Blvd., Bradenton, FL

66B. GREEN BRIDGE PIER/RIVERSIDE PARK—*Boat, Bank, and Pier – Ramp*
Description: The pier, which originates along the north shore, is part of the old

US 41 bridge across the river. Bait and tackle are available on-site.

Directions: From US Business 41 in Palmetto, turn westbound onto Riverside Dr. at the north end of the Green Bridge over the Manatee River. The park and pier are just west of the US Business 41 bridge.

Address: 833 Riverside Dr., Palmetto, FL

For more information: Call Green Bridge Pier Bait and Tackle at (941) 722-5700.

66C. Braden River Ramp—*Boat – Ramp*

Description: This county ramp is on the Braden River, a tributary of the Manatee River.

Directions: From the I-75 exit to FL 64 (Manatee Ave.), drive west on FL 64 for 3.5 miles to the bridge over the Braden River. Turn left onto 29th St. S.E. and then turn left onto the access road to the ramp. The ramp is on the west side of the bridge on the south side of FL 64.

Address: 3020 Manatee Ave. E., Bradenton, FL

66D. Ellenton—*Boat – Ramp*

Description: This small county ramp is on the north shore of the Manatee River.

Directions: From the intersection of US 41 and 301 in Palmetto, drive east on US 301 1.8 miles to Linden Dr. (29th Ave. E.) Turn right and drive 0.3 mile to Shore Dr. Bear left and follow Shore Dr. 0.2 mile to the ramp on your right.

Address: 353 Shore Dr., Ellenton, FL

66E. Fort Hamer—*Boat – Ramp*

Description: This county ramp is a good access point for small boat and canoe or kayak anglers. It marks the official dividing line between fresh water and salt water. Make sure you have the correct fishing license for the area you plan to fish.

Directions: Exit I-75 onto US 301 and drive north for 5.6 miles to 60th St. E. Turn right onto 60th St. E. and drive 0.1 mile to Fort Hamer Rd. Turn right and drive 3.0 miles to the end of the road and the ramp.

Address: 1605 Ft. Hamer Rd., Parrish, FL

67. LAKE MANATEE STATE PARK
Fresh – Boat, Bank, and Pier – Ramp – $

Description: The park extends along the south shore of Lake Manatee, a 2,500-acre impounded part of the Manatee River. There is a 20-horsepower limit for outboard motors on the lake.

Fishing Index: A good place to fish for largemouth bass, shellcrackers, sunshine bass, and crappie. The lake is periodically stocked by the FWC.

Directions: Exit I-75 onto FL 64 and go 8.0 miles east on FL 64 to the park entrance on your left.

Address: 20007 SR 64, Bradenton, FL

For more information: Call the park office at (941) 741-3028.

68. KEN THOMPSON PARK AT NEW PASS
Salt – Boat and Bank – Ramp

Description: This Sarasota County park is on City Island just north of the upscale shopping district on St. Armand's Key. Mote Marine Laboratory, a private marine research and education facility, is adjacent to the park. The lab is open to the public and has an excellent marine center filled with large saltwater aquaria, a touch tank, and other exhibits.

Fishing Index: From the bank in the park, and in New Pass for snook, mangrove snapper, and seasonally for tarpon and flounder. Land-bound anglers can also fish around the embankments of the bridge over New Pass. Boaters have access to the grassflats inside the pass and to several fish havens within a few miles of shore. These sites attract cobia, grouper, Spanish and king mackerel, and mangrove snapper.

Directions: From US 41 in Sarasota or by exiting at Fruitville off I-75, go west on Fruitville Rd. At Sarasota Bay, the road becomes the Ringling Causeway and signs lead to St. Armand's Key. From the roundabout on St. Armand's Key, take Ringling Parkway northfor 1.0 miles. Just before crossing the bridge over New Pass, turn right onto Ken Thompson Pkwy. and the park.

Address: 1700 Ken Thompson Pkwy., Sarasota, FL

For more information: Call New Pass Bait Shop at (941) 388-3050. For more information about Mote Marine Laboratory, call (941) 388-4441.

69. CENTENNIAL PARK, CAUSEWAY PARK, AND TONY SAPRITO PIER
Salt – Boat, Bank, and Pier – Ramp

Description: The three sites are clustered within a few blocks of each other. At the City of Sarasota's Causeway Park, anglers can fish from the seawall. Hart's Landing, inside the park, has bait and tackle and a dock for boaters. The pier is on the mainland side at the base of the Ringling Causeway Bridge over Sarasota Bay. A few blocks away Sarasota County's Centennial Park has a six-lane ramp and plenty of parking.

Fishing Index: Best fishing at the pier is at night for snook. Boaters can fish around the causeway bridges, on the grassflats, and around many other places in Sarasota Bay. New Pass is also nearby. Throughout the area, fishing is good year-round for snook and redfish, with flounder in summer.

Directions: Centennial Park—From the intersection of US 41 and Fruitville Rd. (CR 780) in downtown Sarasota drive north on US 41 for 0.6 mile to the intersection with 10th St. Turn left onto 10th and the park entrance is on your right.
   Causeway Park and Tony Saprito Pier—From the intersection of US 41 and Fruitville Rd. (CR 780) in downtown Sarasota, drive south on US 41 for 0.2 mile and turn right onto Ringling Causeway. Drive 0.3 mile on the causeway and turn onto the service road just before crossing the bridge.

Address: Causeway Park—420 John Ringling Causeway, Sarasota, FL
Centennial Park—1059 N. Tamiami Trail, Sarasota, FL

For more information: Call Hart's Landing at (941) 995-0011.

Other nearby access points:

Bird Key Park—*bank fishing* – 200 John Ringling Causeway, Sarasota, FL
Bay Island Park—*bank fishing* – 946 Siesta Dr., Sarasota, FL

A pinfish makes a great bait for snapper and grouper.

70. TURTLE BEACH PARK
Salt – Boat, Bank, and Surf – Ramp

Description: A Sarasota County park just north of Midnight Pass, an inlet that is now completely filled with sand. The ramp provides boaters with access to Little Sarasota Bay. The park has picnic shelters, a campground, and a playground.

Fishing Index: Anglers can surf fish for snook, wade in the bay, or fish from boats for snook, redfish, mangrove snapper, and seatrout.

Directions: Exit I-75 onto Clark Rd. (FL 72) and drive west 4.0 miles. The road bears to the left and becomes Stickney Point Rd. Continue another 1.8 miles until Stickney Point Rd. ends at Midnight Pass Rd. (CR 789). Turn left and drive south for 2.6 miles to the park on your right.

Address: 8918 Midnight Pass Rd., Sarasota, FL

For more information: Call the park campground at (941) 349-3839.

71. BLACKBURN POINT PARK AND VICINITY ───────
Salt – Boat, Bank, and Wade – Ramp

Description: This Sarasota County park on Casey Key is a good place to access the flats of Little Sarasota and Blackburn bays. The bridge from the mainland to the islands is one of the few operating swing bridges left in Florida.

Fishing Index: Mangroves line Blackburn Bay and create very good cover for snook, redfish, spotted seatrout, and big sheepshead.

Directions: From Venice, take US 41 north about 5.8 miles, or from Sarasota take US 41 south about 10 miles to the intersection with Blackburn Point Rd. (CR 789). Take this road west 0.8 miles and cross the swing bridge. The park and ramp are on the island side on your left.

Address: 800 Blackburn Point Rd., Osprey, FL

72. NOKOMIS BEACH PARK ──────────────
Salt – Boat, Bank, and Surf – Ramp

Description: This Sarasota County facility is on Casey Key. The ramp is on the bayside and provides access to Blackburn Bay and Venice Inlet.

Fishing Index: Fish for snook, redfish, and seatrout in the bay and snook and small tarpon in the surf.

Directions: From US 41 in Venice, turn onto CR 789 (Albee Rd.). Go 1.1 miles to the end of the road and the intersection with Casey Key Rd. and the park. To reach the ramp, turn right onto Casey Key Rd. and then make your first right onto the access road to the ramp.

Address: North Jetty Park—100 Casey Key Rd., Nokomis, FL

For more information: Call North Jetty Fish Camp at (941) 488-2408.

73. VENICE INLET ────────────────────
Salt – Boat and Bank – Ramp

Description: While not as large of an inlet as Big Sarasota Pass to the north, Venice Inlet is a good place to fish. The inlet has rock groins on both sides that attract and hold many fish. Boaters should be mindful of their position relative to the marked channel so as not to interfere with boats in transit.

Fishing Index: Fish close to the rocks for snook, sheepshead, mangrove snapper, and redfish. Tarpon and sharks will be found in the deeper portions of the inlet. Live baits are the preferred choice among anglers fishing for snook, mangrove snapper, and redfish along the rocks, but a dead catfish, ladyfish, or chunk of mullet fished close to the bottom is a good way to attract a large tarpon.

Access Points:

73A. NORTH JETTY BEACH PARK—*Bank*
Description: This Sarasota County facility is on Casey Key and provides access to the north side of Venice Inlet.
Directions: From US 41 in Venice, turn onto CR 789 (Albee Rd.). Drive 1.1 miles to the end of the road and the intersection with Casey Key Rd. Turn left onto Casey Key Rd. and drive 0.8 mile to the park.

73B. HUMPHRIS PARK— *Bank*
Description: This City of Venice park provides access to the south side of Venice Inlet
Directions: From the intersection of US 41 and Venice Ave., drive west on Venice Ave. for 1.6 miles to the end of the road and the intersection with The Esplanade. Turn right and drive north for 0.3 mile to the intersection with Tarpon Center Dr. Turn left onto Tarpon Center and follow it 0.7 mile to the park.

73C. HIGEL PARK—*Boat – Ramp*
Description: The ramp at this park provides anglers with access to the shallow waters of Dona and Roberts bays and Venice Inlet. It is the closest public access boat ramp to the inlet.
Directions: From the intersection of US 41 and Venice Ave., drive west on Venice Ave. for 1.6 miles to the end of the road and the intersection with The Esplanade. Turn right and drive north for 0.3 mile to the intersection with Tarpon Center Dr. Turn left onto Tarpon Center and follow it 0.2 mile to the park.

Address: 1300 block of Tarpon Center Dr., Venice, FL

74. MARINA BOAT RAMP PARK
Salt – Boat – Ramp

Description: This Sarasota County park, located in Venice, provides access to Dona and Roberts bays and the Gulf of Mexico via the Venice Inlet.

Fishing Index: Fish the bays for snook and redfish or head offshore in search of grouper, cobia, and snapper.

Directions: From the intersection of US 41 and Venice Ave., drive west 0.3 miles and turn left onto the access road on east side of the bridge over the Intracoastal Waterway. Follow the road the 0.3 miles to the park which is on the north side of Venice Ave.

Address: 301 East Venice Ave., Venice, FL

75. VENICE PIER
Salt – Pier

Description: This 740-foot municipal pier is part of Brohard Park and is open 24 hours.

Fishing Index: Spanish mackerel migrate through the area in spring and good

Learn to tie the loop and use it to tie the lure to the leader.

catches come off the pier. Snook and redfish are usually present except during the coldest months. Sheepshead action is good in fall and winter. In summer, mangrove snapper and a few cobia move in around the pier.

Directions: From the intersection of US 41 in Venice and Venice Ave., drive west on Venice Ave. 1.0 mile to the intersection with Harbor Dr. Turn south on Harbor Dr. and go 1.8 miles to the park and pier.

Address: 1600 Harbor Dr. South, Venice, FL

For more information: Call the pier bait shop at (941) 488-9713.

Other access points: Caspersen Beach—surf fishing, 1.3 miles south of Venice Pier on Harbor Dr.

76.   MANASOTA BEACH
Salt – Boat, Bank, and Surf – Ramp

Description: The beach is a Sarasota County facility on Manasota Key, near Englewood, south of Venice. It is recognized as a good shelling beach. The ramp provides access to the upper portion of Lemon Bay.

Fishing Index: Surf fish for snook and redfish or fish from the shoreline of Lemon Bay near the boat ramp.

Directions: From the intersection of US 41 and Venice Ave., drive south on US 41 for 3.9 miles to the intersection with FL 776 (Englewood Rd.). Take FL 776 south 2.3 miles to Manasota Beach Rd. Turn right and follow this road about 1.8 miles to the park at road's end.

Address: 8570 Manasota Key Rd., Manasota Key, FL

77.   ANGER PIER
Salt – Pier

Description: This site is in Charlotte County just across the Sarasota County line. Across the road from the pier is Englewood Bait House. The pier is parallel to the bridge to Englewood Beach.

Fishing Index: A good place to fish for snook day or night. There are plenty of submerged structures between the pier and the road bridge. Use a stout rod and reel if you're going after the big snook.

Directions: From US 41 in Murdock, go west 16.1 miles on McCall Rd. (FL 776) to Beach Rd., just before Englewood. Turn left onto Beach Rd. (toward Englewood Beach) and go 0.3 mile. The pier is on the left before crossing the bridge.

Address: 1385 Beach Rd., Englewood, FL

For more information: Call Englewood Bait House at (941) 475-4511.

78. MYAKKA RIVER STATE PARK
Fresh – Boat/Canoe/Kayak, Bank, and Pier – Ramp – $

Description: In addition to fishing in the upper Myakka River, this 30,000-acre park has miles of hiking and backpacking trails and is a great place for wildlife watching, especially birds. The river is also popular for canoeing. A campground, cabins, and interpretive exhibits round out the amenities here. Canoes and kayaks are available for rent.

Fishing Index: The river has two wide spots known as Upper and Lower Myakka lakes. Both are good places to fish for largemouth bass, crappie, redear sunfish, and warmouth. The upper lake is in the developed part of the park and is where you will find the ramp. On the river, anglers target largemouth bass and bluegills. Occasionally snook wander up into the freshwater regions of the river up to Lower Myakka Lake.

Directions: In Sarasota, exit I-75 onto FL 72 and drive east 8.7 miles to the park entrance.

Address: 13208 State Rd. 72, Sarasota, FL

For more information: Call the park office at (941) 361-6511 or go to *www.floridastateparks.org.*

POLK, HARDEE, DESOTO, AND HIGHLANDS COUNTIES

Lake fishing is a major activity in these four counties, especially Polk and Highlands, which have almost 550 and 100 lakes, respectively. All lakes support at least a fair fishery, but some have a much better reputation than others and the quality of fishing in any of these lakes can and does change over time. Most of Florida's lakes will experience changes in water levels going up and down

Polk, Hardee, DeSoto and Highlands Counties

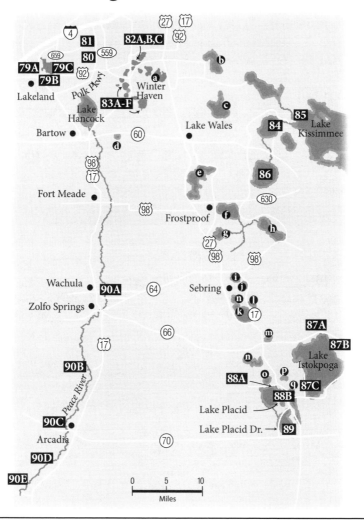

over various periods of time with fishing conditions changing in response to differeing water levels. Many lakes also have a problem with hydrilla, and if lake levels are low, navigation can be a challenge or simply impossible.

It is not practical to list detailed information about every lake with a boat-ramp access. What follows is intended to be a representation of what the lakes in this part of the state have to offer and to mention some of the better-known places to fish.

The Central Florida Convention and Visitors Bureau has some useful information about fishing in this part of the state on their website. This is also the place to go if you want to learn more about a part of Florida's fishing heritage—the fish camp. Many of the lakeside facilities have been in business for 40 years or more and are part of the state's cultural history. To get more information about fishing in this part of the state or to get more information about the fish camps, call the Bureau at (800) 828-7655 or go to *http://www.visitcentralflorida.org/do/outdoors/fishing/*.

79. LAKE PARKER
Fresh – Boat and Bank – Ramp

Description: This 2,272-acre lake is a FWC Fish Management Area.

Fishing Index: The lake has a good reputation for producing largemouth bass, especially at the north end of the lake. Crappie fishing is also good in the wintertime.

Access Points:
79A. LAKE PARKER PARK—*Boat and Bank – Ramp*
Description: A City of Lakeland facility with many other amenities just north of the Detroit Tigers spring training facility. The park is on the west side of the lake.
Directions: From the intersection of US 92 and Lakeland Hills Blvd. (FL33) in Lakeland, take Lakeland Hills north for 1.5 miles to Granada St. Turn right and go 0.4 mile to the park entrance.
Address: 910 E. Granada St., Lakeland, FL

79B. SERTOMA PARK—*Boat and Bank – Ramp*
Description: A FWC-maintained ramp at the small city park. The park is on the south side of the lake.
Directions: From the intersection of US 92 and Lakeland Hills Blvd. (FL33) in Lakeland, drive east on US 92 for 1.6 miles to the ramp on the left side of the road.
Address: 1800 E. Memorial Blvd., Lakeland, FL

79C. LAKE PARKER EASTSIDE PARK—*Boat – Ramp*
Description: A Polk County facility on the east side of the lake.
Directions: From the intersection of US 92 and Lake Parker Dr. in Lakeland, drive north on Lake Parker Dr. 1.0 mile to the park on your left.
Address: E. Lake Parker Dr. and Tanglewood St., Lakeland, FL

80. SADDLE CREEK PARK
Fresh – Boat and Bank – Ramp

Description: The park is a flooded 326-acre phosphate-pit lake that was mined in linear strips, creating extensive places to bank fish as well as many isolated and secluded places to fish from a small boat. There are five boat ramps, a place to swim, campground, shooting range and other recreational facilities. This is a good family place.

Fishing Index: Heavily fished but still a better-than-average place for big bass, especially from February through April. Crappie, channel catfish, and bream are also caught year-round.

Directions: From US 92 exit off I-4 in Lakeland, drive east on US 92 for 8.1 miles to Saddle Creek Park Rd. Turn left and follow the road to the park.

Address: 3716 Morgan Combee Rd., Lakeland, FL

For more information: Call the Phillips Bait and Tackle at (863) 666-2248.

81. TENOROC FISH MANAGEMENT AREA
Fresh – Boat, Bank and Pier – Ramp – $

Description: This 7,300-acre site features 14 former phosphate pits ranging in size from 7 to 227 acres. Each lake is managed to produce top-quality largemouth bass fishing. The site is tightly regulated, and all anglers must check in and out of the sites and pay a daily use fee. Each lake has quotas that are designed to afford anglers a quality fishing experience. Reservations are accepted for some lakes. Fishing at Tenoroc is open to the public Friday through Monday. Anglers surrender their fishing licenses when entering the site and are given a daily fishing permit and a creel information sheet that they must fill out. Special rules apply at Tenoroc, and anglers will be informed of the specific regulations in effect. Largemouth bass fishing is either all catch and release or, for a few lakes, catch and release for fish over 15 inches. Additionally, barrier-free fishing sites are available at Derby Lake and Pasture Lakes.

If all the special rules sound harsh, consider this: Tenoroc's lakes consistently produce trophy-size bass. Each lake is managed for this purpose. Because of tightly controlled fishing pressure and rules adapted to enhance the fishery, those who fish here have an excellent chance for a high-quality experience.

Fishing Index: Trophy-sized largemouth bass are the main attraction at Tenoroc. Fishing is good year-round for this species. The lakes also have good populations of crappie, bluegill, redear sunfish, and catfish.

Directions: From the I-4 exit onto Lakeland Hills Blvd., drive 2.7 miles east to the intersection with Combee Rd. (CR 659). Trun right and drive 1.3 miles to the intersection with Ritter Rd. Turn left and follow Ritter Rd. to the site, about 1.8 miles.

Address: 3829 Tenoroc Mine Rd., Lakeland, FL

For more information: Call the Tenoroc office at (863) 499-2421; to make a reservation, call (863) 499-2422 or visit the website at *http://myfwc.com/ Recreation/WMASites_Tenoroc_index.htm.* This is recommended for weekends. A fishing forecast is available at *http://www.myfwc.com/RECREATION/FW_ forecasts_swr.htm.*

82.   NORTH WINTER HAVEN CHAIN ————————
Fresh – Boat, Bank, and Pier – Ramp

Description: The Lakes District Lake Management District (LDLMD), created as the Winter Haven Lake Region Boat Course District in 1919, is responsible for connecting the lakes that make up the Winter Haven Chain of Lakes. Today the district manages 9 lakes in the north chain, 16 lakes in the south chain (see below), and 35 independent lakes in Winter Haven and vicinity. Their emphasis is on providing public access and managing the water levels in the lakes.

Fishing Index: The chain has good bass and bluegill fishing year-round. Crappie fishing is best during the colder months.

For more information: Visit the FWC website at *myfwc.com/Fishing/forecast* and click on the Southwest Region button. Access to other independent lakes (not part of the Chain of Lakes) in the area can be found at www.lakesmgmtdist.com and the Polk County website at *www.polk-county.net/county_offices/leisure_svcs.* Click on the link to boat ramps.

Access Points:
82A. LAKES CONINE, ROCHELLE, AND SMART—*Boat and Pier – Ramp*
Description: A LDLMD-maintained ramp with a small fishing pier on the north shore of Lake Conine.
Directions: From the intersection of US 17 and US 92 in Lake Alfred drive south on US 17 2.2 miles to the intersection with FL 544 (Ave. T N.E.). Turn

left and drive 0.5 mile to the intersection with Lucerne Park Rd. Turn left and follow Lucerne Park Rd. 1.3 miles to the ramp on your left. It is just before you cross the small bridge over the canal connecting Lake Conine to Lake Smart. The canal connecting to Lake Rochelle is at the north end of Lake Conine. There is also a small ramp on Lake Rochelle. It is 0.2 miles past the junction where US 92 and US 17 join near the town of Lake Alfred. From this ramp, you can access the other lakes via canals, water level permitting.

82B. LAKE FANNIE—*Boat and Pier – Ramp*
Description: A LDLMD-maintained ramp with a small fishing pier. The ramp is on the east shore of lake
Directions: From the intersection of US 17 and US 92 in Lake Alfred drive south on US 17 2.2 miles to the intersection with FL 544 (Ave. T NE). Turn left on Ave. T NE and drive 0.5 miles to the intersection with Lucerne Park Rd. Turn left and follow Lucerne Park Rd. 3.7 miles to the ramp on your right.

82C. LAKE HAINES— *Boat and Bank – Ramp*
Description: A LDLMD maintained-ramp with a small fishing pier. The ramp is on the west shore of the lake.
Directions: From the intersection of US 17 & 92 and Haines Blvd. in Lake Alfred, drive east 0.9 miles to the end of Haines Blvd. and the ramp.

83. SOUTH WINTER HAVEN CHAIN
Fresh – Boat, Bank, and Pier – Ramp

Description: The south chain consists of 16 lakes within the city of Winter Haven and south of town.

Fishing Index: The chain has good bass and bluegill fishing. It is heavily fished and there is considerable boat and jet ski traffic. Try fishing during the weekdays.

For more information: Visit the FWC website at *myfwc.com/Fishing/forecast* and click on the Southwest Region button. Access to other independent lakes (not part of the Chain of Lakes) in the area can be found at *www.lakesmgmtdist.com* and the Polk County website at *www.polk-county.net/county_offices/leisure_svcs.* Click on the link to boat ramps.

Access Points:
83A. LAKES CANON, MIRROR, AND SPRING—*Boat – Ramp*
Description: There is a Polk County–maintained ramp at Lake Canon Park. The ramp is on the west shore of Lake Canon. Lakes Mirror and Spring are to the east.

Directions: From the intersection of FL 544 (Havendale Blvd.) and Boys Club Rd., 1.4 miles east of US 17, drive south on Boys Club Rd. for 0.4 mile to the intersection with West Lake Canon Dr. Turn left and follow this road for 0.1 miles to the ramp on your left.

83B. LAKES HARTRIDGE AND IDYLWILD—*Boat and Pier – Ramp*
Description: A LDLMD-maintained ramp with a small fishing pier along the southwest shore of Lake Hartridge. The canal to Lake Idylwild is just north of the ramp along the west shore.
Directions: From the intersection of US 17 and FL 544 (Havendale Blvd.) north of Winter Haven, drive west on FL 544 for 1 mile to the intersection with 20th St. N.W. Turn right and follow this road 0.1 mile to the ramp on your left.

83C. LAKE HOWARD —*Boat and Pier – Ramp*
There are two ramps on this lake. A City of Winter Haven ramp and pier are along the east shore and a LDLMD ramp and pier are along the west shore. The east side site has a multi-lane ramp and plenty of parking.
Directions: East Shore: From the intersection of US 17 and Central Ave. in Winter Haven, drive west for 0.3 miles to the end of the road and the ramp. West Shore: From the intersection of US 17 and Avenue D N.W., turn west onto Avenue D N.W. and drive 0.1 miles to Lake Howard Dr. Turn right onto Lake Howard Dr. and follow it around the lake 1.7 miles to Avenue B N.W. Turn left to the ramp.
Address: Lake Howard East— Lake Howard Dr. and Central Ave., Winter Haven, FL
Lake Howard West— Lake Howard Dr. and Ave. B N.W., Winter Haven, FL

83D. LAKE ROY –*Boat – Ramp*
Description: The Polk County–maintained ramp is along the lake's southeast shoreline.
Directions: From US 17 and CR 540 (Cypress Gardens Blvd.) in Winter Haven, drive east on FL 540 for 1.8 miles to the intersection with Lake Roy Dr. Turn right and follow Lake Roy Dr. for 0.25 mile to the ramp on your right.

83 E. Lakes Shipp, Lulu, May—*Boat – Ramp*
Description: There are two Polk County–maintained ramps on Lake Shipp. The east side site, W.G. Roe Park, has a multi-lane ramp, fishing pier, and plenty of parking. The smaller Sertoma Park on the west side also has a ramp and fishing pier. Lakes Lulu and May are accessed by the canals connecting each lake to Lake Shipp.
Directions: East Shore—W.G. Roe Park: From the intersection of US 17 and Avenue R S.W. drive west on Avenue R S.W. for 0.1 mile (just across the train

tracks) to 7th St. S.W. Turn left onto 7th St. and drive north for 0.3 mile to the ramp on your left. West Shore—Sertoma Park: From the intersection of US 17 and CR 655., drive west on Cr 655 for 0.8 mile to the ramp on your right.
Address: W.G. Roe Park—2403 7th St. SW., Winter Haven, FL
Sertoma Park –1651 Lake Shipp Dr., Winter Haven, FL

83F. LAKES SUMMIT, ELOISE, AND WINTERSET—*Boat and Bank – Ramp*
Description: Lake Summit has a Polk County–maintained ramp with a small fishing pier. The ramp is in the southwest section of the lake. Legoland Florida, formerly Cypress Gardens, is also on Lake Summit. Lake Summit connects to Lake Eloise, and Lake Elosie connects to Lake Winterset.
Directions: From US 17 and CR 540 (Cypress Gardens Blvd.) in Winter Haven, drive east on FL 540 for 1.8 miles to the intersection with Lake Roy Dr. Turn right and follow Lake Roy Dr. until it branches off to the right. Bear left onto Hillcrest Dr. and go approximately 0.5 miles to the ramp on your left.

84. LAKE ROSALIE PARK
Fresh – Boat and Bank – Ramp

Description: Water flows from Lake Rosalie to Tiger Lake and then to Lake Kissimmee. Small boats can make the trip from Rosalie to Tiger and then on to Lake Kissimmee. Camping is allowed at the park.

Fishing Index: The lakes are good for largemouth bass. Tiger Lake also has a reputation for producing nice stringers of crappie.

Directions: From US 27 in Lake Wales, drive east 13.3 miles on FL 60 to Tiger Lake Rd. Turn left and go 1.9 miles to Lake Rosalie Rd. Turn left and follow the road 1.3 miles to the ramp.

For more information: Call Lake Rosalie Bait, Tackle, Taxidermy and Guide Service at (863) 696-7384.

85. LAKE KISSIMMEE STATE PARK
Fresh – Boat and Bank – Ramp

Description: The park's boat ramp provides access to Lake Kissimmee and other lakes in the Kissimmee Chain of Lakes. Land-bound anglers can fish from the banks of the canal connecting lakes Kissimmee and Rosalie. A more detailed listing is provided in the East Central Florida chapter under the Lake Kissimmee site.

86. Lake Weohyakapka
Fresh – Boat and Bank – Ramp

Description: With a name as hard to pronounce as this, no wonder it's usually called Lake Walk-in-the-Water. This is the largest lake in Polk County at 7,528 acres.

Fishing Index: A bass and crappie lake with a reputation for producing trophy bass. Special restrictions on largemouth bass apply. Current rules require anglers to immediately release all bass from 15 to 24 inches. You are allowed to keep up to three bass less than 15 inches or two less than 15 and one more than 24 inches. The rules may change, so check the FWC website, *www.myfwc.com/ RECREATION/FW_forecasts_swr.htm.*

Directions: From Alternate US 27 in Frostproof, go east 4.9 miles on CR 630 to Lake Walk-in-the-Water Rd. Turn left and go 3.8 miles to Boat Landing Rd. Turn right on Boat Landing Rd. and follow it to the end and the Polk County boat ramp.

For more information: Call the FWC regional office at (863) 648-3202.

Other Polk County Lakes

All the following have ramps and/or are accessed by a nearby lake with a ramp. Lakes with a fishing pier are so indicated. While they are not considered top producers, each lake can have periods of good to above-average fishing. Local knowledge, usually available from bait and tackle shops throughout the region, is very helpful in finding a sleeper lake waiting for you to discover its secrets. There is a general location map and table listing the ramps of the independent lakes in Polk County in the Lakes Region Lake Management District website. To see it, go to *www.lakesmgmtdist.com/lakes_map.cfm.* You will also find a listing of Polk County ramps on the county's website at *www. polk-county.net.* Click on the Parks and Recreation link. The lakes are listed alphabetically and include the name of the closest city to help you locate them. DeLorme's *Florida Atlas and Gazetteer* is a good printed reference to help you locate the lakes. Or try Mapquest or Google Earth on the Internet to locate and view aerial photography of these lakes. The locations of a few of the lakes listed below are given in lowercase letters (for example, Lake Hamilton (a)) on the map on page 185.

Banana Lake – Lakeland
Crooked Lake – Frostproof (e)
Crystal Lake – Lakeland
Lake Agnes – Polk City
Lake Alfred – Lake Alfred
Lake Annie – Dundee
Lake Arbuckle – Frostproof (h)
Lake Blue – Winter Haven
Lake Bonny – Lakeland
Lake Buckeye – Winter Haven; fishing pier
Lake Buffum – Fort Meade
Lake Cannon – Winter Haven
Lake Confusion – Haines City
Lake Daisy – Winter Haven
Lake Deer – Winter Haven
Lake Deeson – Lakeland
Lake Echo – Lake Alfred; fishing pier
Lake Elbert – Winter Haven; fishing pier
Lake Garfield – Alturas (d)
Lake Gibson – Lakeland
Lake Hamilton – Winter Haven (a)
Lake Jessie – Winter Haven
Lake Livingston – Frostproof (g)
Lake Mariam – Winter Haven; fishing pier
Lake Mariana – Auburndale
Lake Marion – Lake Hamilton (b)
Lake Martha – Winter Haven; fishing pier
Lake Maude – Winter Haven; fishing pier
Lake Ned – Winter Haven
Lake Pansy – Winter Haven
Lake Pierce – Dundee (c)
Lake Roy – Winter Haven
Lake Sears – Winter Haven
Lake Silver – Winter Haven; fishing pier
Lake Swope – Lake Alfred
Lake Tennessee – Polk City
Mudd Lake – Polk City
Reedy Lake – Frostproof (f)
Surveyors Lake – Alturas

87. LAKE ISTOKPOGA
Fresh – Boat and Pier – Ramp

Description: One of the best-known lakes in central Florida. Some anglers prefer to fish this lake over Lake Okeechobee. The lake, at 27,692 acres, is home to many bass fishing tournaments. It is a shallow lake averaging four to six feet deep. There are several fish camps around the lake that offer a variety of accommodations for anglers.

Fishing Index: The lake has an excellent reputation for largemouth bass and crappie. The catch rate for largemouths is among the highest in the state. Crappie fishing is best in the winter months. Special restrictions on largemouth bass apply. Current rules require anglers to immediately release all bass from 15 to 24 inches. You are allowed to keep up to three bass less than 15 inches or two less than 15 and one more than 24 inches. The rules may change, so check the FWC website, *www.myfwc.com/RECREATION/FW_forecasts_swr.htm,* for updates.

For more information: The FWC lists this lake in its regional forecasts for the Southwest Region. You will find these reports at *www.myfwc.com/RECREATION/FW_forecasts_swr.htm#istokpog.*

Access Points:

87A. ISTOKPOGA PARK—*Boat and Pier – Ramp*
Directions: From the US 27 and US 98 intersection south of Sebring, take US 98 east along the north shore of the lake for 8.2 miles. Turn right into the park and ramp.
Address: 720 Istokpoga Park Access Rd., Sebring, FL

87B. LAKE ISTOKPOGA EAST—*Boat – Ramp*
Directions: To reach this FWC ramp on the east side of the lake, drive 11.5 miles east on US 98 from the US 17 and US 98 intersection south of Sebring. Turn right onto Cow House Rd. and drive 1.3 miles to Lake Blvd. Turn right and go 0.7 mile to the ramp.
Address: 2011 Lake Blvd., Lorida, FL

87C. WINDY POINT PARK—*Boat – Ramp*
Directions: The ramp is at the south end of the lake. From US 27 in Lake Placid, turn onto CR 621 and go west 2.8 miles to Highlands Lake Dr. Turn left and go 0.7 mile to Boat Ramp Rd. Turn right and drive 0.3 miles to the ramp.
Address: 65 Windy Point Rd., Lake Placid, FL

88. LAKE JUNE IN WINTER
Fresh – Boat, Bank, and Pier – Ramp

Description: Everyone refers to this 3,500-acre lake as Lake June, although the official name includes the "in Winter." Some old-timers may refer to the lake as Lake Sterns, its former name.

Fishing Index: A good lake for largemouth bass. The lake has numerous deep holes, good places to fish for largemouth in summer when the surface water is hot. Anglers should fish these locations throughout the year except for the spawning period in early spring, when the fish move into the shallows. Also, try crappie fishing at night in summer.

Access Points:
88A. H.L. BISHOP PARK—*Boat, Bank, and Pier – Ramp*
Directions: From US 27 in Lake Placid, turn west onto CR 621 (Lake June Rd.) at the north end of the lake and go 0.5 mile to the park entrance on your left.
Address: 10 Lake June Clubhouse Rd., Lake Placid, FL

88B. LAKE JUNE PARK —*Boat – Ramp*
Directions: From US 27 in Lake Placid, turn west onto Roy Pendarvis Rd. and drive west 1.1 miles to the intersection with N. Tangerine Dr. Turn right into the park and the ramp will be on your right.

89. LAKE PLACID
Fresh – Boat – Ramp

Description: This is a clear-water lake just south of Lake June.

Fishing Index: This lake is also very productive for crappie (specs) in late winter and early spring and is an excellent place to fish for bluegills in summer.

Directions: From the intersection of Lake Mirror Dr. and US 27 south of Lake Placid, turn onto Lake Mirror Dr. and head southwest for approximately 0.9 miles. The road ends at Placid View Dr. Turn left and drive 1.6 miles to the ramp on your left.

For more information: Call Lake Placid Bait and Tackle (863) 699-0102.

OTHER HIGHLANDS COUNTY LAKES

All the following have ramps and/or are accessed by a nearby lake with a ramp. While they are not considered top producers, each lake can have periods of good to above-average fishing. Local knowledge, usually available from bait and tackle shops throughout the region, is very helpful in finding a sleeper lake waiting for you to discover its secrets. There is a general location map and table listing the ramps around Lake Placid at *www.lpfla.com/lakes.htm*. You can also get some information on Highlands County ramps by going to *www.hcbcc.net/ ParksBoatRamp.html*. The lakes are listed alphabetically by city. The locations of a few of the lakes listed below are given in lowercase letters (for example, Lake Letta (i)) on the map on page 185.

Dinner Lake – Sebring (l)
Crews Lake – Lake Placid
Lake Adelaide – Avon Park
Lake Apthorp – Lake Placid (p)
Lake Carrie – Lake Placid
Lake Childs – Lake Placid
Lake Clay – Lake Placid
Lake Damon – Avon Park
Lake Denton – Avon Park
Lake Francis – Lake Placid (o)
Lake Glenda – Avon Park
Lake Henry – Lake Placid
Lake Hill – Lake Placid
Lake Huntley – Lake Placid (q)
Lake Jackson – Sebring (k)
Lake Josephine – Sebring (n)
Lake Lelia – Avon Park
Lake Letta – Avon Park (i)
Lake Lotela – Avon Park
Lake Olivia – Avon Park
Lake Persimmon – Lake Placid
Lake Pioneer – Avon Park
Lake Sebring – Sebring (j)
Lake Viola – Avon Park
Little Lake Bonnett – Avon Park
Little Lake Redwater – Lake Placid
Red Beach Lake – Sebring (m)
Red Water Lake – Lake Placid
Wolf Lake – Sebring

90. PEACE RIVER ─────────────────────
Fresh – Boat and Bank – Ramp

Description: This river originates from the waters of Lake Hancock, one of the more polluted lakes in the region. From the lake, the river flows a little more than 100 miles until it empties into Charlotte Harbor near Punta Gorda. Tannins from trees along the riverbanks give the water a tea-colored look. Despite its start from a polluted lake and the fact that it flows through areas of active phosphate mining, the Peace River is fairly clean and healthy south of Bartow. It is a very scenic river and popular with canoeists. River levels do fluctuate; thus, access via the sites listed below may be limited at times of low water.

Fishing Index: The upper part of the river is an excellent place to fish from a canoe, kayak, or small jon boat for largemouth bass and catfish. South of Fort Meade, anglers have a chance of catching a saltwater snook during the winter and spring. The further south you go, the more snook there are. Flip a lure under some brush along the river bank or in one of the deep holes to entice a bass or snook to take the bait. Closer to the mouth of the river you may also hook up with a small tarpon.

For more information: Check out the FWC's regional forecast at *www.myfwc. com/RECREATION/FW_Sites.htm* and click on Southwest Region, or call the Southwest Region office at (863) 648-3200.

Access Points:
90A. CR 652 RAMP—*Boat and Bank – Ramp*
Directions: From US 17 in Wachula, turn onto Main St. (CR 636) and go east 0.6 mile to CR 652 (Griffin Rd.). Turn right and go 1.0 mile to the bridge over the river and the ramp on your right.

90B. GARDNER RAMP—*Boat and Bank – Ramp*
Directions: From US 17 in Gardner, turn onto River Rd. and go west 1.5 miles to the end of the road and the ramp.

90C. ARCADIA RAMP—*Boat and Bank – Ramp*
Directions: The ramp is on FL 70 1.5 miles west of the intersection of US 17 and FL 70.

90D. NOCATEE RAMP—*Boat and Bank – Ramp*
Directions: The ramp is on CR 760 1.3 miles west of US 17 in Nocatee.

90E. Fort Ogden Ramp—*Boat – Ramp*

Directions: This ramp is downriver and on the opposite shore from Fort Ogden. From I-75 take the Kings Hwy. exit (one of the Port Charlotte exits) and drive north on Kings Hwy. for 3.2 miles to the intersection with Peace River Rd. Turn right and follow Peace River Rd. 1.4 miles to the end of the road and the ramp.

91. Gulf of Mexico
Salt – Boat and Surf

Description: There are two distinct types of shoreline along this part of Florida's west coast. From Crystal River to Tarpon Springs the coastline generally lacks the sandy beaches that attract tourists. It is replaced with mangroves and salt marshes with dense seagrass beds in the shallow offshore waters. South of Tarpon Springs begins a series of barrier islands that separate much of the mainland from the Gulf. In between are a string of shallow bays surrounded by intense development. The beaches of the barrier islands in this region are popular for sunbathers and swimmers. They also offer excellent fishing in early morning or whenever there aren't a lot of people in the water.

Fishing Index: Surf fishing is very good along most of the beaches south of Tarpon Springs. Fish for snook, redfish, and whiting in the trough that lies just a few feet off the beach. In addition, Spanish mackerel and tarpon make a showing in spring and fall. For offshore species, try one of the party boats or sportfishing boats (up to six anglers). Popular targets are grouper, snapper, Spanish and king mackerel, amberjack, and cobia for the boats that fish inside the 100-foot line. Beyond that, the charters may go after these same species or look for dolphin and sailfish. Several party boats make overnight trips to the middle grounds, where big catches of bottom dwellers such as grouper and snapper are usually the rule.

One of the most exciting nearshore fisheries is the late spring and early summer run of jumbo tarpon. These fish, some in excess of 200 pounds, migrate up the Gulf coast to breed. You can find them along the shoreline, sometimes within 100 feet of the shoreline and in the major passes. While your best chance of catching one of these fish is from a boat, some 100-pound and larger tarpon are so close to the shore that anglers fishing from the surf have a chance for a hookup. Look for these opportunities early in the morning. Wear polarized sunglasses to help you see into the water and locate the fish.

Anglers with boats capable of going offshore and who are not familiar with the region can visit any of the numerous artificial reefs, well-known wrecks, and natural hard-bottom areas. GPS coordinates to the most popular sites are also widely available from local marinas and bait and tackle stores.

Directions: Anglers can reach the beach at numerous public access sites or by staying at a beachfront hotel and walking out the door. A list of local fishing guides offering offshore or backcountry trips is usually available at your hotel, or you can find them online or in the local phone directory. If you talk to a bait and tackle shop, the owners will usually recommend several guides that would be the best for the type of fishing you want to do. The offshore boats tend to congregate at the marinas around the passes. Look for their brochures in hotels and other tourist spots.

Month by Month in West Central Florida

Note: Offshore is defined as greater than 2 miles from the coast. Coastal waters include open waters inside of 2 miles, including surf fishing, and all brackish water areas such as bays, the saltwater regions of rivers, and lagoons. Fresh water includes lakes, ponds, reservoirs, and rivers.

January

Offshore: This is a tough month for offshore anglers because of the high number of bad-weather days. When the fronts aren't blowing through and stirring up the seas, grouper grabbers will find keeper-sized fish 10 to 30 miles offshore. Local knowledge is necessary to find these fish closer to shore.

Coastal: This is one of the months when anglers head up the region's tidal creeks and rivers. That's where the snook, spotted seatrout, and redfish go to escape the cold, windswept waters of the bays and coastline. On warmer days, you may find good numbers of trout on the grass flats. Another good bet is to fish around one of the power plant discharge canals. The warm water attracts a wide variety of fish. Bridge anglers will find a good supply of sheepshead and flounder this month and next.

Fresh water: Largemouth bass start to spawn in the shallow waters of the region's many freshwater lakes. Live wild shiners are the bait of choice for trophy-sized fish. This is also a top month for crappie.

February

Offshore: The rough winter will peak this month, so anglers must resign themselves to heading out between the northwesters. When the weather is good, so is the fishing. Grouper are always biting, but the season is closed this month so what you catch must be released. Look for tripletail hanging around any fixed or floating structures. When you see one, toss a live shrimp its way and hang on.

Coastal: Look for the warm water this month. Anything above 70 degrees is where you want to be. Snook, redfish, and seatrout lurk in these warm spots. Late in the day, after the sun has warmed the water on the flats, look for some fish to move in and feed. There will also be plenty of fish around the power plant outfalls.

Fresh water: This is peak time for the big bass. The fish are spawning in the shallows around the lakes and the females are on their nests. Live wild shiners are as surefire a bait as you'll ever find this time of year. If you have to use artificials, try something that looks like a shiner or shad. Also expect great crappie action.

MARCH

Offshore: The Gulf water begins to warm up in March and by the end of the month, offshore action will be in high gear. Grouper season is still closed but will open next month. Expect the Spanish and king mackerel to arrive following the schools of baitfish moving up from the south.

Coastal: This is the time when fishing along the coast picks up. Baitfish move into the area and are the apple of every fish's eye and mouth. Hoping to avoid becoming a meal, the baitfish will seek what cover they can get. The huge number of bridge and dock pilings in the region attracts the bait and bring along mackerel, snook, redfish, and tarpon. Best places to go for this action are the Gulf fishing piers and the Sunshine Skyway.

Fresh water: The last month for female largemouths to spawn and for good big-bass fishing. Live shiners are the preferred bait. Crappie action will begin to slow as the water warms up, but this is still usually a good month.

APRIL

Offshore: King and Spanish mackerel are at the peak of the spring run. Sometimes you must set several lines out at different depths to find where in the water column the fish are congregating. Lines set closer to the bottom will also find grouper, cobia, and snapper. Those closer to the surface might be hit by a blackfin tuna. Use what locals call whitebait, an encompassing name for several species of white-sided baitfish.

Coastal: The snook, redfish, and seatrout that were up the creeks over the winter are moving closer to the coast and the open water of Tampa Bay. Tarpon are more numerous than last month. You can always count on sheepshead and mangrove snapper around the bridges and piers this time of year. If it has been a warm winter, some of the big tarpon may arrive early.

Fresh water: Largemouth bass are entering the post-spawn period and some veteran anglers say that while there are plenty of fish around, getting them to bite takes more work than in the previous three months. Look for bluegill and redear sunfish action to pick up as their spawning time approaches.

MAY

Offshore: Depending on how warm the Gulf water is there may be some king mackerel around, but chances are most are farther north by now. Anglers can return to the reliable grouper and snapper fishing or look in the water column for summer's pelagic fish: cobia, blackfin tuna, amberjack, sailfish, and maybe a marlin.

Coastal: Anglers are looking for big tarpon to appear. The site of a 150-pound fish leaping out of the water is something that die-hard anglers and novices will remember for a long time. Look for the big fish along the coast, within a few miles of shore. Toward the north end of the region, the fish will move onto the flats around Homosassa and anglers will be waiting for them with fly rods in hand. This is also a great time for snook and redfish. Seatrout are on the flats, and there are plenty of cobia in Tampa Bay. With the rainy season not quite in full swing, this is a good month to fish in west central Florida.

Fresh water: Bluegills and shellcrackers (redear sunfish) are spawning and it's easy to catch your limit of these fish. Largemouth bass seek deeper water during the day and move into shallower water to feed during the early and late hours of the day.

JUNE

Offshore: Offshore anglers have to start moving farther offshore for good grouper action. Gag grouper tend to move to deeper water in summer. Forty miles out and farther will get you into the best dolphin, wahoo, sailfish, blackfin tuna, and marlin fishing there is along the west central coast. It's not as convenient as fishing in the Atlantic, but the experienced charter boat operator knows how to bring these fish to the boat.

Coastal: Tarpon, tarpon, tarpon. Now is the time for the monsters. The biggest fish, in excess of 200 pounds, are on the flats around Homosassa. That's also where you will find some of the best guides in the state taking their clients in search of record fish. If tarpon aren't your bag, this is a prime month for snook, but it's catch and release only; the season is closed June, July, and August. The fish will be in the passes and along the beach, making them accessible to surf anglers.

Fresh water: Worm fishing for largemouths early in the morning or late in the day is a standard tactic this month. In midday the bass are down deep, and anglers willing to use deep-diving crank baits or live shiners down deep will catch fish.

JULY

Offshore: The bluewater fish—dolphin, wahoo, sailfish, and blackfin tuna—are the target of anglers with open-water boats that can make the trip more than 40 miles out. This is the peak month for these species. Grouper are in at least 70 feet of water. For a change of pace, try night fishing for snapper. Mangroves, yellowtails, and a few reds are active feeders after dark.

Coastal: Along the shore, usually within 0.5 mile, 50- to 125-pound tarpon cruise the channels paralleling shore. They're looking for a whitebait breakfast so use some fresh cast-netted fish. Toss your bait ahead of the direction they're heading and hold on. Cobia are plentiful in Tampa Bay both around the shipping lane markers and in the open sandy holes in the grassflats. Redfish will also be on the flats and along mangrove shorelines, but look for them during the cooler parts of the day.

Fresh water: If you want largemouth bass, either fish the shallow waters of the lakes very early in the morning or just as the sun sets. The rest of the time go to the deepest spots in the lake and fish deep. You will also find some crappie there.

AUGUST

Offshore: Those bluewater fish, in 100 feet of water and deeper, continue to provide good summer action. Grouper are in at least 70 feet of water. Chumming them out of their holes may help increase your chances of getting one to the boat. If you fish the bottom, it's essential to turn their heads up as quickly as possible. If you don't, the fish will duck into a hole and you will never muscle it out. At this point, just leave the rod alone for a half hour and then try again. Maybe the fish will move back into open water.

Coastal: Shark anglers like to fish in the passes at night during summer. Sharks are abundant in west central Florida. The traditional flats fish—snook, redfish, and seatrout—move to the deep side of the flats now that it's hot. Fish early and late in the day, especially when the tide is moving.

Fresh water: Look for lakes with deeper water and fish for bass and crappie there. Local anglers don't take advantage of this enough and may tell you not to bother fishing in the middle of the day. But if you can stand the heat, give it a try. Otherwise consider night fishing for bass and crappie. It works.

September

Offshore: Anglers will be watching the water to the north and looking for signs that the Spanish and king mackerel will be arriving. This will be the last good month for the bluewater species. Dolphin like to travel with anything that's floating in the water. Grass or algae lines are ideal places to look but so is any piece of debris. Grouper will start to move slightly closer to shore if the water starts to cool a bit. Trolling a big lure 5 to 10 feet above the bottom will attract the fish. Mangrove snapper fishing should continue to be consistent throughout the month.

Coastal: Redfish are the top inside fish this month, but snook aren't far behind. Sight fishing reds on the flats is a popular way to catch these fish. You will need a shallow draft boat to reach them or be prepared to get wet and wade. This is also the time when snook season reopens.

Fresh water: It is still hot this month so the bass will continue to hole up in the deeper waters. A few may head towards the shallower water early in the morning or if a cool front passes through the area.

October

Offshore: King and Spanish mackerel traditionally make their return trip through the area this month, coming down from their summer home along the north Gulf coast. They move in schools, so not every day will be great, but you'll have more action than you can handle if you find the fish. Grouper are getting closer to shore, and that makes them more accessible to smaller boats.

Coastal: This is a great month for coastal and backwater anglers because there is top action for redfish, snook, cobia, flounder, and Spanish mackerel. The snook and reds start to move out of the passes and coastal areas and head toward the rivers, where they eventually move whenever the weather turns cold.

Fresh water: Activity starts to pick up as there are more bass spending more time in the shallow waters that anglers like to fish. Crappie fishing will still be better in the deeper waters.

NOVEMBER

Offshore: Grouper have anglers excited this month. The Gulf populations of gag grouper are as close to shore as they will get, and that means the fish are in 20 to 40 feet of water. The fastest way to find the fish, unless you have a book full of GPS numbers of secret grouper holes, is to troll a lure along the bottom. Try this along stone crab trap lines because crabbers set their traps along edges where the bottom drops onto a hard bottom area. The king mackerel run continues through this month before most of the fish disappear until the following spring.

Coastal: The creeks and rivers are still bringing warm water to the Gulf and Tampa Bay and that's why snook, redfish, and seatrout are attracted to these areas. Fish the seagrass beds around any of these places; the action will be hot. This is also a great month for flounder. Fish for them on open sandy patches in the seagrass beds or around the edges of oyster bars.

Fresh water: Crappie action should turn on toward the end of the month. The quicker it gets colder, the better the fishing will be. Live Missouri minnows are a favorite, reliable bait. Bass anglers will find fish around the edges of aquatic weeds and shorelines, and the number of bigger fish being caught will increase. The females are preparing for the spawn, which can begin in December in mild-weather years.

DECEMBER

Offshore: This is one of the best months for gag grouper. The only problem is the weather. Fronts sweep down from the northwest, kicking up the seas and making it impossible to get offshore. On calm days there's very good fishing within 10 to 20 miles off the coast. Live bait works best, but you may want to refrain from using it until you slow-troll up a good location.

Coastal: The fish are up the creeks and around the power plant outfalls now. You can fish inside even on windy days. There's always a lee side of an island or the mainland where the water will be calm and you can fish in relative comfort. Cobia, pompano, and permit join redfish, snook, and spotted seatrout around the power plants. Freelining a shrimp is a good tactic to use in winter.

Fresh water: Crappie are spawning, and the fish bite readily. All you need to catch these fish is a cane pole, and that's what many anglers use. Simple still works when it comes to fishing. The first largemouth bass of the season will begin to spawn in the shallower, warmer lakes. They won't be the biggest females, but it does make this a better-than-average month.

West Central Florida Fish Availability Chart

NOTE: The information contained in this chart represents the seasonal patterns observed over the past two or three years. For saltwater species, the arrival of the migrant species and the peak times for each species is heavily dependent on water temperature. Unusually warm or cold periods will affect the patterns described above. Bream is the local name for bluegills and shellcrackers. Speckled perch or specs are crappie. Speckled trout is another name for spotted seatrout.

■ signifies a reasonable chance of catching this species in that month.

□ signifies the optimal months for catching the species.

Species	Jan	Feb	Mar	Apr	May	Jun	Jul	Aug	Sep	Oct	Nov	Dec
Snook	■	■	■	□	□	□	□	■	□	□	■	■
Redfish	■	■	■	■	□	□	□	□	□	□	■	■
Spotted trout	□	□	■	■	■	■	■	■	■	■	□	□
Sheepshead	□	□	□	■	■	■	■	■	■	■	□	□
Mangrove Snapper	■	■	■	□	□	□	□	□	■	■	■	■
Gag and Red Grouper	□	□	□	■	■	■	■	■	■	■	□	□
Amberjack	■	■	■	■	■	■	■	■	■	■	■	■
Flounder	□	■	■	■	■	■	■	■	■	□		
Crevalle Jack	■	■	■	■	■	■	■	■	■	■	■	■
Shark(all species)	■	■	■	■	■	□	□	□	■	■	■	■
Black Sea Bass	■	■	■	■	■	■	■	■	■	■	■	■
Spanish Mackerel	■	□	□	□	■	■	■	□	□			
Whiting	□	□	■	■						■	■	□
Blackfin Tuna	■	■	■	■	■	■	■	■				
King Mackerel		■	□	□	□	■	■	■	□	□		
Tarpon	■	■	■	□	□	■	■					
Cobia	■	□	□	■	■	■	□	■	■			
Dolphin		■	■	■	■							
Tripletail	□	□	□	■	■	■	■	■	■	■	■	■
Sailfish	■	■	■	■	■	■						
Wahoo	■	■	■	■	■							
Largemouth Bass	□	□	□	■	■	■	■	■	■	■	■	■
Catfish	■	■	■	■	■	■	■	■	■	■	■	■

FLORIDA FRESHWATER RECORD FISHES

Downloaded from http://myfwc.com/RECREATION/FW_record.htm July 2010 Note: Species listed with an * are uncertified state records. These records are believed to be accurate but for one or more reasons cannot be certified. To be eligible for a record, a fish must exceed the certified records listed below

SPECIES	WEIGHT	PLACE	COUNTY	DATE	ANGLER
Largemouth bass	17.27	unnamed lake	Polk	07/06/86	Billy O'Berry
*Largemouth bass	*20.13	Big Fish Lake	Pasco	05/00/23	Frederick Friebel
Redeye bass	7.83	Apalachicola River	Gadsden	02/18/89	William Johnston
Spotted bass	3.75	Apalachicola River	Gulf	06/24/85	Dow Gilmore
Suwannee bass	3.89	Suwannee River	Gilchrist	03/02/85	Ronnie Everett
Striped bass	42.25	Apalachicola River	Gadsden	12/14/93	Alphonso Barnes
Butterfly peacock bass	9.08	Kendall Lakes	Dade	03/11/93	Jerry Gomez
Oscar	2.34	Lake Okeechobee	Palm Beach	03/16/94	Jimmy Cook
Skipjack herring	VACANT	*Qualifying Weight is 2.5 pounds*			
White bass	4.69	Apalachicola River	Gadsden	04/09/82	Richard Davis
Sunshine bass	16.31	Lake Seminole	Jackson	05/09/85	Thomas Elder
Black crappie	3.83	Lake Talquin	Gadsden	01/21/92	Ben Curry, Sr.
Flier	1.24	Lake Iamonia	Leon	08/14/92	William Lane Jr.
Bluegill	2.95	Crystal Lake	Washington	04/19/89	John LeMaster
Redbreast sunfish	2.08	Suwannee River	Gilchrist	04/29/88	Jerrel Dewees, Jr.
Redear sunfish	4.86	Merritts Mill Pond	Jackson	03/13/86	Joseph Floyd
Spotted sunfish	0.83	Suwannee River	Columbia	05/12/84	Coy Dotson
Warmouth	2.44	Yellow River	Okaloosa	10/19/85	Tony Dempsey
Chain pickerel	6.96	Lake Talquin	Gadsden	06/11/04	Jep Dove
*Chain pickerel	*8.00	Lake Talquin	Gadsden	07/05/71	Jimmy James
Redfin pickerel	1.06	New River	Bradford	06/06/93	Mike Wilkerson

Species	Weight	Location	County	Date	Angler
Common Carp	VACANT	*Qualifying Weight is 35 pounds*			
*Common Carp	40.56	Apalachicola River	Gadsden	05/24/81	Bernard Rowan
Channel catfish	44.50	Lake Bluff	Lake	05/19/85	Joe Purvis
Flathead catfish	49.39	Apalachicola River	Gulf	04/10/04	Tommy Fowler
*Flathead catfish	*57.50	Hillsborough River	Hillsborough	12/09/75	Tom Norman
White catfish	18.88	Withlacoochee River	Marion	09/21/91	Jim Miller
Blue catfish	64.50	Choctawhatchee River	Washington	08/04/08	James Mitchell
Brown bullhead	5.72	Cedar Creek	Duval	03/28/95	Robert Bengis
Yellow bullhead	2.91	Withlacoochee River	Levy	03/07/07	Michael Pace
Black bullhead	VACANT	*Qualifying Weight is 2 pounds*			
Bowfin	19.00	Lake Kissimmee	Osceola	11/05/84	Jim Brown
American shad	5.19	St. Johns River	Seminole	02/15/90	Bud Dankert
American shad	5.19	St. Johns River	Volusia	03/18/92	Albert Judy
Longnose gar	41.00	Lake Panasoffkee	Sumter	04/14/85	Evan Merritt
Alligator gar	123.00	Choctawhatchee River	Walton	07/08/95	Zachary Phillips
Florida gar	9.44	Lake Lawne	Orange	03/25/01	Patric A. McDaniel
Blue tilapia	VACANT	*Qualifying Weight is 10 pounds*			

FLORIDA FISH AND WILDLIFE CONSERVATION COMMISSION SALTWATER RECORD PROGRAM

Conventional Tackle   July 1, 2010

SPECIES	SCIENTIFIC NAME	WEIGHT	LOCATION	DATE	ANGLER
Amberjack, greater	*Seriola dumerili*	142 lb	Islamorada	Feb. 3, 1979	W. A. Colbert, Jr.
Barracuda, great	*Sphyraena barracuda*	67 lb	Islamorada	Jan. 29, 1949	Harold K. Goodstone
Bass, black sea	*Centropristis striata*	5 lb 1 oz	Panama City	July 21, 1956	Mrs. R.H. Martin
Bass, striped (saltwater)	*Morone saxatilis*	43 lb 9 oz	Indian River	Jan. 3, 2004	Carl R. Jackson
Bluefish	*Pomatomus saltatrix*	22 lb 2 oz	Jensen Beach	Mar. 19, 1973	Liz Yates
Bonefish	*Albula* spp.	16 lb 3 oz	Islamorada	Mar. 19, 2007	Robert Schroeder
Bonito, Atlantic	*Sarda sarda*	6 lb 8 oz	Boca Raton	Feb. 15, 2009	Derrick Salim Jaradi
Catfish, gafftopsail	*Bagre marinus*	8 lb 14 oz	Titusville	Sept. 21, 1996	Larry C. Jones
Catfish, hardhead	*Arius felis*	3 lb 5 oz	Sebastian	Apr. 18, 1993	Amanda A. Steed
Cobia	*Rachycentron canadum*	130 lb 1 oz	Destin	Mar. 21, 1997	Peter McCollester
Croaker, Atlantic	*Micropogonias undulatus*	4 lb 15 oz	St. Lucie	Dec. 15, 2002	Anthony de Foster
Dolphinfish	*Coryphaena hippurus*	81 lb	Lantana	June 9, 2007	Robert Vail
Drum, black	*Pogonias cromis*	96 lb	Fernandina Beach	April 12, 2001	James E. Cartwright
Drum, red	*Sciaenops ocellatus*	52 lb 5 oz	Cocoa	Feb. 24, 1996	George E. Hogan, Jr.
Flounder	*Bothidae or Pleuronectidae*	20 lb 9 oz	Nassau County	Dec. 23, 1983	Larenza W. Mungin
Grouper, black	*Mycteroperca bonaci*	113 lb 6 oz	Dry Tortugas	Jan. 27, 1990	Donald W. Bone
Grouper, gag	*Mycteroperca microlepis*	80 lb 6 oz	Destin	Oct. 14, 1993	Bill Smith
Grouper, goliath	*Epinephelus itajara*	680 lb	Fernandina Beach	May 20, 1961	Lynn Joyner
Grouper, Nassau	*Epinephelus striatus*	9 lb	Marathon Key	Jan. 28, 2007	Nicholas F. Grecco
Grouper, red	*Epinephelus morio*	42 lb 4 oz	St. Augustine Inlet	Mar. 9, 1997	Del Wiseman, Jr.
Grouper, Warsaw	*Epinephelus nigritus*	436 lb 12 oz	Destin	Dec. 22, 1985	Steve Haeusler
Grouper, yellowfin	*Mycteroperca venenosa*	34 lb 6 oz	Key Largo	Dec. 7, 1988	Roy Hogrebe
Grunts, margates,	*Haemulon,* spp.	15 lb 8 oz	Key West	May 6, 2001	Carman Nichols

Sailors choice, white margate					
Hind, speckled	*Epinephelus drummondhayi*	52 lb 8 oz	Destin	Oct. 21, 1994	Russell George Perry
Hogfish	*Lachnolaimus maximus*	19 lb 8 oz	Daytona Beach	Apr. 28, 1962	Robert E. Batson
Jack, bar	*Caranx ruber*	7 lb 12 oz	Miami	Dec. 18, 1999	Martin Arostegui
Jack, crevalle	*Caranx hippos*	57 lb	Jupiter	May 18, 1993	Gerald John Washburn
Jack, horse-eye	*Caranx latus*	25 lb 12 oz	Palm Beach	Oct. 31, 1997	David Leavitt
Jack, yellow	*Caranx bartholomaei*	Vacant			
Ladyfish	*Elops saurus*	6 lb 4 oz	Cocoa Beach	Aug. 2, 2005	Lorie Elliot
Mackerel, cero	*Scomberomorus regalis*	17 lb 2 oz	Islamorada	Apr. 5, 1986	G. Michael Mills
Mackerel, king	*Scomberomorus cavalla*	90 lb	Key West	Feb. 16, 1976	Norton I. Thomton
Mackerel, Spanish	*Scomberomorus maculatus*	12 lb	Ft. Pierce	Nov. 17, 1984	John F. Colligan
Marlin, blue	*Makaira nigricans*	1046	Panama City	July 14, 2001	Conrad E. Hawkins
Marlin, white	*Kajikia albida*	161 lb	Miami Beach	Mar. 20, 1938	L. F. Hooper
Permit	*Trachinotus falcatus*	56 lb 2 oz	Ft. Lauderdale	June 30, 1997	Thomas Sebestyen
Pompano, African	*Alectis ciliaris*	50 lb 8 oz	Daytona Beach	Apr. 21, 1990	Tom Sargent
Pompano, Florida	*Trachinotus carolinus*	8 lb 4 oz	Port St. Joe	Oct. 16, 1999	Barry Huston
Runner, blue	*Caranx crysos*	8 lb 5 oz	Pensacola	June 16, 1995	Kevin Siverly
Runner, rainbow	*Elagatis bipinnulata*	23 lb	Boynton Beach	Sept. 28, 2003	Alan Richbell
Sailfish, Atlantic	*Istiophorus platypterus*	126 lb	Big Pine Key	June 13, 2009	Larry Maier
Scamp	*Mycteroperca phenax*	28 lb 6 oz	Mayport	April 3, 2002	Braden Douglas Pursell
Seatrout, spotted	*Cynoscion nebulosus*	17 lb 7 oz	Ft. Pierce	May 11, 1995	Craig F. Carson
Shark, blacktip	*Carcharhinus limbatus*	152 lb	Sebastian	Oct. 29, 1987	Darlene Rees
Shark, bull	*Carcharhinus leucas*	517 lb	Panama City Beach	October, 1981	Gregory K. Burnett
Shark, dusky	*Carcharhinus obscurus*	764 lb	Longboat Key	May 28, 1982	Warren Girle
Shark, hammerhead	*Sphyrna* spp.	1060 lb	Boca Grande	May 5, 2009	Capt. Bucky Dennis
Shark, lemon	*Negaprion brevirostris*	397 lb	Dunedin	Apr. 29, 1977	Richard M. Guccione
Shark, mako	*Isurus* spp.	911 lb 12 oz	Palm Beach	Apr. 9, 1962	Audrey Cohen
Shark, spinner	*Carcharhinus brevipinna*	190 lb	Flagler Beach	Apr. 3, 1986	Mrs. Gladys Prior
Shark, thresher	*Alopias* spp.	544 lb 8 oz	Destin	Sept. 15, 1984	James Weil

Common name	Scientific name	Weight	Location	Date	Angler
Shark, tiger	*Galeocerdo cuvier*	1,065 lb	Pensacola	June 20, 1981	Richard Baggs
Shark, white	*Carcharodon carcharias*	686 lb	Key West	Apr. 30, 1988	Richard P. DeAngelis
Sheepshead	*Archosargus probatocephalus*	15 lb 2 oz	Homosassa	Jan. 29, 1981	Eugene Lechler
Snapper, cubera	*Lutjanus cyanopterus*	116 lb	Clearwater	July 26, 1979	Billy Graham
Snapper, gray	*Lutjanus griseus*	17 lb	Port Canaveral	June 14, 1992	Steve Maddox
Snapper, lane	*Lutjanus synagris*	6 lb 6 oz	Pensacola	Apr. 18, 1991	Ken Jones
Snapper, mutton	*Lutjanus analis*	30 lb 4 oz	Dry Tortugas	Nov. 29, 1998	Richard Casey
Snapper, red	*Lutjanus campechanus*	46 lb 8 oz	Destin	Oct. 1, 1985	Lane Nichols III
Snapper, yellowtail	*Ocyurus chrysurus*	8 lb 9 oz	Ft. Myers	Sept. 13, 1996	Capt. William M. Howard
Snook	*Centropomus undecimalis*	44 lb 3 oz	Ft. Myers	Apr. 25, 1984	Robert De Cosmo
Spearfish, longbill	*Tetrapturus pfluegeri*	61 lb 8 oz	Islamorada	April 29, 1981	Ted Damiano
Spot	*Leiostomus xanthurus*	Vacant			
Swordfish	*Xiphias gladius*	612 lb 12 oz	Key Largo	May 7, 1978	Stephen Stanford
Tarpon	*Megalops atlanticus*	243 lb	Key West	Feb. 17, 1975	Gus Bell
Triggerfish, Gray	*Balistes capriscus*	12 lb 7 oz	Pensacola	July 15, 2001	Kenneth Morris
Tripletail	*Lobotes surinamensis*	40 lb 13 oz	Ft. Pierce	Mar. 4, 1998	Thomas D. Lewis
Tuna, bigeye	*Thunnus obesus*	167 lb	Miami Beach	Jan. 18, 1957	Jerry Mills
Tuna, blackfin	*Thunnus atlanticus*	45 lb 8 oz	Key West	May 4, 1996	Sam J. Burnett
Tuna, bluefin	*Thunnus thynnus*	Vacant			
Tuna, skipjack	*Euthynnus pelamis*	33 lb 8 oz	Islamorada	July 21, 1998	Frank Digiovanni
Tuna, yellowfin	*Thunnus albacares*	240 lb	Key West	Dec. 5, 2002	Michael Delph
Tunny, little	*Euthynnus alletteratus*	27 lb	Key Largo	April 20, 1976	William E. Allison
Wahoo	*Acanthocybium solandri*	139 lb	Marathon	May 18, 1960	George Von Hoffman
Weakfish	*Cynoscion regalis*	10 lb	Port Canaveral	Dec. 30, 1987	George R. Mizell, Jr.

Florida Fish and Wildlife Conservation Commission
620 South Meridian Street
Mailbox MF-OAE
Tallahassee, Florida 32399
(850) 488-6058 Fax: (850) 488-7152

International Game Fish Association
Fishing Hall of Fame & Museum
300 Gulf Stream Way
Dania Beach, Florida 33004
(954) 927-2628 Fax: (954) 924-4299

FLORIDA FISH AND WILDLIFE CONSERVATION COMMISSION
SALTWATER RECORD PROGRAM

Fly Fishing Tackle

July 1, 2010

SPECIES	SCIENTIFIC NAME	WEIGHT	LOCATION	DATE	ANGLER
Amberjack, greater	*Seriola dumerili*	103 lb 12 oz	Key West	Jan. 28, 1977	Dr. Wm. J. Munro
Barracuda, great	*Sphyraena barracuda*	37 lb 12 oz	Key West	Dec. 19, 1978	Joe Machiorlatti
Bass, black sea	*Centropristis striata*	Vacant			
Bass, striped (saltwater)	*Morone saxatilis*	1 lb 9 oz	Milton	Sept. 8, 2003	Steven P. Peake
Bluefish	*Pomatomus saltatrix*	18 lb	Miami Beach	Apr. 2, 1983	Steve Melvin
Bonefish	*Albula spp.*	15 lb 8 oz	Key Biscayne	Feb. 27, 1997	Joe Pantorno
Bonito, Atlantic	*Sarda sarda*	Vacant			
Catfish, gafftopsail	*Bagre marinus*	7 lb 8 oz	Port Canaveral	Dec. 26, 1989	Dave Chermanski
Catfish, hardhead	*Arius felis*	2 lb 8 oz	Placida	May 11, 1996	Louis Herrero
Cobia	*Rachycentron canadum*	83 lb 4 oz	Key West	Jan. 2, 1986	Jim Anson
Croaker, Atlantic	*Micropogonias undulatus*	2 lb 4 oz	Cape Canaveral	Feb. 8, 2008	Dave Chermanski
Dolphinfish	*Coryphaena hippurus*	51 lb 8 oz	Islamorada	March 25, 2001	Nicholas Stanczyk
Drum, black	*Pogonias cromis*	50 lb 4 oz	Merritt Island	July 12, 1986	Mark R. Marconi
Drum, red	*Sciaenops ocellatus*	43 lb	Banana River	May 7, 1995	Greg Braunstein, MD
Flounder	*Bothidae or Pleuronectidae*	6 lb 15 oz	Sebastian Inlet	May 4, 2005	Dave Chermanski
Grouper, black	*Mycteroperca bonaci*	11 lb 15 oz	Key West	Feb. 26, 2008	Dave Chermanski
Grouper, gag	*Mycteroperca microlepis*	20 lb 15 oz	Ft. Pierce	Nov. 30, 2005	Dave Chermanski
Grouper, goliath	*Epinephelus itajara*	356 lb	Islamorada	Mar. 15, 1967	Bart Foth
Grouper, Nassau	*Epinephelus striatus*	Vacant			
Grouper, red	*Epinephelus morio*	23 lb 8 oz	Sebastian	May 5, 2005	Dave Chermanski
Grouper, Warsaw	*Epinephelus nigritus*	11 lb 7 oz	Sebastian	Sept. 10, 2007	Dave Chermanski
Grouper, yellowfin	*Mycteroperca venenosa*	Vacant			
Grunts, margates, sailors choice	*Haemulon, spp.*	Vacant			
Hind, speckled	*Epinephelus drummondhayi*	Vacant			
Hogfish	*Lachnolaimus maximus*	7 lb 8 oz	Key West	Feb. 14, 2008	Dave Chermanski

Common name	Scientific name	Weight	Location	Date	Angler
Jack, bar	*Caranx ruber*	Vacant			
Jack, crevalle	*Caranx hippos*	37 lb 8 oz	Dry Tortugas	Feb. 11, 1994	Carlos B. Solis
Jack, horse-eye	*Caranx latus*	14 lb 8 oz	Key West	Sept. 7, 1986	Joseph M. Stehr III
Jack, yellow	*Caranx bartholomaei*	Vacant			
Ladyfish	*Elops saurus*	5 lb 4 oz	Port St. John	Oct. 3, 1994	H.P. Woodham
Mackerel, cero	*Scomberomorus regalis*	9 lb	Key West	Dec. 11, 1991	George L. Foti
Mackerel, king	*Scomberomorus cavalla*	55 lb	Key West	Mar. 20, 1995	Ben Bergeron
Mackerel, Spanish	*Scomberomorus maculatus*	6 lb 13 oz	Tarpon Springs	Nov. 7, 1995	Capt. James P. Wisner
Marlin, blue	*Makaira nigricans*	Vacant			
Marlin, white	*Kajikia albida*	68 lb	Ft. Pierce	Dec. 23, 1972	Dave Chermanski
Permit	*Trachinotus falcatus*	41 lb 8 oz	Key West	Mar. 13, 1986	Del Brown
Pompano, African	*Alectis ciliaris*	33 lb 8 oz	Palm Beach	Dec. 21, 1968	Gil Drake, Jr.
Pompano, Florida	*Trachinotus carolinus*	6 lb 8 oz	Cocoa Beach	Jan. 14, 1978	Dave Chermanski
Runner, blue	*Caranx crysos*	3 lb 14 oz	Fowey Rock	July 1, 1987	Capt. Dan Kipnis
Runner, rainbow	*Elagatis bipinnulata*	8 lb 10 oz	Key West	Jan. 18, 1980	John M. Ahearn
Sailfish, Atlantic	*Istiophorus platypterus*	55 lb 8 oz	Palm Beach	Feb. 4, 1980	(Mr.) Pat Ford
Scamp	*Mycteroperca phenax*	12 lb 12 oz	Ft. Pierce	Nov. 30, 2005	Dave Chermanski
Seatrout, spotted	*Cynoscion nebulosus*	12 lb 7 oz	Stuart	Mar. 5, 1984	Sidney Freifeld
Shark, blacktip	*Carcharhinus limbatus*	122 lb	Key West	March 13, 2003	Martin Arostegui
Shark, bull	*Carcharhinus leucas*	389 lb 4 oz	Key West	Mar. 29, 1980	Pete Peacock
Shark, dusky	*Carcharhinus obscurus*	Vacant			
Shark, hammerhead	*Sphyrna Rom.*	353 lb	Key West	April 19, 2004	Rick Gunion
Shark, lemon	*Negaprion brevirostris*	288 lb 8 oz	Key West	Mar. 15, 1978	Pete Peacock
Shark, mako	*Isurus Rom.*	Vacant			
Shark, spinner	*Carcharhinus brevipinna*	Vacant			
Shark, thresher	*Alopias Rom.*	220 lb	Key West	Jan. 25, 1995	Gary Spence
Shark, tiger	*Galeocerdo cuvieri*	Vacant			
Shark, white	*Carcharodon carcharias*	8 lb 14 oz	Jacksonville	Oct. 1, 2008	Bob Moore
Sheepshead	*Archosargus probatocephalus*	Vacant			
Snapper, cubera	*Lutjanus cyanopterus*	10 lb 12 oz	Key West	June 8, 1998	Jerome N. Matthews
Snapper, gray	*Lutjanus griseus*	Vacant			

Common name	Scientific name	Weight	Location	Date	Angler
Snapper, mutton	*Lutjanus analis*	11 lb	Sebastian	May 5, 2005	Dave Chermanski
Snapper, red	*Lutjanus campechanus*	4 lb 12 oz	Key West	Feb. 15, 2008	Dave Chermanski
Snapper, yellowtail	*Ocyurus chrysurus*	30 lb 4 oz	Chokoloskee	Apr. 23, 1993	Rex Garrett
Snook	*Centropomus undecimalis*	Vacant			
Spearfish, longbill	*Tetrapturus pfluegeri*	Vacant			
Spot	*Leiostomus xanthurus*	Vacant			
Swordfish	*Xiphias gladius*	Vacant			
Tarpon	*Megalops atlanticus*	202 lb 8 oz	Chassahowitza	May 11, 2001	James J. Holland
Triggerfish, gray	*Balistes capriscus*	Vacant			
Tripletail	*Lobotes surinamensis*	21 lb 2 oz	Port Canaveral	Apr. 17, 1988	Dave Chermanski
Tuna, bigeye	*Thunnus obesus*	Vacant			
Tuna, blackfin	*Thunnus atlanticus*	34 lb 3 oz	Islamorada	Dec. 17, 1977	Rip Cunningham
Tuna, bluefin	*Thunnus thynnus*	Vacant			
Tuna, skipjack	*Euthynnus pelamis*	Vacant			
Tuna, yellowfin	*Thunnus albacares*	Vacant			
Tunny, little	*Euthynnus alletteratus*	19 lb	Dry Tortugas	Apr. 12, 1995	Philip Caputo
Wahoo	*Acanthocybium solandri*	28 lb 12 oz	Key West	Apr. 15, 1982	Jim Anson
Weakfish	*Cynoscion regalis*	Vacant			

Florida Fish and Wildlife Conservation Commission
620 South Meridian Street
Mailbox MF-OAE
Tallahassee, Florida 32399
(850) 488-6058 Fax: (850) 488-7152

International Game Fish Association
Fishing Hall of Fame & Museum
300 Gulf Stream Way
Dania Beach, Florida 33004
(954) 927-2628 Fax: (954) 924-4299

Government Agencies

Florida Fish and Wildlife Conservation Commission (FWC)
www.myfwc.com

The FWC's purpose is: Managing fish and wildlife resources for their long-term well-being and the benefit of people. To accomplish this, the FWC employs nearly 2,000 men and women. They work from the headquarters in Tallahassee, five regional offices, the Fish and Wildlife Research Institute in St. Petersburg, and 73 field offices around the state.

The Fish and Wildlife Conservation Commission was created on July 1, 1999, by combining the staffs of the former Game and Fresh Water Fish Commission and Marine Fisheries Commission along with much of the Department of Environmental Protection's Divisions of Marine Resources and Law Enforcement.

Headquarters
620 South Meridian Street
Farris Bryant Building
Tallahassee, FL 32399-1600
(850) 488-4676

Regional Offices
Northwest Region
3911 Highway 2321
Panama City, FL 32409-1658
(850) 265-3676

Southwest Region
3900 Drane Field Road
Lakeland, FL 33811-1207
(863) 648-3200

North Central Region
3377 E. U.S. Highway 90
Lake City, FL 32055-8795
(386) 758-0525

South Region
8538 Northlake Blvd.
West Palm Beach, FL 33412
(561) 625-5122

Northeast Region
1239 S.W. 10th Street
Ocala, FL 34471-0323
(352) 732-1225

The FWC's responsibilities include management of the state's fish and wildlife resources, enforcing the rules designed to protect fish and wildlife, keeping the state's waterways safe for boaters, conducting research to provide the FWC with information on which to make management decisions, and an extensive outreach program to educate and inform the public about conducting their responsibility to protect Florida's natural resources.

The research arm of the FWC, the Florida Marine Research Institute, is based in St. Petersburg. The staff is involved in a variety of research projects that, according to their website, includes "assessment and restoration of ecosystems and studies of freshwater and marine fisheries, aquatic and terrestrial wildlife, imperiled species, and red tides." To learn more, visit their website: *http://research.myfwc.com*

One of the most important ways in which the public can help the FWC protect fish and wildlife is by participating in the Wildlife Alert Program. Anyone suspecting a wildlife or boating law violation can report it to the Wildlife Alert Reward Program by calling (888) 404-FWCC (3922). Depending on your cell phone provider, you may also report violations by calling *FWC or #FWC. You may be eligible for up to a $1,000 reward.

Department of Environmental Protection
www.dep.state.fl.us

Prior to creation of the FWC, the Florida Department of Environmental Protection (DEP) was responsible for managing the state's marine resources, including saltwater fishing. This role was reassigned to the new FWC, leaving the DEP with the role of environmental management and stewardship. This includes regulatory activities such as environmental permitting and managing state parks and other state-owned lands.

Department of Environmental Protection
3900 Commonwealth Boulevard
Tallahassee, FL 32399
(850) 245-2118

Water Management Districts

The state has five water management districts. Their mission is to manage the state's ground and surface waters. Although the districts are not directly involved in maintaining recreational facilities, they do own land from which anglers can access places to fish. The water management district websites contain a wealth of interesting information, including listings of the recreational opportunities available on the District's lands. Some of these areas are not used much and might make the perfect place for your next outdoor adventure. To find out more about the various programs each district offers:

Northwest Florida Water Management District
81 Water Management Drive
Havana, FL 32333-4712
(850) 539-5999
www.nwfwmd.state.fl.us

Suwannee River Water Management District
9225 County Road 49
Live Oak, FL 32060-9573
(386) 362-1001
(800) 226-1066
www.srwmd.state.fl.us

St. Johns River Water Management District
P.O. Box 1429
Palatka, FL 32178-1429
(386) 329-4500
(800) 451-7106
www.sjrwmd.com

Southwest Florida Water Management District
2379 Broad Street
Brooksville, FL 34604-6899
(352) 796-7211 or (800) 423-1476
www.swfwmd.state.fl.us

South Florida Water Management District
3301 Gun Club Road,
West Palm Beach, Florida 33406
(561) 686-8800 or (800) 432-2045
www.sfwmd.gov

National Marine Fisheries Service/Fisheries Management Councils

The National Marine Fisheries Service (NOAA Fisheries Service) is an agency of the National Oceanic and Atmospheric Administration (NOAA). Its role is to use science-based research to provide stewardship of living marine resources. Florida is within the Southeast Regional Office located in St. Petersburg, Florida. To learn more about what this agency does, visit the NOAA Fisheries Service's website, *www.nmfs.noaa.gov*, or the southeast Regional Office website at *http://sero.nmfs.noaa.gov.*

In addition to this agency, the South Atlantic and Gulf of Mexico Fisheries Management Councils manage fisheries from where state waters end (9 nautical miles offshore in the Gulf and 3 nautical miles offshore in the Atlantic) out to the 200-mile limit in the Atlantic and Gulf, respectively. The Councils regulate recreational and commercial harvesting of a wide range of fish. Anglers who fish in federal waters should keep up to date on the current regulations which include the dates of open and closed seasons. To learn more, contact:

South Atlantic Fishery Management Council Office
4055 Faber Place Drive, Suite 201
North Charleston, SC 29405
www.safmc.net
(843) 571-4366
(866) 723 6210

Gulf of Mexico Fisheries Management Council
2203 N. Lois Avenue Suite 1100
Tampa, Florida 33607 USA
www.gulfcouncil.org
(813) 348-1630
(888) 833-1844

Additional Sources of Information

Counties

The following links are to the home page for each county's website and the county's property appraiser website. Each county website is a bit different, but if you search each site for the Parks and Recreation Department, boat ramps, or fishing, you will get to the pages with that information. The property appraiser websites (except for Sarasota County) have links to the local Geographic Information System (GIS). These are high-resolution searchable maps.

Brevard
www.brevardcounty.us
www.brevardpropertyappraiser.com

Citrus
www.citruscountyfl.org
www.pa.citrus.fl.us

DeSoto
www.co.desoto.fl.us
www.desotopa.com

Hernando
www.co.hernando.fl.us
www.hernandocounty.us/pa

Indian River
www.ircgov.com
www.ircpa.org

Pasco
http://portal.pascocountyfl.net/portal/server.pt
http://appraiser.pascogov.com

Pinellas
www.pinellascounty.org
www.pcpao.org

Hardee
www.hardeecounty.net
www.hardeepa.net

Hillsborough
www.hillsboroughcounty.org
www.hcpafl.org

Manatee
www.mymanatee.org
www.manateepao.com

Polk
www.polk-county.net
www.polkpa.org

Sarasota
www.scgov.net

Volusia
www.volusia.org
www.volusia.org/property

Florida Sea Grant
www.flseagrant.org

According to its website, "Florida Sea Grant uses academic research, education and extension to create a sustainable coastal economy and environment. We are a partnership between the Florida Board of Education, the National Oceanic and Atmospheric Administration and Florida's citizens, industries, and governments." Based at the University of Florida, the staff and faculty include a cadre of Sea Grant Agents found in most coastal counties in Florida. Sea Grant also has several publications that may be of interest to anglers. For more information, contact:

Florida Sea Grant
PO Box 110400
Gainesville, FL 32611-0400
(352) 392-5870

Other Sources of Information

International Game Fish Association (IGFA) – www.igfa.org
You can check on the current all-tackle records, learn more about the IGFA, and download the International Angling Rules.

Tides

In addition to software programs that you can purchase, here are two sites that also have tide information for Florida.

http://www.softseas.net/
http://www.rodnreeltides.com/

Angling Publications (Print and/or Online)

These publications have useful articles and other information that anglers will find helpful. *Florida Sportsman* magazine is the best-known printed and online magazine for sports in Florida. *Florida Wildlife* magazine is published by the FWC. Both are highly recommended.

Florida Sportsman magazine - *www.floridasportsman.com*

Florida Wildlife magazine - *www.floridawildlifemagazine.com*

Florida Sport Fishing magazine - *www.fsfmag.com*

CapMel - *www.capmel.com*

Florida Game and Fish magazine - *www.floridagameandfish.com*

Woods 'n Water magazine - *www.woodsnwater.net*

CyberAngler - *www.cyberangler.com*

Index to Fishing Sites by County

Here are some other books from Pineapple Press on related topics. For a complete catalog, visit our website at www.pineapplepress.com. Or write to Pineapple Press, P.O. Box 3889, Sarasota, Florida 34230-3889, or call (800) 746-3275.

Fishing North Florida by Kris Thoemke. Second in a series of three books to replace and update the classic guidebook *Fishing Florida*. Covers northeast Florida, the Panhandle, and the Big Bend. For each of the 125 sites, there is a detailed description of the site; information about whether you can fish by boat, bank, pier, bridge, ramp, or surf; a heads-up about the species you can expect to catch and the kinds of bait to use as well as the best particular spots to find the fish; directions to get there; access points; and an address for GPS. Also featured are tips, maps, fish drawings, site photos, and month-by-month regional summaries of species in each area. (pb)

Fishing South Florida by Kris Thoemke. Third in a series of three books to replace and update the classic guidebook *Fishing Florida*. This comprehensive regional guidebook provides anglers with the information they need to find 120 of the best places to fish in south Florida from Port Charlotte on the west coast and Stuart on the east coast south through the Keys. The book covers places to fish from the land or by boat along with tips, maps, photos, fish identification illustrations, and plenty of insider information that will help any angler look like a pro wherever he or she decides to drop a line in the water. (pb)

Fishing Adventures in Florida: Sport Fishing with Light Tackle by Max D. Hunn. Join the author as he steers through twisted mangrove channels of the Ten Thousand Islands, searching for the "big one." Brawl with tarpon and angle with snook; if there's a cure for snook fever, Max Hunn hasn't found it. (pb)

Tales from a Florida Fish Camp by Jack Montrose. Join Jack Montrose, a fish camp regular since 1965, as he reminisces about the good old days fishing on the St. Johns River. Captures the atmosphere and humor of fish camps, where fishermen gathered to tell tales of their fishing exploits, play practical jokes, and relax with a cold beer. (pb)

Sea Kayaking in Florida, Second Edition, by David and Mark Gluckman. The latest information on boats, camping, clothing, and gear for both the novice and experienced kayaker. Maps and campsite guides to the Big Bend Sea Grasses Saltwater Paddling Trail, a trail itinerary of the Nature Coast, and maps and campsite locations for the open water of the Everglades. (pb)

Bicycling in Florida: The Cyclist's Road and Off-Road Guide, Second Edition, by Tom Oswald. Complete directions, maps, and tips for over 70 rides throughout the state from the highest point in Florida (345 feet) through the horse farms in the center of the state and out to Key Biscayne. Information on Florida's cycling laws and important safety issues. List of bike associations. (pb)

Running in Florida by Mauricio Herreros. The author has run every course in this book and gives you the best places in each region. Complete directions, mileage, where to find facilities and parking, whether there are fees, the condition of the terrain, safety tips. Includes running clubs, general references, and a pace chart. (pb)